IMAGINATION FROM FANTASY TO DELUSION

In this book, Lois Oppenheim illustrates the enhancement of self that creativity affords, the relationship of imagination to the self as agent. The premise of the book is twofold: first, that the imaginary is real, differing from what we commonly take to be reality in structure and in form; second, that enhancement of the self through an increase in agency is facilitated by the biology of reward: The pleasure of increased self-cohesion is ultimately the *sine qua non* of imaginative thought.

She emphasizes the idea that imagination generates knowledge: Our sensory systems, like our higher cognitive functions, give us knowledge to maintain the balance required for survival and to enrich the sense of self required for agency; imagination is a function of their doing so. Moreover, she explores the construct by which we apprehend the workings of imagination—fantasy—and considers how fantasy may be transmitted transgenerationally, and how delusion can be an impediment to imagination while also being a product of it.

Lois Oppenheim, Ph.D., is Distinguished Scholar, Professor of French, and Chair of the Department of Modern Languages and Literatures at Montclair State University, where she teaches courses in both literature and applied psychoanalysis. She has published over 80 papers and authored or edited 10 books, the most recent being *A Curious Intimacy: Art and Neuro-Psychoanalysis* and *The Painted Word: Samuel Beckett's Dialogue with Art*. She is Scholar Associate Member of the New York Psychoanalytic Society and Institute and Honorary Member of the William Alanson White Society. She has also been a Visiting Scholar at the New York State Psychiatric Institute at the Columbia University Medical Center, on the Boards of The Philoctetes Center for the Multidisciplinary Study of Imagination and the UK Network for Modern Fiction Studies, and a past president of the international Samuel Beckett Society. Her interview series, "Conversations with…," at the New York Psychoanalytic Society and Institute is a popular forum for discussions on creativity. She is co-creator of the documentary film on mental health stigma (currently in production) called *The Madness Project*.

PSYCHOANALYSIS IN A NEW KEY BOOK SERIES

DONNEL STERN
Series Editor

When music is played in a new key, the melody does not change, but the notes that make up the composition do: change in the context of continuity, continuity that perseveres through change. Psychoanalysis in a New Key publishes books that share the aims psychoanalysts have always had, but that approach them differently. The books in the series are not expected to advance any particular theoretical agenda, although to this date most have been written by analysts from the Interpersonal and Relational orientations.

The most important contribution of a psychoanalytic book is the communication of something that nudges the reader's grasp of clinical theory and practice in an unexpected direction. Psychoanalysis in a New Key creates a deliberate focus on innovative and unsettling clinical thinking. Because that kind of thinking is encouraged by exploration of the sometimes surprising contributions to psychoanalysis of ideas and findings from other fields, Psychoanalysis in a New Key particularly encourages interdisciplinary studies. Books in the series have married psychoanalysis with dissociation, trauma theory, sociology, and criminology. The series is open to the consideration of studies examining the relationship between psychoanalysis and any other field—for instance, biology, literary and art criticism, philosophy, systems theory, anthropology, and political theory.

But innovation also takes place within the boundaries of psychoanalysis, and Psychoanalysis in a New Key therefore also presents work that reformulates thought and practice without leaving the precincts of the field. Books in the series focus, for example, on the significance of personal values in psychoanalytic practice, on the complex interrelationship between the analyst's clinical work and personal life, on the consequences for the clinical situation when patient and analyst are from different cultures, and on the need for psychoanalysts to accept the degree to which they knowingly satisfy their own wishes during treatment hours, often to the patient's detriment.

PSYCHONALYSIS IN A NEW KEY BOOK SERIES

DONNEL STERN
Series Editor

Vol. 16
Imagination from Fantasy to Delusion
Lois Oppenheim

Vol. 15
Still Practicing: The Heartaches and Joys of a Clinical Career
Sandra Buechler

Vol. 14
Dancing with the Unconscious: The Art of Psychoanalysis and the Psychoanalysis of Art
Danielle Knafo

Vol. 13
Money Talks: In Therapy, Society, and Life
Brenda Berger & Stephanie Newman (eds.)

Vol. 12
Partners in Thought: Working with Unformulated Experience, Dissociation, and Enactment
Donnel B. Stern

Vol. 11
Heterosexual Masculinities: Contemporary Perspectives from Psychoanalytic Gender Theory
Bruce Reis & Robert Grossmark (eds.)

Vol. 10
Sex Changes: Transformations in Society and Psychoanalysis
Mark J. Blechner

Vol. 9
The Consulting Room and Beyond: Psychoanalytic Work and Its Reverberations in the Analyst's Life
Therese Ragen

Vol. 8
Making a Difference in Patients' Lives: Emotional Experience in the Therapeutic Setting
Sandra Buechler

Vol. 7
Coasting in the Countertransference: Conflicts of Self Interest between Analyst and Patient
Irwin Hirsch

Vol. 6
Wounded by Reality: Understanding and Treating Adult Onset Trauma
Ghislaine Boulanger

Vol. 5
Prologue to Violence: Child Abuse, Dissociation, and Crime
Abby Stein

Vol. 4
Prelogical Experience: An Inquiry into Dreams & Other Creative Processes
Edward S. Tauber & Maurice R. Green

Vol. 3
The Fallacy of Understanding & The Ambiguity of Change
Edgar A. Levenson

Vol. 2
What Do Mothers Want? Contemporary Perspectives in Psychoanalysis and Related Disciplines
Sheila F. Brown (ed.)

Vol. 1
Clinical Values: Emotions That Guide Psychoanalytic Treatment
Sandra Buechler

IMAGINATION FROM FANTASY TO DELUSION

Lois Oppenheim

Routledge
Taylor & Francis Group
NEW YORK AND LONDON

First published 2013
by Routledge
711 Third Avenue, New York, NY 10017

Simultaneously published in the UK
by Routledge
27 Church Road, Hove, East Sussex BN3 2FA

Routledge is an imprint of the Taylor & Francis Group, an informa business

British Library Cataloging in Publication Data
A Catalogue record for this book is available from the British Library

Library of Congress Cataloging in Publication Data
Oppenheim, Lois.
Imagination from fantasy to delusion / Lois Oppenheim. – 1st ed.
p. cm. – (Psychoanalysis in a new key; 16)
Includes bibliographical references and index.
1. Imagination. 2. Creative ability. 3. Psychoanalysis. I. Title.
BF408.O67 2012
153.3–dc23
2011052049

ISBN: 978-0-415-87570-7 (hbk)
ISBN: 978-0-415-87571-4 (pbk)
ISBN: 978-0-203-85995-7 (ebk)

Typeset in Garamond
by Cenveo Publisher Services

FOR SARAH AND KEITH

CONTENTS

ACKNOWLEDGMENTS

A great many people are to be thanked, some for providing me with various materials, others for discussing matters of mutual interest that led to further exploration here. They include, most especially, Irwin Badin, Rosa Berland, Geneviève Chevallier, Hallie Cohen, Sidney Feshbach, Jules Kerman, Brian Koehler, Francis Levy, Sarah Nettleton, Shani Offen, Léone Seltzer, Terry Tolk, and Lynne Van Voorhis. I wish to thank Dr. Cheryl Corcoran, Director, The Center of Prevention and Evaluation (COPE), Assistant Professor of Clinical Psychiatry at Columbia University, and Research Scientist V at the New York State Psychiatric Institute for my appointment as Visiting Scholar in 2008 which gave me access to many first-hand accounts of those at increased risk for psychosis. I sincerely thank as well all those interviewed for their time, insight, and, in some cases, exceptional courage. Comments on the manuscript by Donnel Stern were invaluable and Kristopher Spring's editorial expertise was also much appreciated. I am deeply grateful to my husband, Ellis Oppenheim, for his patience and a great deal more.

INTRODUCTION

At the end of his 1942 essay *The myth of Sisyphus*, Albert Camus asks us to imagine his philosophical "hero" happy. "Each atom of that stone," he writes, "each mineral flake of the night-filled mountain, in itself forms a world. The struggle toward the heights is enough to fill a man's heart" (p. 91). Many a creative person would agree. But why? What is it that fills the heart as the struggle toward the heights of imaginative expression begins anew? And how do shifts in our thinking on the workings of the mind—changes in how we think about the mind in relation to the brain and in how we think about the mind/brain in relation to other mind/brains—alter our response to those questions?

In a previous book, *A Curious Intimacy: Art and Neuro-Psychoanalysis*, my primary objective was to show that the purpose served by the making of verbal and visual art was homeostatic. Homeostasis (broadly conceived) is the end product of creativity, I argued, inasmuch as the creative endeavor augments the very awareness of self on which the regulation of our internal environment depends. In the present volume, I aim to go further by illustrating not the *consciousness* of self but the *enhancement* of self that creativity affords. More precisely, I aim to investigate *the relationship of imagination to the self as agent*.[1] The fundamental premise of this study is twofold: It is, first, that the imaginary is real. Where it differs from what we commonly take to be reality is in structure and in form. The imaginary of art, for example, is not illusionary for it is phenomenologically describable and even depictable, as demonstrated by the self-reflexive efforts of modernist painters and writers. No less real than the imaginary of art, and thus fantasy, is the imaginary of delusion, ascertainable in the very function it serves. Although fundamentally different, fantasy and delusion do share a

1 Insofar as psychoanalytic metapsychology has not fully clarified how self and ego are related, following Pinchas Noy (1979) I will proceed in this study in agreement with Frances, Sacks, and Aronoff (1977), who "regard the self as an intrapsychic structure and the ego as a group of functions that differentiates and integrates the self" (p. 330).

significant feature: A preoccupation with agency. The second premise is that change, the enhancement of self through an increase in agency, is facilitated by the biology of reward: The pleasure of increased self-cohesion—of efficacy acquired though knowledge of, and the attribution of meaning to, the world—is ultimately the functional *sine qua non* of imaginative thought.

This is not to say that imagination is reducible to the neural substrates of gratification as provided either by fantasy or delusion. Rather, the brain itself has intentionality; it differs from all other bodily organs by being not just a chemical and structural machine, but by having mechanisms that are epiphenomenal. In a word, the brain is intrinsically psychological.[2] And it is the intrinsic psychology of the brain, not the neural correlates, that calls for an investigation of imagination within the context of its expression, which may or may not be aesthetic. Psychoanalysis, for instance, not an explicitly aesthetic endeavor, is analogous to the making of art in a number of important ways, not least of which is the role played by fantasy. Fantasy in art (art as fantasy) entails the externalizing of emotion, desire, and conflict, conscious and unconscious. So, too, does psychoanalysis, with its foundation in the fantasy of both transference and, in its overlap with memory, reconstruction. Operative in the making of art, as in the psychoanalytic situation, moreover, is the objectification of subjective experience such that first- and third-person perspectives (subjectivity and objectivity) are intertwined. At its best, the artistic process, like the analytic, deepens one's sense of identity and empowers the self.

Evidence of the brain's intentionality and its intrinsic psychology is found in individuals with disorders of the brain that limit their sense of agency, such as the severely autistic and the psychotic. Not free to shape their lives, such individuals are incapacitated by a lack of self-governance. Central to their dysfunction is, precisely, imagination—whether its inhibition or its misappropriation. By this I mean that creative thinking—which is *not* to say artistic talent—may be so impoverished as to result in automatism of thought and behavior; it may be so misguided as to derail the reality of the self–world relation. In fact, imagination is at the crux of the delusional thinking associated with some forms of psychosis. Delusions are creative (if not "reality-oriented") means of making theoretical sense of a world that is otherwise nonsensical, but in creatively giving meaning to what is otherwise incomprehensible, they diminish the dynamic dimension of the self and thereby the capacity to adapt and change that is agency.

2 This idea was articulated at length by Mark Solms in a commentary at the June 6, 2009, meeting held at the Arnold Pfeffer Center for Neuropsychoanalysis at the New York Psychoanalytic Institute.

And yet, as we shall see, delusional thinking may, at times and however paradoxically, be therapeutic. Trauma may be mastered and features of psychosis controlled precisely by an imaginative reinforcing of the role of self as agent. In the aim of uncovering *how* the imagination interacts with the self as agent (or, perhaps more accurately, with the ego in its effort to maintain the cohesiveness of self required by agency), this study will focus both on art and mental illness—not, I wish to stress from the outset, for the purpose of advancing any notion of an underlying correlation between them. On the contrary!

My point of departure is that perception, inherent within both fantasy and delusion, however different their imaginative registers—is in itself creative and a strong determinant of how we think. We know this from the allusionary contours of literary and visual art that stimulate the reader/viewer to add his or her own expectations and associations to the work. We know it also from the disambiguating of all we perceive visually and aurally every day as we creatively structure our world. How we think and learn *about ourselves* and what we feel within has everything to do with what we perceive from without.

Although it is not generally conceived as such, the making of art is similarly a two-way occurrence—which is to say that the transmission of mental imaging into art is a reciprocal event: *An internal stimulus is processed in the act of externalization, but also reprocessed as an external stimulus once transmitted to the canvas, page, or stage.* In other words, the occurrence in the mind is coupled with the metabolization of the sensory perception of its expression; feed-forward is always feed-back dependent.

Moreover, what happens in the work of psychoanalysis is comparable to aesthetic experience by virtue of the psychodynamic function served by perceptual processing: Self-discovery is stimulated through the reciprocity of the treatment relationship. Just how that relationship is to be conceptualized has increasingly become the focus of controversy with representatives of the Freudian and post-Freudian (primarily the relational and interpersonal) perspectives on transference, self-disclosure, and related matters remaining, for the most part, on opposite sides of the theoretical fence.[3] But the dichotomies—between drive theory and object relations, say, or between a one- and two-person psychology in the clinical setting—may actually be less real than apparent: In its comparability to aesthetic experience (whether the making or observing of art), psychoanalysis unveils both instinctual drive and object relations (whose significance for Freud is all too often underestimated) at its core. Similarly, the therapeutic alliance,

3 See the publication of the conference "Minding the gap: Freudian and relational/interpersonal psychoanalysts in dialogue" held at the New York Psychoanalytic Institute on February 28, 2009, in *Contemporary Psychoanalysis*, 46(1).

when conceived not hierarchically but in terms of equality, deconstructs the schism. As Samuel Abrams (1996) has articulated the distinction, in the former conception the analyst interprets from an authoritative position of knowing and the patient comes to accept the analyst's offering; in the latter, it is an "independent capacity for discovering" that is enriched as, guided by the analyst, the patient comes to see, to relate, and to integrate differently than before. In short, in the non-hierarchical model the patient does not *acquire* insights, but practices what Abrams calls "insighting" (p. 77). "Insighting" is the *act* of creating new ways of knowing and discovering the self. It is based on a kind of give-and-take I would contend is endemic to the artistic process as well.

However unconscious or conscious the new paths of self-discovery, however painful the Sisyphean task of traveling them, a sense of well-being is present too. The following exchange between a person with schizophrenia participating in a research study and the researcher is telling:

Participant: Every night [I paint] and I get away from the voices.
Interviewer: How does that work? What happens when …
Participant: It rests me, and every time I seem to make a picture, it always comes out and turns out like a face and I don't know why [but] I feel good afterwards.

(cited in Davidson, 2003, p. 197)

Why is the subject of this book.

Imagination: Feed-forward as feed-back dependent

Imagination is the basis of aesthetic visualization and of transference—to the analyst, to the work of art even—indeed, it is the foundation of any mental act that engages fantasy. A vexed concept, fantasy obliges us to give ourselves to a perceptuo-cognitive and affective dialogue with its objectification. Is this a dialogue engaging differing *states of self* (as Philip Bromberg and Donnel Stern would argue) or differing *structures* of the "mental apparatus" outlined by Freud? The question is a timely one given the polarization in theoretical perspectives that has characterized the mental health field for some years now, the dichotomy between those who rely heavily on unconscious conflict and those focused exclusively on relational capacities, on developmental deficits and trauma in the etiology of psychological disturbance. The question is timely given the schism between those who look to the interrelation of conflict and fantasy and those who are calling for a re-examination of the notion of enduring unconscious images or templates that determine the more ephemeral shape of conscious experience (as we find in the writings of Jacob Arlow or Sander Abend, for example). Fantasy thinking, as Arlow (1969b) has said, "exerts an unending influence on how reality is perceived and responded to" (p. 29). Yet, it is less the *influence* exerted by fantasy than the *interplay* with it, less the way in which fantasy implicitly bears on our constitution of reality than its interaction with agency, that is the referential context of this study.[4]

As the basis of delusion, a disorder of thinking where a process of mentation is no longer served but in control, imagination assumes power over the self as agent, although in the denial of reality there is also the creation of new meaning that is no less real for being less true. Much research of late focuses on dissociation as the essence of delusion and yet post-Freudian, which is to say post-drive, theory of mind has been used to delineate the creative act of the artist as fundamentally dissociative as well. Is the age-old linking of art to psychopathology, therefore, still to be perpetuated? Or is there, rather, a creative adaptation of the mind inherent in dissociation that serves to disinhibit imagination in the service of art? If so, how might this adaptation be operative? And what distinguishes it from the dissociation that occurs in conjunction with delusional thought? These are among the questions that will aid in the investigation of the creative struggle that carries within it its own reward.

As has been noted by D. J. Treffinger in a 2002 monograph, imagination is a multi-faceted construct for which there is no universally accepted definition. Over 100 meanings are cited in a 1996 review of the literature (p. vii). Treffinger's model, however, clusters its many characteristics into four comprehensive categories, the first three of which are relevant to the art-psychoanalysis analogy and its basis in "insighting":

1 The generation of ideas (what cognitivists call "divergent" thinking and also metaphorical thinking)
2 The willingness to dig deeper into them ("convergent" or critical thinking, which involves analyzing, synthesizing, the seeing of relationships, and the like)
3 The courage to remain open to their exploration (which takes in a number of personality traits, such as aesthetic sensitivity, playfulness, risk-taking, tenacity, and tolerance for ambiguity among others) (pp. 7, 11–17).

Given the knowledge of the mind gained over the past two to three decades and of the brain from which it is inseparable, however, it no longer suffices to consider imagination outside the neurophysiological domain. And given what that knowledge of the mind–brain may reveal of a relational disposition (a neuronal capacity for empathy, for instance), neither does it suffice

4 I am grateful to Donnel Stern for his incisive comments on my own and others' usage of the term *fantasy*.

to consider it outside the social realm. Clearly, it is a psycho-socio-biological phenomenon.

It is for this reason that studies of imagination, which, in the past, had focused primarily on measures of divergent thinking, volition, and intelligence, are now looking at hemispheric asymmetry (the complementarity of hemispheric function), perceptual variation, body chemistry, and gender as well. And the significance of the role played by memory (particularly working memory) in the measurement of these capacities is recognized in addition. So too considerations of psychopathology (schizotypy, paranoid ideation, hyper-defensiveness, and hyper-anxiety) have begun to enter the literature with tests measuring levels of blood flow in particular regions of the brain and of chemical activity in addition to tests of inventiveness and personality being used to identify markers of creativity. Yet lacking in the search for determinants of imaginative capacity is sensitivity to the role of *psycho-physical responsivity*. Feed-back—whether from the visual perception of one's own artistic production and the processing of that visual apprehension fundamental to creativity in the aesthetic arena, or from the perceptual precipitates of the transferential/counter-transferential relationship fundamental to creative growth (therapeutic action) in analysis—is a determinant that cannot be ignored. In fact, it is precisely what allows for the organizational features, the regulating mechanisms, and the "insighting" that are the subjectively felt components of the creative act. This we shall see as we resituate the phenomenology of imagination at the very crossroad between visual neuroscience and the psychodynamic functioning of the mind–brain, at that juncture where the brain reveals itself not as the machine that drives behavior, but as the sentient, motivated, subjective agent itself.[5]

Visualization and the neurobiology of creativity

I am reminded here of the oft-cited question posed by author Wallace Stegner (1967): "How do I know what I think till I see what I say?" (p. 3). The word "see"—which may be taken in its figurative sense to mean "cognitively discern" or in its literal sense to mean "visually perceive"—allows for an ambiguous play: Are we to understand the question as "How does one subjectively *know* their own mind prior to articulating the thoughts therein"? Or, alternatively, as "how does knowing depend upon a *visual acquisition* of what is expressed"? What should become clear in my inquiry into the structure and function of imagination is that the two in reality are

5 Mark Solms has made a compelling argument for this perspective on the brain in his many writings on neuro-psychoanalysis, a now commonly used term that, in fact, is owed to him.

one and the same. As an innately *creative* species, the only animal species that is so (when "creativity" is used in the aesthetic context as opposed to the evolutionary context of adaptation), we may be said to create precisely to apprehend what it is we think and feel.

I create and in creating I "see"; I externalize my internal representations and use my visual perception as a means of grasping—cognitively or affectively, consciously or subliminally—something of the subjective experience of "me." I thereby gain what we refer to, without regard for its etymology, as "insight" (in-sight). Thus creativity has much to do with identifying for oneself not only *how* one is but *who* one is and increasing one's sense of agency. This thesis begs the question, of course, of what we mean by a number of terms—agency, self, identity, fantasy, and representation not least among them—and how they relate to what appears to lie at the antipodes of their conceptualization: self to other, identity to anonymity, fantasy to reality, and representation to the unformulated. But just how antithetical are they?

To approach an answer, we need to think about what it is we do when we turn an imprint on the mind into a visually perceptible work of art. And we need to reflect on the perceptual processing that occurs when we bear witness to what we are creating. Perception, it must be said, is not a passive recording, but an active process in and of itself (see Offen, 2008, p. 3) and it is only when one considers the many cognitive and emotional factors that exercise control over the process that the complexity of imagination is revealed. Shani Offen has recently posited a number of points with regard to the significance of cognition for visual perception; namely, that stimuli appear different when attended to directly, that expectation influences what is seen, that the association between visual working (or short-term) memory and human cognitive encoding mechanisms impacts the processing of visual stimuli, and that object memory differs from spatial memory (pp. 3–6, 53). A painter studying his work as he paints will thus process the composition in its entirety differently from its detail; will judge the relevance or irrelevance of features of the work (color, content, form) in relation to the desired expression of the mental representation; and will retain in memory aspects both of what *is to be* and of *what has been* transmitted onto the canvas in accordance with the internal and external localization and configuration of an image.

The emotional control of visual perception—whether the processing of external stimuli (the painting in progress itself) or internal stimuli (the mental representation)—is no less formidable. This should become evident throughout this book, particularly in the discussion of artistic inheritances from artist parents where the relationships of offspring to parent will inform the conscious and unconscious links between artistic subject matter and style and in the discussion of evidence for the neuronal basis of empathy and related feelings. In fact, it is there, and in the consideration of the relation of fantasy to overvalued ideas, obsessions, and delusions, that the question of just how antithetically we ought to conceive of the above terms will be most relevant.

To cite but one brief example, it has been suggested (Pally, 2008) that self and other, insofar as there is evidence of their representation occurring within the very same regions of the brain, are not to be conceived of as truly independent phenomena. This is not to say that you and I are not two, but that the boundaries of self and other are blurred by shared circuits within the brain of each individual; that the representation of an other's behavior, emotion, and the like—in sum, their subjective experience—occurs in those areas used for the representation of our own subjectivity. Both the philosophic and psychoanalytic implications of such findings in neuroscience are tremendous: Our understanding of the very notions of reality and truth, for example, reflects them in our ever-evolving theory of mind and in the clinical setting to which such theory gives rise. As Regina Pally put it, "shared circuits contribute to clinical issues *outside* of conscious awareness"; "empathy, internalization, projection, transference and countertransference, and enactment" are all implicated and bear heavily upon the interpretations made by the clinician.

The concept of agency

The psychoanalytic literature on the concept of agency is large and diverse. "Causal agency," with its implication of responsibility; "executive agency," as a feature of personality; "repressing agency," as in superego function; "human agency," the subjectivity of experience; "defensive agency," whereby a perceived threat is unconsciously subverted—the list of agency descriptors is endless (Abelson et al., 1978; Abrahams, 2005; Alexander, 1926; Anscombe, 1986; and we have not neared the Bs!). Agency and autonomy, agency and gender, agency and efficacy, agency and passivity, agency and volition, agency and self-reflection—there is no lack of relevant topics for the investigator of agency. How does agency relate to the self? How does it develop (or fail to)? And what do we mean by the "sense of agency" as opposed to "agency" proper (cf. Kafka, 2011, p. 43, fn. 7)? Such questions, essential to the study of agency, are beyond the scope of this volume. Nevertheless, I wish to be clear on my own usage of the word: Agency, as I will use it, is the feeling of empowerment that is enhanced by understanding, understanding in the form of knowledge that is the creative constitution of meaning (either through the direct apprehension of how things are, phenomenologically speaking, or their indirect apprehension through the likeness of metaphor).

Indeed, what I wish to contribute to the study of imagination—whether it be the imagination of the creative artist, the fantasizing individual, or the delusional person seeking to extend the "hegemony of the self" over "intense and intrusive affects" (as Arnold Modell has said in a somewhat different context; Modell, 1993, p. 54)—is the idea that *imagination imparts knowledge*. And that as the agent of imaginative activity or thinking, the self is rendered more cohesive for being more effective in its dealings with the world. Modell (2008) has written: "Imagination always carries a touch of omnipotence, inasmuch as imagination creates the illusion that, by creating a meaningful internal narrative, external events can be controlled" (p. 359). To that I would add that the drive to master, with results illusionary or real, entails another: the drive to understand. The drive for knowledge, which—when one considers drive as the striving to meet one's needs—is a source of pleasure when comprehension, through the attribution of meaning by the agency of the self, is achieved. Modell defines a "two-phase process"—first an unconscious perception that is involuntary and "by definition outside the agency of the self" (p. 364). It is meaning assigned in a second phase to perception which is within that agency. Thus the *capacity for the creation of meaning is where the feeling of agency resides*. But I would also say that in psychoanalysis, as in the making of art, agency is not expanded, the self not made cohesive, only by the enhancement of this capacity, itself an achievement of knowledge-satiating drive for perception, is multi- or over-determined, with affect, expectancy, and desire contributory features. Gratification in the form of enhanced agency results, therefore, from the *perceptual give-and-take embedded in association*, in the questioning and answering, conscious or unconscious, that occurs in the practice of free association (cf. Bollas, 2009) that has its place in art making too. If one could "imagine" a congruence of the classical and relational approaches, it would be precisely here: In the *drive* for knowledge that *is* the creation of meaning, in the *pleasure* of the generation of meanings, and in the *relation* between the subjective experience of agency and the object of perception, a relation grounded in interaction necessarily bio-psycho-social in its core.

Pluralism in psychoanalysis

As noted earlier, the duality in our conception of the human mind has become increasingly apparent in recent years. Just as the burgeoning interest in neuroscience is no longer at the antipodes of psychoanalysis, however, but returning through neuropsychoanalysis to where Freud himself began, the rift between drive and relational theory may indeed be less schismatic than we think. Those who advocate sociability as inherent within the mind-brain are determined to unseat the hegemony of the intrapsychic over the interpsychic in our understanding of mental function. In fact, by study of the brain, adherents of the relational perspective are now seeking to prove that the brain is indisputably a social organ and endemically object related, just as adherents of classical drive theory seek neurobiological confirmation of the unconscious, of the role played by instinct in psychic processes, of the workings of repression and other defenses. But there is a bridge: It has been said that "the human faculty which enables [the] dialogic process to take place between the inner and the outer, the instinctive and the social, the private and the public Self, is the imaginative faculty" (Kahn & Sutherland, 1968, p. viii). My objective here is to show how that is so.

Psychoanalysis as initially established by Freud was based upon the proposition of two determinants of human motivation: unconscious mental processing and instinctual urge. While he was limited by the technology of his time to offer sufficient non-clinical evidence of their existence (and that of the principles of repression and pleasure from which they emerged), and while subsequent approaches to understanding motivation (from the perspective, say, of object relations or cognitive science) derailed the popularity of his thought, neuroscience has now offered the confirmation he knew would come. Imaging, deep brain stimulation, medications—all have contributed to the identification of both unconscious mentation and instinctual forces.

With regard to the former, research on implicit memory by Eric Kandel, Daniel Schacter, and Larry Squire, to name but three, has significantly advanced the unconscious–conscious demarcation along distinctly neurophysiologic lines. Others (Howard Shevrin, for instance), in demonstrating that neither memory processes outside nor those within the parameters of conscious awareness are necessarily non-mental simply because the neuroscientific evidence is fundamentally physiological and anatomical and, further, that subjects under general anesthesia can form episodic memories outside of consciousness, suggest that their findings are evidence of the existence of a dynamic (or motivated and representational) unconscious. The cognitive "unbinding" or disintegration of any number of cognitive processes necessary for consciousness seen in anesthesia studies has supported this evidence as well (see Bunce et al., 2001; Mashour, 2008; Shevrin, 2002). And neurophysiological markers for unconscious conflict have been identified through time-frequency analysis of event-related potentials and shown to correlate in social phobics with personality measures associated with repression (see Shevrin et al., 1992; see also Bazan et al., 2007).

With regard to the latter, affective neuroscience (as undertaken most famously by Joseph LeDoux and Jaak Panksepp) has uncovered what promotes and energizes the pursuit of pleasure in its various forms. Panksepp's SEEKING system, for instance, the neuro-emotional system (regulated by the neurotransmitter dopamine) that prompts many of our human strivings from the most primitive to the most complex, provides a stunning paradigm for the motivational behavior intrinsic to all mammals and bears a striking similarity to Freud's understanding of libidinal drive (see Solms, 2004).

Existing research in neurobiology, however, also offers evidence of the kind of thinking put forth by a number of post-Freudian psychoanalytic thinkers. As Brian Koehler (2008a) has noted, "human interactionality" is a part of human biology: "Relationships impact on gene expression and neural morphology," he has explained, citing "the neurological signature to social defeat and social status" as an example. In fact, Koehler (2008b) has gone so far as to claim (with a wink to Winnicott) that "There is no such thing as a brain," by which he means there is only this person's brain or that one's, the brain of someone always in negotiation with an Other. "Many contemporary neuroscientists," offers Koehler, "besides studying what is traditionally called 'bottom-up' processing, i.e., the effects of genes and neurophysiological processes on subjective experiences, are also studying 'top-down' processing, i.e., the effects of psychological and social experience on gene expression and neurobiology." Indeed, this is the *raison d'être* of several newly developed fields, among which are molecular social neuroscience, epigenetics, and developmental psychobiology (Koehler, 2008a).

Moreover, among the many today who consider human relatedness "the key element in both normal and therapeutic development of self," as Bromberg (2008, p. 414) has put it, there are those for whom the dissociation of self-states (which may be normal or pathological) is essential to an understanding of mental function. What these relationalists emphasize—and they are known as "relationalist" because their point of departure is the *inter*actional as opposed to the *intra*psychic patterns of thinking, feeling, and behavior—is the process whereby thoughts, emotions, and memories associated with different self-states are kept from mutual awareness, the process whereby the "I" of "I am in this moment" finds the "I" of "I am in a different kind of moment" alien. The capacity for self-reflection is what allows for the perception of disjunctions between self-states and of the risk to stability posed by non-communication between them. Though the neurobiology of dissociation is still limited, cognitive neuroscience appears to provide non-clinical evidence of what a number of relationalists consider to have been amply determined clinically: Namely, that insofar as there are mental processes which are part of the self and accessible to consciousness at any given moment, the operative force is not repression into the unconscious but dissociation from the current perception of "me."

Pluralism is neither new to nor unhealthy in psychoanalysis, but the degree of divergence (both in theory and practice) between relationalists and those who adhere more closely to the classical tradition need not be so significant. Winnicott famously proclaimed "there is no such thing as a baby," implicating in infantile development the nurturer (who generates, it is hoped, an environment facilitating of growth), and he contributed to the view that reality is always and indisputably *co*-created. This is the basis for the clinical work of those who, however different in their treatment ideology and methodology from each other they may be, characteristically seek not to reconstruct in psychoanalysis historical truth as determinant of a present reality so much as negotiate the subjective truths at play in the clinical setting. What comes to the fore, then, is the existentially and interactively "real" that is distinguishable in its mutability from narrative fact while being no less legitimate. But neuroscience, in addition to offering empirical confirmation of the relational perspective and, thereby, of the negotiations at play in the creative process, both in the artist's work place and the analyst's consulting room, also confirms the classical view of creativity as drive driven, for we are beginning to understand the biological function of motivation and to account for the physiological and anatomical origins of motivation and "pleasure." And just as we are beginning in neuropsychoanalysis to delimit the interdependence of the objectively verifiable and the subjectively felt, we are beginning in neuroesthetics to regard imagination in terms of its usefulness, through the attainment of the knowledge, to the body's chemical, neurological, musculoskeletal, and visceral systems.

Sublimation versus interrelation in art

Freud insisted that dreams are merely a form of thinking and he extended this idea to include waking dreams and the fantasies of art. Like the dreamer, the literary or visual artist, he maintained, shapes his wishful thoughts into a representation of fantasy, one that evades the repressive forces of the ego. This liberation from inhibition, from ego censorship, is a source of pleasure to the dreamer/artist precisely to the extent that the fantasy is in some way fulfilled. Freud established the idea that art emanates from within needs of the psyche and that it serves psychic aims. His own pathographic studies attempted to reveal how art is used to master the conflict that arises between unacceptable urges of the id and their repugnancy to the ego. Others (most notably, Phyllis Greenacre) have studied the dependence of imagination on the developmental phases of the individual; the service rendered the ego by the regressive pull of the imagination (Ernst Kris); and the neutralization of drive, the notion of a deinstinctualized energy (Heinz Hartmann) as opposed to the libidinally charged sublimation originally espoused by Freud. Hans Loewald objected to the implication that "neutralization" was altogether non-instinctual, a function of the autonomous ego. Substituting a "reconciliation" between object-oriented libidinized energy and narcissistic libido, Loewald defended the dynamic quality of the sublimatory process against the debiologizing tendency of ego psychology. At the same time, however, he refused the idea of sublimation as a purely biological force. Maintaining that it was not to be viewed as a defense against the id, he situated it on the order of internalization and ego development. In so doing, he did away with the view that a reduction of tension, a discharge of object libido, was endemic to the sublimatory act. Instead, he stressed the faculty of object relatedness, the capacity to form new connections with the world, which developed out of the psychic matrix of the infant's symbiotic union with its mother: "Sublimations," he wrote, "are progressing differentiations that culminate in new synthetic organizations of such unitary experiences" (2000, p. 453). He thereby proved significantly closer, in the matter of sublimation, to Winnicott than to Freud, for Winnicott situated his thinking on creativity within the me/not me dialectical frame of transitional experience.

Also closer to Winnicott is the relational theoretician who rejects the idea that culture derives from the vicissitudes of instincts. The self–other context in which the mind is shaped enhances or inhibits, in this perspective, individual differences in endowment but also, however, ultimately renders the concept of sublimation irrelevant to relational thinking. Stephen Mitchell's (1991) overview of the reformulation of the role of the instincts clarifies the point:

> The key transition to postclassical psychoanalytic views of the self occurred when theorists began thinking … of the repressed not as disorganized, impulsive fragments but as constellations of meanings organized around relationships, and they began to conceive of the id as involving a way of being, a sense of self, a person in relation to other persons.
>
> (p. 127)

Construed in the relational perspective, the psychoanalytic truth of art (in other words, the psychodynamic validity attributed to its meaning) would be said to reside in the interactivity between the artist and his work. This, according to Bromberg (1998), is precisely what renders art analogous to psychoanalysis:

> Like the analyst, the painter must permit an interactive process to take place through which the painter's understanding of what he or she wants to create and how it is to be created, changes as it is expressed on canvas … Each painting must be allowed to possess a changing identity of its own as it is being painted, and this identity must be free to instruct and inform the painter as to how it is to be painted in an evolving rather than a preconceived way.
>
> (p. 20)

Similarly, Stern (2004) likens psychoanalysis to the creative process of the writer who must assume the stance of simultaneously experiencing himself as "illusory critic" and creator. To write something useful, Stern maintains that he must "be able to think creatively at the same time that [he] think[s] critically *about* thinking creatively" (p. 211).

What Bromberg and Stern describe lends itself to a concept of creativity in which it is not a privileging of primary over secondary process thinking that defines the making of art, as the classical theoretician would have it, so much as a give and take between the two modes of mentation whereby each may be said to inform the other. Neither is the making of art a transformation of unacceptable impulses into other forms so much as an interplay, a negotiation, between different self-states. Dissociation has been described by Bromberg (2003) as both a healthy capacity of the mind and a pathological structure that operates defensively. The aim of psychoanalytic treatment, as he sees it, is the creation of a link between the mental representation of dissociated experience and the "*mental representation of the self as the agent or experiencer*" (p. 709). This is very much in line with Stern's (2004) description of what must take place for the artist (in this case, Stern himself as writer) to be productive: He needs to be able to negotiate the conflicts between self as creator and self as critic; he needs "to be able to evaluate each purpose in the light of the other" and "either be able to revise his manuscript or to answer his illusory critic in a way that satisfies him." In a word, he needs to be able to create "the experience of conflict" rather than withdrawing into "one or the other of these self-states," which would impede the formulation of "the perspective that would be offered by the other" and result in dissociation (p. 211), a profound inhibitor of creativity.

Is creative process as experienced by the artist, then, intrapsychic and sublimatory or interpsychic and relational in essence? Or both? And if not the former but the latter, are we to see it in terms of a fundamentally dissociative phenomenon wherein the artist relates defensively by keeping alternative self-states out of communication with each other? Or is it to be viewed, rather, in terms of a shift via the imagination toward intersubjective function, the artist relating through the work to the reader or spectator, to any and all others inhabiting his inner fantasy life, and even drawing his own self-states into dialogue? Much has been said about the classical model of sublimation. Much has been said about creativity with to regard object relations. But what might imagination look like on the coexisting spectrums of drive and relational theory? Might a theory of creativity be conceivable that privileges neither drive over object relations nor the reverse?

"The choice of one psychoanalytic theory over another," Donald Kuspit (1991) has observed, "is a heroic intellectual—and political—act, but piety toward one theory is likely to foreclose some area of understanding" (p. 1). Whether or not one accepts the role assigned by Freud and others to the ego in creative process, the body (already implicated by Freud in the concept of ego) is implicated by the very construct we refer to as self.

And affect, now known to have distinct neurophysiological components, is the primary source of the implication. Indeed, the subjective "I" is constituted precisely through the transmission of information from within the viscera of the body to the brain (a process that occurs by way of nerve impulses, cerebral spinal fluid, and the circulatory system controlled by the heart). What this information reveals is the *feeling* state or subjectivity of the individual. Current trends in neuroscientific research on aesthetic experience emphasize the significance of those areas of the brain controlling mood and motivation. The dorsolateral prefrontal cortex, for instance—the area of the brain under the forehead whose importance for mood is well documented—has been shown to be active during problem solving and creativity and magnetic stimulation to this region has shown an increase in creative function. Additionally, the role in creativity of neurotransmitters—the molecules that mediate the transmission of chemicals in the brain—is receiving progressively more attention. Dopamine, for example, would appear to have much to do with creativity thinning the line between normal fantasizing and delusional thought.

The creative endeavor, however sublimatory or relational the context in which it is viewed, is rooted in the neurobiology of humankind. Indeed, creativity, its identification of the self to the self and consequent augmentation of agency, depends upon the physiology of the faculty, imagination, through which it emerges. Listen to David Beres (1960): "Without imagination, reality is only sensed and experienced; with imagination, reality becomes an object of awareness. With his imagination man participates in reality, alters it, and even to some extent controls it" (p. 334). If creativity in art is akin to analytic treatment, it is that the analyst, as Abrams (2004) has said, is a "servant of creative adjustment." As Abrams sees it, analysis is not a matter of "resultants" but of "emergents," not a matter of exposing structures of the past but of tapping into "the forward pull" of the patient's creative, as reorganizational, capacity. The "transformational potential" of an analytic interpretation, more precisely, is realized when the interpretation is made less in the interest of problem resolution (which implies a focus on the past) than in the interest of change (that is, with an eye to the future). And I would contend that the "transformational potential" of art is not dissimilar. Art destabilizes the absolute quality of the self–world relation to constitute a new such relation—whether by way of dissociation, by way of the intersubjectivity of the artist and his viewer/reader, or by way of the interconnectedness that occurs between differing self-states of the artist that reciprocally act on and result from the perceptual interplay of the artist with his art.

This will become evident as we investigate imagining—its origins in the mind/brain, its psychosocial or developmental endowment, its projection in fantasy and, potentially, in delusion. The objective of this inquiry into imagination is thus to be seen, on the one hand, as an exploration of the commonality between art and psychoanalysis—for therein the rift between drive theory and the relational perspective truly narrows—and, on the other hand, as an inquiry into the transformational power of creative process, of that process for which, in both psychoanalytic practice and the making of art, representation is pivotal: Once imaged, subjective experience is necessarily altered allowing for the unique opportunity for the blind spots of self-perception to diminish.

Part I

"IMAGINATION DEAD IMAGINE"

> Being has a form. Someone will find it someday. Perhaps I won't but someone will. It is a form that has been abandoned, left behind, a proxy in its place.
>
> Samuel Beckett

1

WHENCE THE IMAGE?

The setting is the Groote Schuur Hospital in Cape Town, South Africa. The patient, whom I will call Ms. P., has suffered a stroke and remains unable to move her left arm. Neuropsychologist Mark Solms approaches the bedside of Ms. P. and begins to converse with her:

Dr. S.: Do you remember our discussion yesterday?
Ms. P.: Yes.
Dr. S.: Do you remember what we spoke about?
[*Patient nods affirmatively.*]
Dr. S.: Can you tell me?
[*No reply.*]
Dr. S.: We spoke about how you came to be here in hospital.
[*Seemingly disinterested, Ms. P. withdraws with her right hand a Q-tip from under her blanket and begins to clean her ears.*]
Dr. S.: You don't feel like talking this morning?
[*Patient shakes her head.*]
Dr. S.: Why not?
Ms. P.: I just want to go home. I'm not sick.

Solms says he understands that Ms. P. feels well and that she has her mind on things at home, but wonders why she thinks others brought her to the hospital. Ms. P. utters a few words revealing, significantly, that she is the caregiver of others (her husband and teenaged son) and that being sick and thus cared for is not a role she wants to play. *She does not want to be treated as sick*:

Dr. S.: You have no symptom of any kind?
[*Patient nods in agreement.*]

To Solms' further questioning, Ms. P. persists in denying that any part of her body is not working. Although willing to hear that her file contains information on her stroke and interested, even, in hearing the causes of stroke, she is unwilling to hear that a blocked artery in the right side of *her* brain was responsible for the paralysis on *her* left side. Solms then demonstrates the non-functioning of her left arm by lifting it for her and letting it fall gently to her side. To his additional questions, Ms. P. simply shakes her head, shuts her eyes, and tries to sleep.

Rejection of such evidence of paralysis is not uncommon. Anosognosia, or the disavowal of physical disability, may present in a lesser form wherein the patient displays a cognitive acceptance of the deficit, but no affective concern about it (anosodiaphoria). Or it may take on any one of a number of other strange, if more severe, features, such as the attribution of the limb to someone else (somatoparaphrenic delusion) or disgust before or even hatred of the paralyzed limb (misoplegia). To account for the phenomenon, theorists have implicated disorders of spatial perception and cognition and, more recently, those of attention arousal (the restricting of attention to the right hemispatial field that is operated by the brain's intact left hemisphere) and negative emotion (the limiting by damage to the right hemisphere of the positive emotions located therein) (see Kaplan-Solms & Solms, 2000, p. 154). But what of the psychological factors that are irreducible to hemispheric lateralization? The case of Ms. P. seems to illustrate that something psychodynamic is at play.

Near the end of the session, when asked to move her left arm, she does so by using her right arm. Solms points this out to her and asks with regard to the immobilized arm:

Dr. S.: Is this arm working normally or not?
Ms. P.: No.
Dr. S.: What is wrong with it?
Ms. P.: There is nothing wrong with it because I can touch it.

After showing the patient that she is able to lift her right arm but not her left, explaining that that is called "paralysis" and that paralysis is the result of the stroke she has suffered, he asks the patient what he had said. She repeats his words verbatim and seems to "know" that her arm is paralyzed, just as she had come to "know" it in the session of the preceding day, although she was unable at the start of the current session to articulate her memory of what she had come to "know" the day before. Solms then asks what she will answer when doctors come to see her and inquire if there have been any symptoms resulting from her stroke. The patient tellingly returns to the idea that she did not *want to be treated as a sick person*. And this is how the session concludes:

Dr. S.: So let's discuss it one last time; this arm, is it working properly or not?
Ms. P.: It's working properly.
Dr. S.: But a moment ago you agreed with me that it was paralyzed.

Forced to confront the contradiction, the patient tells Solms that in her "*mind's eye*" she sees her arm moving, while with her *physical eyes* she sees that her arm is not lifting as it should. She is also aware that Solms, not seeing from within her, sees something other than what she herself sees:

Dr. S.: So which is right? Your "mind's eye" sees something that is more real than what your actual eye sees?[1]

The roadblock faced by doctor and patient is precisely that: The *internal image* of the moving arm *is* "more real" to the patient than the perception of her paralyzed limb. Three primary questions emerge from this session: What is an image? Why might an internal representation take precedence over the actuality of perception? And what do the "what" and the "why" tell us about the relationship of imagination to the self as agent?

Affinities

One way in which psychoanalysis is analogous to art is that each offers a way of seeing a *this* as if it were a *that*. To acknowledge the affinity between them is to acknowledge the mechanism of similitude at work in each: Therapeutic action resides, in part, in the emerging into consciousness of the comparability of the analytic dyad to earlier relations. But this bringing to awareness of likeness is simultaneously recognition of difference, just as identification of the "real" in visual or verbal art is not identification *with it*, but the projection at once of semblance and the "unreal"—in the sense of incongruent—status of art. The discrepancy between what Ms. P. saw internally and externally may be conceptualized as of the same order and thus the task of her physicians was to make her aware that what she "saw" in her mind's eye was *like seeing*, but *not seeing*, and that the moving arm she envisioned was incompatible with, if comparable to, the arm to which she was habituated.

In a seminal work on imagination that dates to 1940, Jean-Paul Sartre probed from a purely philosophical perspective a number of issues whose neuropsychological complexities we are finally beginning to unravel. These include spatial consciousness and intentionality (the substituting for the represented object in the mind one's emotional regard for an object existing outside it). One in particular to which he called attention has begun of late to draw much notice, namely, the relation between perception and interpretation. While claiming the imaginary to be entirely distinct from perception, well ahead of his time Sartre wrote, "*L'imaginaire représente à chaque instant le sens implicite du réel*" [the imaginary represents at every

1 I am grateful to Mark Solms for providing me with the videotaped session cited here.

moment the implicit meaning of the real] (p. 360; translation mine). Sartre's point is that *the process of imagining, while separate from that of perceiving, carries within it the ascription of meaning to perceptual experience.* Constructing what he called an "analogon," an equivalent to the object of perception, he observed that, in "seeing" (visualizing) without seeing, consciousness mentally represents the real both as it is and as it is not. Sartre owed to philosophical traditions other than his own—the metaphysical idealism of Kant, for instance—the dissimilarity between the appearance and reality of phenomena, but he extended the divergence to the imagination and the inherence within it of interpretation. In today's world of neuroscience, Sartre's idea of the imaginary as informed by expectation (the "implicit meaning of the real") is proving true, even if his Kantian proposition on the imaginary's disjunction from perception as the sensorial provider of *pure* data—data separate from visual, auditory, and other forms of bodily memory and the cognitive and affective associations they evoke—is faring less well.

Ms. P. did not appear to visually perceive her left-sided immobilization. Given, however, that there was no apparent ophthalmological reason for her lack of visual perception and that any cognitive explanation for her lack of understanding would have to be limited, for she did have moments of acknowledging the paralysis, one is obliged to ask if some sort of interference between those systems in the brain that allow for motoric and visual imaging was at play. Or was some sort of bias as yet not fully understood by researchers influencing her incapacity to remain cognizant of her left-sided deficit, something on the order of choice blindness, right-side bias, or other observable phenomena that bear upon perceptual preferences individuals are unaware of having? Perhaps, though, it was that the perception itself carried within it extraordinary meaning, meaning made of memory and affect, meaning that made the perception too difficult to bear.

Ms. P.'s visualization of her immobilized self was unequivocally at odds with her proprioceptive awareness, her kinesthetic representation of her bodily self in action. Body image is an integral part of identity and any motor handicap can gravely alter one's self-representation (see Morin & Thibierge, 2004), throwing into question the ego ideal and inflicting narcissistic injury. As Jaak Panksepp (1998) has written, "the self-schema provides input into many sensory analyzers, and it is also strongly influenced by the primal emotional circuits" (p. 309). Ms. P's affective awareness (or more accurately pre-awareness) of her condition would seem to have had a significant effect on her self-representation that, in turn, generated the need for rejection of that awareness. Psychodynamically speaking, her anosognosia may thus be seen as a defensive response wherein extreme denial or even a regressed state of primary narcissism was struggling to protect a fragile psyche from the threat of damage.

Somatic disorders of self- and body representation are often the models on which the explanations of anosognosia are based, along with some sort of neurobiological disturbance in the emotion systems entailing a reduction of "negative" emotions. Yet the role played by "implicit awareness," the idea that anosognosia is a defensive denial motivated by the need to protect the self from the emotional pain that full awareness would bring, is significant and illustrative accounts of subliminal awareness are compelling. V. S. Ramachandran (1996), for one, has described the case of a patient who was offered a justificatory explanation of his deficit that would deter any potentially negative emotional response to it. Ramachandran suggested to his patient, Mr. C., that an injection of anesthesia into his left arm would temporarily paralyze his limb. In truth, there was but a saline solution in the syringe. Following the injection, the patient, now cognizant of his immobilized arm, fully acknowledged its immobility and did so in a matter of fact way. He was no longer anosognosic simply because his condition had been legitimized and the negative emotional implications of the paretic limb were removed. As has been noted by Oliver Turnbull:

> This finding does not, in itself, demonstrate that the patient was implicitly aware of his deficit. However, the sudden and dramatic fluctuation in his awareness, on the basis of a simple (but ingenious) psychological manipulation, suggests that it is the emotional *consequences* of the awareness that are central in the production of the anosognosia, rather than a deficit in some form of somatic awareness.
>
> (personal communication)

Alternatively, one might consider the anosognosia of Ms. P. in terms neither of the neurological deficits brought on by the stroke nor of the emotional fallout from awareness of her altered state. Rather than an absence of cognition, it may be seen as the presence of a firmly held alternate belief. A recent study undertaken by Michael Garrett et al. (2011) found that patients deny illness not because of lack of awareness (the absence of insight) but because of strongly held beliefs contrary to what is known (the presence of competing ideas).

A yet somewhat different perspective is this: "The brain uses the process of *normal dissociation*," Bromberg (2009) has written, "to routinely inhibit simultaneous consciousness of *unadaptively* discrepant self-states ... In emotionally heightened unanticipated situations, the conditions are ripe for self-states to become *traumatically* discrepant, triggering *defensive dissociation* when an attempt is made to hold them simultaneously in consciousness" (p. 353). In this respect, it could be said that what Ms. P. could not maintain concurrently was a self-state whose component self-representation was as it had been and a self-state in which that representation was altered. To the extent that she could not tolerate the image of herself as helpless and no longer the caretaker of her family and, moreover, the depressive affect stemming from her sense of loss (her loss of physical function and her loss of identity as thriving wife and mother), she dissociated her paralysis in her apparent disinterest in the session with Solms. Primary narcissistic regression or dissociation into a "not-me" self-state, anosognosia clearly provided the patient with a defensive means of protecting her self-image, of preserving some degree of integrity of her self-representation. Perceiving her left side as immobilized threatened her fundamental sense of autonomy, an autonomy deriving in part from the integrity of that self-image, and her sense of identity was therefore at stake.

At the crux of the matter, however, is how expectation and interpretation are linked to perception generally and to visual perception more specifically. Indeed, the affinity between Ms. P.'s seeing while not seeing and art's being a seeing of some *this* as though it were *that* (an affinity analogous to that between art and psychoanalysis) is determined precisely by the shaping of perception by emotional memory and the investment of emotional energy in the perceived object. We tend to think of visual perception simplistically, as light bouncing off the surface of objects and scenes to transmit to our eyes a complete picture of what lies before us. Vision, of course, is far more complicated than that: "There are infinitely many possible arrangements of surfaces and light sources consistent with any given pattern of light on the retina," Rebecca Saxe and Shani Offen (2010) explain. "The input to vision is ambiguous and sparse, containing many gaps; yet these inputs are somehow transformed into a perception of a stable and highly detailed reality" (p. 14). How? The goal of the visual system is to provide the seer with information on which to base action and in conformity with that goal "the inputs are disambiguated and completed by processes that take advantage of the system's cumulative knowledge, encoded as prior expectations" (p. 14). Acquired over time by an individual, or structurally incorporated into our brains through evolution, the visual representation that is seeing is highly inferential—which both leaves room for error and tells us something of our physiognomy:

> Naively, one might conceive of "input processing" and "interpretation" as two separate components of the visual system, housed in distinct brain regions and arranged serially. By contrast, experimental evidence from both humans and animals suggests that *interpretation of the visual input is built into the architecture of the visual system at every level.*
>
> (p. 17; emphasis added)

In fact, it is precisely the anticipatory and interpretive dimensions of visual perception that render the distinction between vision and visualization—that is, between seeing and imagining—significantly more complex than might be assumed. It is generally supposed (à la Hume) that the dissimilarity between perception and imagination is merely a matter of the content of the latter being of lesser intensity than the former (cf. Byrne, 2010, p. 18). But when expectation is put back into the perceptual hopper, so to speak, when we dispel the "naïve intuition that we 'just see' the world" and acknowledge with Saxe and Offen (2010, p. 21) that visual perception is a process of inference, what is implicated immediately as a vital feature of perception is memory. Memory, moreover, is inextricably linked with emotion, as we know not only from Freud's metapsychological illustration of the powerful force that is repression, but from Proust's (1928) powerful depiction of the other side of that same coin: The writer's famous story of the madeleine that, once dipped in tea, yielded a texture and taste that, like the scent of hawthorns that overtook him on a walk and the view of church steeples as he rode from them, is remarkable for the delineation of the intense emotion potentially brought forth by recollection. The association of the perceptual moment with memory itself, perception by the very nature of expectation and inference being a moment of remembrance, has dramatic (obliterating) consequences for the distinction between imagination and perception that Sartre, however elegantly, put forth.

Furthermore, there are experimental data supporting the idea that visual imagery and perception share a common neural substrate. As Marc Jeannerod (1994) has explained, "The pattern of cortical activation during visual imagery seems to match, at least in part, that observed during visual perception." Activation of occipital and inferior temporal regions has been shown by regional cerebral blood flow analysis to occur in subjects performing visual perceptual tasks or tasks requiring the use of visual imagery whereas "tasks requiring a different sort of imagery (e.g., motor imagery) or tasks involving non-imaginal thinking did not activate the same areas." Electrical brain activity mapping during visual perception and imagery has produced very similar results (p. 188).

"Cognitive contact," Alex Byrne (2010) makes clear, "is the point of overlap between perception and recollection" (p. 21). This, in fact, is precisely what Proust puts in high relief in insisting upon the mental effort required for the sensory perception eliciting memory to culminate in an epiphanous and intensely joyful finish. It is as if we are observing in slow motion the cognitive contact Byrne defines as the crossroads of perception and recall when Proust (1928) elongates the very point of overlap:

> I retrace my thoughts to the moment at which I drank the first spoonful of tea. I find again the same state, illuminated by no

> fresh light. I compel my mind to make one further effort, to follow and recapture once again the fleeting sensation. And that nothing may interrupt it in its course I shut out every obstacle, every extraneous idea, I stop my ears and inhibit all attention to the sounds which come from the next room. And then, feeling that my mind is growing fatigued without having any success to report, I compel it for a change to enjoy that distraction which I have just denied it, to think of other things, to rest and refresh itself before the supreme attempt. And then for the second time I clear an empty space in front of it. I place in position before my mind's eye the still recent taste of that first mouthful, and I feel something start within me, something that leaves its resting-place and attempts to rise, something that has been embedded like an anchor at a great depth; I do not know yet what it is, but I can feel it mounting slowly: I can measure the resistance, I can hear the echo of great spaces traversed.
>
> (p. 64)

"Palpitating in the depths of [his] being" is "the image, the visual memory" linked to the taste. And this is accompanied by enlightenment, the realization that the "object of [his] quest ... lies not in the cup but within [himself]" (pp. 64, 62).

This is equivalent to saying, as Jonah Lehrer (2008) has, that a "painting emerges, not from the paint or the light, but from somewhere inside our mind" (p. 98). What is also discovered by Proust's narrator, however, is that what emerges from within the mind does not do so of its own accord. Rather, the emergence of form (ultimately, the novel itself) results from stimulation of what has been projected onto consciousness (that is, mapped onto the brain). If in the making of art feed forward is always feed-back dependent, it is that creative output is always input based.

I liken to each other such unlikely candidates for resemblance as anosognosia, psychoanalysis, and art, then, because *what generates form, what allows the image to emerge, is the integration of sensory input from what is external to the body with what is internal within it*. It is, moreover, because representation has valence; it has affective value derived from previously encoded experience (however conscious, preconscious, or unconscious awareness of that valorization may be) and affective value is intimately linked to meaning. This is what is remarkable about the neuropsychological phenomena associated with anosognosia, its delusional form and related disturbances: Meaning is evidenced in the repressive or dissociative mechanism tied to the implicit awareness of disability, in the emotional aversion to it, just as it is evidenced in the defensive mechanisms that come to light in psychoanalysis. And the implications of that meaning—with regard to transference, self-object distinctions, the shaping of perception by cathexis, and more (cf. Zellner, 2009)—are significant both clinically and aesthetically.

Another way to conceptualize the commonality between the three—and my reason for putting it in high relief—is this: Framing anosognosia is the relationship between self-representations; the healthy one delusionally disavowing the one with the deficit. Yet a deeper frame is to be found in the repressive or dissociative "not-me" self-state that characterizes the disorder. In Ms. P.'s case, as we saw, her sense of identity (me) was clearly dependent upon the integrity of her self-image as it related to her husband and son. So, too, the relationship between self and other frames the analytic setting and not only by establishing the boundaries within which the therapeutic process takes place but by being integral to that process itself (see Bass, 2007). However neutral or interpersonal the stance of the analyst, there is always interaction with the (real and transferential) other framing the analysis and the relationships with the many other others at play in the therapeutic picture as well. No less elastic for the ever changing parameters of analysis is the framing that takes place in the making and viewing of art.

Modern art, most notably, attempts to depict where frame and process meet, where self and other and self and object are intertwined. Merleau-Ponty wrote of "reversibility," "chiasma," and other notions meant to delineate that area where, as João A. Frayze-Pereira has put it, subject and object "imply" and "complement one another." In striving to reveal that zone, modern art gave up the model for the matrix, Frayze-Pereira rightly observed, and, in so doing, "de-centered spectators in relation to themselves and their little world and opened them as their necessary Others, who could behold new dimensions of Being. In this context, body and work of art, artist and viewer, one and an Other are complementary terms, not dichotomies." Merleau-Ponty's phenomenology showed us thinking as incarnate; art shows us that this thinking is not set as subject or object, frame or content; and psychoanalysis displays a similar aesthetic: In its clinical work with transference, "idea and expression, content and form, interior and exterior, subject and object are inseparable" (Frayze-Pereira, 2007, pp. 497–498).

Throughout his career, but especially in the Grid and the ideas expressed in *Transformations* (1965), Wilfred Bion was preoccupied with communicating the interrelation of association and interpretation in psychoanalytic praxis. Seeking to accurately convey the dynamic interaction between analysand and analyst and the change and growth that occur in each as a result of the interactive experience, he compared psychoanalysis to art. The psychoanalytic process aims to wrest verbal meaning, coherent narrative-like links, from the illogical, pictorial images of which dreams and fantasies are made. So striking is its similarity to the visual arts that Bion was led to invoke the latter as the very model for the representation of psychoanalytic experience itself. Even his well-known model of the container-contained was a visual means of relating the idea that parts of the patient are projected into the analyst forming a connection susceptible, via emotional vitality, to growth.

More recently, Edgar Levenson (2003) has described psychoanalytic praxis in terms of "a visual-spatial modality" and defined the basics of that praxis as the square, the plane, the circle, and the helix: The square, Levenson tells us, is the space within which one analytically works while the plane is the horizontal line above which "material is organized, made more coherent, abstracted" and "understood" and below which "material is extended, deconstructed, allowed to branch out, without reference to meaning or clarity of purpose." The cyclical movement from the "present through the transference-countertransference and then to the past and back to the present" is viewed as the circle, and the helix as the process of working-through. The helix is what "reminds the therapist that the praxis consists of revisiting the same material, over and over again, but at a higher level of awareness and with a wider grasp of pattern" (pp. 233, 240). Like Bion's, Levenson's effort is *to image* the subjective and intersubjective experience of psychoanalysis, *to give visual form to what is lived*. But just how "innocent" is the image?

Image as interlocutor

Oscar Wilde, who reportedly said "Life imitates art far more than art imitates life," knew whereof he spoke, although undoubtedly he knew not why. Only recently have the creation of images within the mind, of internal representations on the order of Ms. P.'s, begun to be understood. And it is not surprising that they resemble the formation of the image by the artist, the external representation we view on the canvas, though they underscore the process of artistic creation as fundamentally dialectical, not expressive, as it is my aim in this book to show.

In fact, seeing itself has been said to resemble painting to the extent that a painter, working from life, continually refers to the external world, then to the canvas, back again to the world, and again to the canvas. "Seeing, like painting," philosopher Alva Noë (2004) has written:

> [I]nvolves the temporally extended process of reaching out and probing the scene. The causally sufficient substrate of the production of the picture is surely not the internal states of the painter, but rather the dynamic pattern of engagement among the painter, the scene, and the canvas. Why not say the same thing about seeing? Seeing, on this approach, would depend on brain, body, and world.
>
> (p. 223)

Insofar as how we see is the very paradigm that underlies my thesis of art making as feedback dependent and thereby agency enhancing, let us return for a moment to what seeing entails. Simply if briefly put, vision is a twofold process: There is the transmission to the brain of images perceived by the eye as light passes through the cornea to the lens and then the retina and there is the brain's processing of those images according to pattern recognition. Visual perception, as noted earlier, is not merely a matter of taking in what is present before the eye. Rather, it is the synthesizing by the visual association cortex of very small amounts of data in accordance with the ensemble of information that has already been encoded and is best described as anticipatory. The development of visual acuity in children illustrates the point: If the child's perceptual intake is weak, the brain's processing will be weak and that weak processing of the brain will make for less visual acuity. Suppression by the brain of weakly transmitted imagery, in fact, is a blueprint for the legal determination of blindness (such is the condition called amblyopia), for the development of strong visual acuity requires adequate stimulation of the brain. Input and output are necessary for vision, then, just as they are in painting.

Cézanne's genius resided precisely in his capacity to capture on the canvas the dual process of seeing in its illusory form as unitary, what Merleau-Ponty (1945) termed the "lived perspective" or "indivisible whole" of seeing: "When the overall composition of the picture is seen globally, perspectival distortions are no longer visible in their own right but rather contribute, as they do in natural vision, to the impression of an emerging order, an object in the act of appearing, organizing itself before our eyes" (pp. 64–65). Rendering a scene from life in all its density was for Cézanne to render it in the act of *being perceived*, as "a mass without gaps, a system of colors across which the receding perspective, the outlines, angles, and curves are inscribed like lines of force," a plenitude, a "spatial structure [that] vibrates as it is formed" (p. 65). The plenitude that defines for the viewer the real in a Cézanne still life is the plenitude that defines our perception of the coherent and stable reality of the world. The object is not a rediscovery by the viewer. Rather, in Merleau-Ponty's phenomenological appreciation of Cézanne, the qualities of objects—the defining properties that determine their very feel to the touch—are *seen*, yet we also disambiguate those qualities by previously encoded knowledge, just as we do when perceiving objects in the world (see Saxe & Offen, 2010).

But what of paintings that are not made from life, art that is something other than an abstraction from or emergence of the real—the all-blue, monochromatic paintings of Yves Klein, say, or the non-representational, color-filled canvasses of Mark Rothko? How is seeing paradigmatic of such work? And what, moreover, do Cézanne, Klein, or Rothko have to do with the non-sensory image making (i.e., the internal representation) and the steadfast mental image holding of Ms. P.?

For much of his career, Yves Klein (1928–1962)—sometimes thought of as a neo-Dadaist, but more accurately associated with what the critic Pierre Restany named *Nouveau Réalisme* (mid-20th century France's counterpart to American Pop Art)—worked with a meticulously mixed shade of deep blue. Some of his work (not only canvasses, but human models as well!) was uniformly covered in what came to be called International Klein Blue (IKB) as the artist sought an aesthetic purity of color and texture and annihilated the subject altogether. So too Rothko (1903–1970), in his mature work, purged content from his art leaving the viewer before the shaping of lyrical and ever expansive, however luminous or hazy, hues. In the late 1940s Rothko's blocks of pure color, or "multiforms," began to evolve toward what, from 1949 on, would be paintings devoid of any definable figuration, human or other.

It is all too easy to impose upon the work of Klein or Rothko a way of looking that gratifies our need for meaning, narrative or symbolic. Looking, for instance, psychobiographically at Rothko's late art, one is tempted to see emptiness, the void that may derive from early loss; he did know parental abandonment as a child. One is inclined also to see isolation and withdrawal; attachment was problematic for Rothko throughout his life. And one is disposed to interpreting the deeper tones and the blackening even of his work over time in terms of the preoccupation with tragedy and the despair to which he was prone; following great and persistent torment, he did, after all, finally take his own life. But such "understanding"—approaching the art from outside it, so to speak—is not about *seeing* (by which I mean *visually experiencing*) the work.

Neither, though, is what might be considered approaching it from within, finding meaning through some sort of unembodied, unarticulated symbiotic merging of the spectator's self-state with that presumed to be the artist's. Cohabitation of this sort is nothing short of self-referential reverie, sightlessness in the face of the unacknowledged specificity of the art. With regard to a 1949 painting described by Rothko biographer Dore Ashton (2005) as "an early essay into limitless space, with huge areas of yellow and orange interrupted only by a horizontal red band, in which he had scraped, with the handle of his brush, three horizontal lines," the painter remarked that "most people, upon seeing the bright yellow and red" thought the work "optimistic" (p. 14). (For him it was tragic.) The "undeniably soothing quality" of the pictures is how one critic wrote of the "multiforms" while another observed that, though enveloping, like the transitional object they ultimately leave the viewer very much alone (see Elderfield, 2005; Rich, 2005). Such meaning making tells us more about the viewer than the experiencing of the image at hand.

Perhaps it is from those working in the area of research called "neuroesthetics" that we have the most to learn about what happens when one looks at art, figurative or non-figurative, for however much we "think" a work optimistic, tragic, or anything else, how we respond is less cognitively informed than that. I will return to the neurobiology of aesthetic response in Chapter 7. For the moment, however, it suffices to say that of interest to neuroscientists is our apprehension of the image (object filled or objectless) by the signaling of stored representations brought to awareness (conscious or unconscious) by the expectancy or predictability—motoric and affective—that constitutes visual perception itself.

To say Wilde was right that life imitates art is to recognize that how we see is interpretive from the start and this is precisely the conceptual point made by non-figurative paintings and texts. Research has shown that we are not to conceive of vision as sequential—input followed by interpretation. Rather, interpretation is constituted within the visual system itself; more precisely, in the posing by the image of a fundamental question to the visual cortex concerning its familiarity. The cumulative knowledge (both learned and evolutionary) encoded in the brain links expectancy with perception—meaning that sensory visual perception is inferential and that it is so in response to the inquiry: How known is what is seen? In de-objectifying the image, abstract painting opened for inspection that interrogative process, with the result that seeing itself was rendered communicative.

Consider the grids of Piet Mondrian (1872–1944), which reveal a deliberate inhibition of affect. Unambiguous, ascetic even, his use of color was an aesthetic determination whose achievement was a purity of plasticity undisturbed by the disorder of feeling. Reminiscent of the absolutism Samuel Beckett was after in his "painterly" writing (his stage images were exceedingly "painterly" even if he repeatedly told his muse, the actor Billie Whitelaw, that what he wanted from her was *less* "color"), Mondrian's bold coloration reveals the intelligibility and immediacy of communication that the writer was after in equating, as he did, life itself with the envisioning mind. Indeed, Beckett's reduction of characters to voices and his denial of the symbolic attribution of meaning to objects ("no symbols where none intended" is how Beckett famously ended his novel *Watt*) are about removing what might stand between artist and work and work and viewer obscuring the *communicative seeing of thought*.

Beckett, whose ironic title for the 1965 short prose piece *Imagination Dead Imagine* provides the heading for Part I, once castigated the Viennese symbolist painter Max Klinger for making art that offered "the optical experience post rem." This, the disapproving Beckett wrote in 1937, was "a hideous inversion of the visual process, the eye waiving its privilege" (cited by Maude, 2009, p. 84).[2] The "privilege" to which Beckett referred

2 Pages 84–85 of Maude's intelligent essay stimulated some of my thinking here.

is the kind of *seeing* a painting should afford. It is a seeing devoid of *knowing*, a seeing that offers a visual—as opposed to conceptual—input to which the painter must be attentive in making art, much as the viewer who experiences it. Beckett's own deepest desire as a writer was to find a mode of expression that would leave even the preconceived aside, for increasingly his use of language appeared to him "like a veil that must be torn apart in order to get at the things (or the Nothingness) behind it." To an acquaintance he wrote, "As we cannot eliminate language all at once, we should at least leave nothing undone that might contribute to its falling into disrepute. To bore one hole after another into it, until what lurks behind it—be it something or nothing—begins to seep through; I cannot imagine a higher goal for a writer today." For the most part, it seemed to him that music and painting had already abandoned the "old lazy ways" to which literature clung in its respect for grammar and style. "Is there something paralysingly holy in the vicious nature of the word that is not found in the elements of the other arts?" he went so far as to ask. "Is there any reason why that terrible materiality of the word surface should not be capable of being dissolved, like for example the sound surface, torn by enormous pauses, of Beethoven's seventh symphony, so that through whole pages we can perceive nothing but a path of sounds suspended in giddy heights, linking unfathomable abysses of silence?" In his search for a "literature of the unword," what Beckett was seeking was a means of displaying perception. Dependent upon neither preconception nor received modes of configuration, his ideal is more accurately described as a sensorial apperception, an apprehension by means of the senses that is essentially interrogative. For the image throws into question the relation of the subject (whether artist or reader/viewer) to an objectively "real." What Beckett envisioned was literature as interlocutor, as much music and some visual art had already revealed themselves to be (1984, pp. 172–173, Appendix).

The "privilege" of non-conceptual imaging Beckett found lacking in Klinger is comparable, then, to the concept-less imaging Beckett was after in unworded literature. For, visual or literary, art's legitimacy (its "privilege") resided for him in the absence of inherent meaning. This is a "privilege," however, that comes at a cost, one best defined by the risk the artist, like the viewer, is obliged to take in constituting an image, in giving it meaning: that of being unsettled by the unfamiliar, the strangeness, or peculiarity even, of the unknown. This is the price paid for the truly subjective experience of an image, the experience of being somewhere *between seeing and knowing* (cf. Didi-Huberman, 1990, pp. 5, 120 [trans. 2005]). Cézanne is celebrated for having avoided in his work representation as a re-presentation of the known. The consequence of his daring was precisely an emphasis on seeing versus knowing as a dichotomy inherent within the image itself. Cézanne directed the eye to an essential schism that rendered the provenance of the image as depiction of an a priori reality irrelevant. In so doing, he paved the way for all the minimalist art that followed, about which more later.

But let us return to Ms. P. In her session with Mark Solms, the internal representation of her arm as mobile is illustrative of the very same schism highlighted by a non-representational landscape or still life by Cézanne. At least in part because of the *affective* resonance of her arm perceived as it was in reality, Ms. P. held steadfastly to the visual image of the arm as it no longer was. Clearly, she was compelled to do so by the loss the sight of her immobilized limb implied. Seeing was threatening for not being congruent with the identity Ms. P. assumed in life, with an otherwise sustainable self-image, and the external perception had therefore initially to be denied. Ms. P. *saw* her limb as it now was, but hers was a *troubled seeing*, a seeing constituted of *affective meaning* that inhibited her transition to full awareness and acceptance of her plight. *But just how untroubled is the seeing of any image, one painted or otherwise staged? Does Ms. P.'s disturbed viewing of her arm and need to retain the internal representation over the perception of the real not point to the potential power of the image more generally? Was Ms. P. not thrown into that very same "between" that separates seeing and knowing, the "between" that the creative image as interlocutor implies?*

The viewer of a painting, so too the reader of fiction, habitually seeks to undo the unsettling schism between the sensorially perceived image and the presupposed real by attributing to the image a familiar subject–object relational mode—be it symbolic, iconographic, or other signaling of the known. The aim is to render the image more normative. But why? For no reason other than to render seeing less unsettling. As art historian Georges Didi-Huberman (1992) has insightfully written: "*Donner à voir, c'est toujours inquiéter le voir, dans son acte, dans son sujet. Voir, c'est toujours une opération de sujet, donc une opération refendue, inquiétée, agitée, ouverte*" ("Showing always troubles seeing, in its act, in its subject. Seeing is always the operation of a subject, an operation therefore that is split, troubled, shaken, open"; p. 51; translation mine).

Merleau-Ponty famously wrote of the trope of the hidden and the revealed, the visible and the invisible, that has to do neither with a Kantian metaphysical constraint on the knowable nor an aesthetic constraint on the representable. Rather it relates to Didi-Huberman's (1990–2005) notion of the knowing and not-knowing emanating from the image's presence and virtuality. Indeed, there is a paradox in the image that obliges us to choose between knowing without seeing and seeing without knowing, as Didi-Huberman explains, which is a matter not of an either/or but of tolerating the ambiguity, remaining "in the dilemma, *between knowing and seeing*" (pp. 140, 143). Interestingly, the "between" in its infinite incarnations is also where Philip Bromberg situates the source of all creation—creativity in art and in life: Tolerating differences in self-states involves, for Bromberg, negotiating or "standing in the spaces," which is akin to remaining in the dilemma imposed by the visual image. In life as in art it is a matter of seeking that integrative point of arrival through the dialectical interplay between the real and the imaginary, the known and the fantasy, the symbolized and the enacted.

The method to our madness

In his *Project for a Scientific Psychology*, Freud (1895) outlined his theory of the primary and secondary processes of mentation:

> Wishful cathexis to the point of hallucination [and] complete generation of unpleasure which involves a complete expenditure of defense are described by us as *psychical primary processes*; by contrast, those processes which are only made possible by a good cathexis of the ego, and which represent a moderation of the foregoing, are described as *psychical secondary processes*.
>
> (pp. 326–327)

Seeking direct gratification and in obeisance to the pleasure principle, the primary process was said to operate by the mechanisms of condensation and displacement while the secondary process was subject to the rules of rational and reality-oriented thinking. Until the mid-20th century when a theoretical controversy arose over the extension of the economic view to knowledge more recent than Freud's of dreams and thought processes, the theory of the primary process remained exclusively an economic formulation, the notion of energy cathexis having been integrated into the structural theory introduced in 1923 without its being revised in accordance with the new psychology of ego function (Noy, 1969, p. 155). Pinchas Noy was among those who argued for a broadening of the concept, especially with regard to "the significance of primary processes in art, creativity, culture and many other 'normal functions'" (p. 155).[3]

Questioning the function of the primary process, Noy traced the association of art theory to dream theory to indicate the meaning of primary process for ego functions not restricted to drive mobility. At first, Noy (1969) explained, "the primary processes in art were considered to have the same function as in dreams—to provide the best modes for transforming drive energy in order to discharge it, through the limited channels allowed by the rules of art." Over time, however, "this view of art as a sublimated

3 For details on the controversy and the implications of the revision as undertaken by some, see Noy, 1969, pp. 155–158.

wish-fulfillment changed gradually to the view which regards art as an ego function in the service of ego mastery." The result was the notion that "Artistic and creative activity is an ego activity which operates by primary processes. As this activity is one of the ego activities in the service of mastery, primary processes are used for mastery, i.e. as a part of the synthetic function of the ego" (p. 161).

I cite Noy at length here for the following reason: If the concept of mastery developed from the insufficiency of the initial view of the ego as "an agent whose role is to control drive discharge in consideration of reality and the superego," if the ego came to be viewed as inducing "stressful situations [to] arouse new stimuli" for it to seek to control, then there is an underlying assumption of feedback in the development and activity of ego function that supports my own thinking on art and agency in an important way. "[B]esides its function of solving conflicts," Noy elaborates, "the ego is always active in creating new ones, in order to be forced to solve them again, an activity which is understandable only as an attempt to train and improve its functions of control and synthesis." The ego functions to regulate drive discharge with an eye to reality but it functions as well for the preservation of "self-continuity and identity by assimilating and integrating any new experience or line of action into the self" (p. 161). Noy's cogently argued position is that primary and secondary process differentiation is dependent on "feedback information," a position based on the assumption that the primary processes are not present at birth "but develop gradually out of the immature infant's attempt to organize his perceptual world and integrate his needs within the given environment" (p. 161). And the development of secondary process, then, would be a function of the environmental feed-back organization of the primary process, a notion it is important to stress is not a denial but a broadening of the economic view.

A final citation from Noy should suffice the make the point:

> My assumption is that every artistic talent involves one or several of the primary processes which for some reason begin to send feedback information, which in turn gradually makes possible their reality-oriented monitoring. By this transformation into a feedback-controlled process they are detached from the rest of the primary processes to develop together with all other secondary processes, and so they are finally integrated with, and used as, logical thought processes. This explains what characterizes artistic talent—from the formal aspect it retains the quality of a primary process, but from the aspect of the level of performance, reality-adaptation, and integration with other logical thought processes, it is like a secondary process.
>
> (pp. 164–165)

The principal conclusion to be drawn from Noy's discussion, then, is that art *is* primary process-related, but that displacement, condensation, and symbolization serve *via the action of their meaning upon the self* a function more wide ranging than the sublimation of drive: the enhancement of agency in its managing of identity and self-preservation.

To ask how Ms. P.'s anosognosia is analogous is to ask how it proves right Wilde's quip that "Life imitates art far more than art imitates life." Ms. P. may be said to be defensively avoiding the trauma of her paralysis by that most primitive of psychic mechanisms: denial. Or by dissociating from the self-state whose affective implications are too much for her to bear. But she does so much like the artist who employs the teleological orientation of primary process mentation in the service of ego mastery, of continuity of self, and of agency: That is, she is responsive to the affective meaning of the perceptual feedback—the sight of her physical state—whose implicit meaning is determined by the effect that perceptual input has on her self. What distinguishes primary from secondary process is the self-centeredness of the organization; reality has not yet assumed dominance in the form of the logic of reason, which is not to say that the more primitive form of thinking is devoid of its own logic (cf. Noy, 1969, p. 171).

Yet, as we saw earlier, the meaning ascribed by Ms. P. to the visual perception of her arm is self-oriented in the context of an immediate association with the other. If we view perception as a dynamic process, then the disavowal of the reality of her illness derives from the relational meaning given her exchange with the world. Clinically speaking, Solms was able to make Ms. P. more aware, which is to say accepting, of her plight by negotiating what Bromberg (1998) calls a "consensually constructed interchange between the timelessness of one's internal 'self-truth' and the immediacy of a discrepant, external perception of oneself as seen by an other." Then, and only then, could her situation be given new meaning, however fragile its tenure, and the hope be maintained that with repeated sessions this meaning would be more securely "accommodated into [her] internal dialogue, self-narrative, or unconscious fantasy, whichever phrase one chooses" (pp. 178–179).

I set out in this chapter to explore three principal questions framed by the encounter of Ms. P. with Mark Solms: What is an image? Why might an internal representation take precedence over the actuality of perception? And what do the "what" and the "why" tell us about creativity and the relationship of imagination to the self as agent? What has become clear so far is that imagery is constructed partially from what has been taken in from the external world and partially from what is generated from within. For this reason I introduced the comparability of imaging to seeing, as vision is not merely an encapsulating of the environment but, in its conversion to neural signaling (the vehicle for the functioning of sight), a drawing upon memory and related forms of association (like expectancy) that supplements the bits and pieces of input to fill out the "picture." Imagining, like seeing, in other words, is a feedback process and from this the following is concluded: Memory, association, and expectancy are both biologically plastic and psychologically dynamic in being neurally driven and in implicating cathexis; imaging, therefore, is an inherently *active* phenomenon the principal implication of which is agency.

The neuroscience of creativity supports the notion of imagery as having agency. In the first place, perception itself is intrinsically active. Perceiving is doing and the notion of a passive perceiver is oxymoronic. It is because of our ability, in perceiving, to abstract from things their essential properties "that the imagining of new things is possible" (Kessler, 2010; cf. Llinás, 2001, p. 228). Perceptual illusions, to be sure, reveal the importance of an agent's cognition in the "reading" (or "misreading") of perceptual content (cf. Ben-Ze'ev, 1993, p. 1; Noë, 2004, pp. 3, 12–13).

Second, there appears to be a common neural substrate for perception and visual imagery. Research on motor actions and the relation between motor and visual images has shown that mental imaging entails the processing of both ingoing and outgoing information: Knowledge from outside contributes to the building of representations, but it is the neural structure and biochemical constraints of the brain that determine their expression. Studying the parameters encoded in motor representation (the representation of force and effort in movement and the representation of temporal duration of action) as well as the interaction between signals, Marc Jeannerod (1994, 2003) has identified the relation between the coding of motor actions and their neural representation at different levels of organization and found that sense of agency can be modulated by distorting how action-related signals relate to each other. Much of his work, in fact, has been dedicated to providing evidence for the shared neural correlates of the perceived and the imaged and the agency inherent within them.

Third, internal representation is affectively constituted and it is so not solely on the basis of perception but consciousness. Moreover, current trends in creativity research emphasize the significance of those areas of the brain controlling mood and motivation. The dorsolateral prefrontal cortex, for instance, has been shown to be engaged during problem solving and creativity and magnetic stimulation to this region has shown an increase in creative function. Neurotransmitters—the molecules that mediate the transmission of chemicals in the brain—are also a focus of interest with regard to creative thinking and aesthetic experience. Critic Norman Holland (2009) has advanced the idea that creativity has to do with a decrease in norepinephrine insofar as inspiration and creative insight appear to involve the very states of mind for which such a decrease is responsible (Heilman, 2005). So, too, Richard Kessler (2010) has noted that creativity "is associated with lower pre-frontal arousal (attention) and cognitive control and lower levels of noradrenaline and dopamine."

Imagery has agency, then, because images—in art no less than in our internal representational world—are real in being not only in existence but performative: Rothko (2004) proclaimed art "action," observing that when art "enters the environment it produces its effects just as any other form of action does" (p. 10). Erich Fromm described creativity as "the ability to see (and to be aware) and to respond" (cited by Anderson, 1959, p. 6). My contention in this volume is that responsivity—the constituting of meaning—is a neglected determinant in the literature on imagination and, furthermore, that it is the very determinant of aesthetic and therapeutic growth that renders them alike. It is also, however, what underlies the delusional convictions in psychopathology (a matter to be treated in Chapter 6). A phrase from *Imagination Dead Imagine* gives pause: "all white in the whiteness." Restoring it to its full context, however, we visualize with the author the imaginative process itself, that without which there is no mind: "Islands, waters, azure, verdure, one glimpse and vanished, endlessly, omit. Till all white in the whiteness the rotunda" (p. 182). When we speak of the mentally disabled we say they have lost their mind. What we mean is that they have lost their reason. But reason is not synonymous with mental function: Imaging is. This is Beckett's point.

The challenge of this chapter has been to illustrate that perceptions are meaningful in and of themselves because they are dynamic and immediately imaginative. Whether construed as neural re-presentations or as phenomena that are not necessarily re-presentational at all, images and imagery, the *sine qua non* of imagining, are visual and motoric embodiments of perceptual stimuli, and what give imagination form. So as to more fully investigate the potential of imagination for self-empowerment, for greater awareness and personal strength, I turn now to that form: the rhythm and structure of imagination we frame in fantasy.

2

THE PHENOMENOLOGY OF FANTASY

"No trace anywhere of life, you say, pah, no difficulty there, imagination not dead yet, yes, dead, good, imagination dead imagine." The meaning of the opening passage of Beckett's text is seemingly simple: The death of imagination, synonymous with life, is unimaginable. The form that supports that meaning, however, is resolutely complex—syntactically, paradigmatically, and syntagmatically. And what expresses the writer's fantasy of the unimaginable is precisely the aesthetic structure. It is in the finding of structure that the Sisyphean task of making art resides. Indeed, many an artist has described the anguish the giving of form to fantasy, or even to the perception of external reality, may entail: Van Gogh's desire to capture either what he felt before the cypresses he viewed in St. Rémy or their own essential reality was of such intensity he despaired greatly of his limitations as an artist (cf. Charles & Telis, 2009). The impossibility of duplicating his visual experience in his art so haunted Giacometti that he suffered severe anxiety as he worked. At times he even felt the object of his perception to be disappearing and feared being left with an empty canvas as a result (see Oppenheim, 2000, pp. 148–155). "[T]here is nothing to express, nothing with which to express, nothing from which to express, no power to express, no desire to express, together with the obligation to express" Beckett (1970, p. 103) famously wrote of making art in his *Three Dialogues with Georges Duthuit*.

Psychoanalytic praxis is similar in that its aesthetic structure, like that of art an organizer of sensory experience, also struggles to remain concealed. As described by Edgar Levenson, the "inquiry into [the] private aesthetic structure" that is psychoanalysis is an inquiry into a "private myth," one analogous to the "melodic line," "the sequential patterning of events (notes)," that is "played out" in the life of the patient and manifested in treatment. Psychoanalysis is by nature highly creative and has much to do with the making of art and art's concretizing of reality in imagining, in fantasies having bearing on the self. In fact, psychoanalysis is conditional upon the same paradox that is the very measure of the existence of art: In revealing, the work of art reveals itself as revelatory; in enlightening, it is artistic process that is itself enlightened (see Garelli, 1966, p. 9). So, too, in effecting change the analytic process displays the very conditions upon which therapeutic change depends. That is to say that in the interaction of analyst and analysand the myth or "melodic line" is unveiled as psychoanalysis' own operative mode is unveiled as well. But how? Simply put, the myth becomes accessible, and only over time, as the analyst *either resists the fantasy exhibited in the transference so as to correct the distortion of reality that fantasy implies or enters the fantasy to effect a change from within* (see Levenson, 2005, pp. 40–41). I would posit that distinction as the most salient to make between the classical and post-classical (or relational) clinical perspectives. And I believe it is that differentiation that leads us to contemplate a post-Freudian understanding of the creative act. But before we explore creativity in that context, before we investigate what the notion of creativity as relational and non-sublimatory might look like, we need to delimit what we mean by fantasy; we need to inquire as to its origin and location and ask what the phenomenology of its structure is.

Where fantasy resides (or the unconscious in "unconscious fantasy")

Levenson (2005) has claimed, with characteristic eloquence, that "fantasies grow in the soil of omission: what is not known is imagined. What is half-known is embellished" (p. 25). Another way of saying this, albeit less lyrically, is that fantasy is the experience of imagination in action. The classical view of fantasy is that its impetus lies in the instinctual drives whose source is the body. Drives appear as representations in the mind distorted by defensive mechanisms determined by the degree of satisfaction associated with the fulfillment of wish. In other words, psychic representations of somatic drive constituted wishes for Freud and fantasies are thus understood in this context as the cognitive seeking of wish fulfillment, the mental satisfaction of those very stimuli responsible for homeostasis. While the character of fantasy is influenced by development, conflict, and the strength and diffusion of its libidinal (and aggressive) motivation, the yield of fantasy, simply put, is gratification (see Abrams, 1984, pp. 83–94).

In keeping with Freud's topology, we would say that fantasy is preconscious ideation, neither perceptually verifiable nor the result of accurate remembrance of the past or reasonable anticipation of the future. In being preconscious, however, it retains both a descriptive and a dynamic relation with the unconscious, a topographical sense and a quality of latency in that it is easily accessible to conscious awareness. In fact, Freud linked the preconscious with the ego, saying they are as intimately connected as the id and the unconscious. Writing of the preconscious state he claimed late in his life "to have found that processes in the unconscious or in the id obey different laws from those in the preconscious ego" (1938, pp. 163–164), the former constituting the primary process, the latter the secondary process with which it is contrasted. Thus when the mental activity that is fantasy evades all influence of secondary process thinking, and by way of regression yields to the primary process alone, it is no longer an act in (or of) the imagination, but a belief held by the subject and dealt with as though in (or of) reality (see Schafer, 1968, pp. 37–38). It is then that the threshold into delusional thinking has been crossed.

Yet "fantasy," a term whose meaning was most famously first thrown into question with the "Controversial Discussions" of 1943 and 1944 when the compatibility of Melanie Klein's perspective on psychoanalysis with Freud's own was deliberated, is commonly used conjointly with "unconscious" and as such has long been a core concept of psychoanalytic thinking and practice. More precisely, it dates to Freud's (1897) oft-cited letter to his friend and confessor, Wilhelm Fleiss, in which he abandoned his seduction theory in favor of symbolic fantasy as the origin of neurosis (pp. 259–260). Although he never devoted a paper or book to it, and although he himself was not always consistent in his use of the term, the concept of unconscious fantasy remained central to Freud's thinking insofar as it denoted a universal disposition to wish-fulfilling mental activity occurring with the frustration of instinctual drive.

Over time, the concept has become increasingly vague. Klein (who distinguished unconscious from conscious fantasy and relied on the *ph* spelling to emphasize the ubiquity and intensity of such mentation, its inherence in all mental growth and psychic function) extended Freud's use of the term to underscore the symbolic representation of instinctual urges. Others have placed greater emphasis on the resolution of conflict. Jacob Arlow, for example, stressed the compromising function of such fantasies with regard to residual childhood conflict, and Jacques Lacan, speaking of the linguistic structure of the unconscious, stressed the narrative of loss and desire inherent within them.

Today unconscious fantasy endures as a slippery construct, one rendered all the more imprecise by the self-psychological, object-relational, and myriad other perspectives on what Freud considered universal themes (such as the primal scene and the family romance, about which more later). Still considered by many essential to the understanding of psychological development, the understanding of psychopathology, and the etiology of creative expression, the usefulness of the construct for treatment has nonetheless increasingly been deemed suspect by some in the relational arena who take to task the idea that unconscious fantasy accounts for much of our behavior and feelings.

Indeed, if the mind is conceived not in accordance with the intrapsychic and drive-determined thinking on which Freud and Klein based their however differing theories of unconscious fantasy, but rather with the view that it is relationally constituted, the usefulness of the construct is effectively weakened. While its authenticity is not denied, its value for the conceptualization of mental function and therapeutic change is. Those adhering to the classical perspective strive to uncover the unconscious fantasies affecting, as Sander Abend (2008) puts it, "a host of symptoms, mood, character traits, and other clinical manifestations" and esteem "the finding that mental functions like perception, memory, thinking, judgment, and reality testing are all influenced by unconscious fantasy function." That their accession is so difficult is evidence enough for the classical analyst of the early repression and powerful influence of these fantasies (pp. 128, 119). Those without allegiance to dual-drive theory and to the mental topography that retained its significance for Freud despite his 1923 shift to the structural model, however, are more and more re-evaluating the centrality of unconscious fantasy in psychoanalytic theory and practice.

Alan Sugarman (2008), for one, has sought to disqualify the significance of interpreting the hidden content of unconscious fantasy as traditionally conceived in favor of recognizing the value of the *process* of fantasizing itself. Claiming the concept of unconscious fantasy no longer relevant to psychoanalytic thinking and working as we know them today, he views fantasizing as a means of developing insightfulness and argues that it is regaining the capacity to fantasize, a function that may be trumped by trauma or conflict if not constitutional limitations, that promotes therapeutic change. So, too, Samuel Gerson (2008) deems the concept of unconscious fantasy as such incompatible with the direction in which psychoanalysis has moved in recent years. But rather than repositioning the analytic focus away from content onto process, he has reflected on the notion from a developmental perspective. Gerson redefines the origin and locus of fantasy as an unconscious shared by mother and infant and has illustrated its structure and content in terms of a narrative re-presentation of that dyad's earliest interpersonal events. Alluding to the differences in meaning of "unconscious" in contemporary psychoanalytic theory from the Freudian era—the actuality of any relationship, he explains, has its own unconscious—and also the implications of the relational perspective for the psychology of the individual, he affirms that:

> Just as we do not study or treat individuals as isolated specimens living independent lives and unaffected by their cultural and interpersonal surrounds, so we must always wonder how it is possible for an unconscious phantasy to exist in an independent mind, unaffected by the other's presence and the reciprocal influences they exert on one another.
>
> (pp. 163–164)

But it is perhaps Philip Bromberg who most explicitly calls into question the usefulness of unconscious fantasy as a clinical concept. The notion of "unconscious fantasy" is not only misguided as Bromberg sees it but fundamentally illusory, for it is un-symbolized affect—not fantasy—that is the raw material of change and fantasy is necessarily a *conscious* mental process in that it is a *symbolization of affective experience in narrative form*. In "'Grown-up' words: An interpersonal/relational perspective on unconscious fantasy," Bromberg (2008a) does not go so far as to reject the "heuristic power" of the concept, but he acknowledges that power only if the notion of "symbolized thought (a daydream) that is repressed in the mind of one person" is relinquished in favor of what he describes as "a coconstructed dissociated experience" (p. 140). In the clinical setting, he explains, the experiential and co-constructed nature of unconscious fantasy is revealed in the light of what constitutes psychic change: Therapeutic action is predicated upon the transition from unprocessed affect to self-reflective insight, a transition that occurs through enactment, an externalization of the relational essence of selfhood whose origin resides in the repudiation of one or another self-state from awareness:

> The ability of different parts of the self to recognize other parts as me is always relative. Consequently, reality (me) for one part of the self will be fantasy (not-me) to another part. What we call "unconscious" will depend on which part of self has access to consciousness at that moment.
>
> (p. 135)

While differences between the classical and post-classical views on the clinical usefulness of fantasy are indeed relevant to our theoretical understanding of imagination, the process of fantasizing itself subsumes other, more fundamental questions: namely, the structure of fantasy and the fantasy of structure as well as the nature of the reality against which fantasy is habitually juxtaposed. For while fantasy, deemed conscious, preconscious, or unconscious, is real in its narrative projection of thinking and feeling, there is also, of course, a sense in which it is imaginary (perhaps best termed a "real imaginary"), which necessitates inquiring as well into the nature of reality as universally and objectively known.

The structure of fantasy/the fantasy of structure

In the biographies of few men and women are the topics of knowing, truth, and fantasy more explicitly intertwined than that of Leonardo da Vinci. We are familiar, in his study of the artist, with Freud's assessment of Leonardo's childhood memory of a vulture coming to the infant in his cradle and opening his mouth with its tail while striking the tail against the child's lips (1910, p. 82). The analyst deemed this not a memory as such but a fantasy constructed from a memory, a fantasy imagined by Leonardo at a later time and then transposed to his infancy. The fantasy serves as the starting point for Freud's reconstruction of the memory it contains, the motivations that subsequently led to its distortion, and the unraveling of Leonardo's childhood as it relates to his later work.[1] In this pathography, however, special attention is paid the artist's "love of truth" and "thirst for knowledge," which are said to be sublimated libidinal curiosity (p. 130).

In brief, Freud argues that memories are not readily distinguishable from fantasies and that the analysis of Leonardo's vulture memory as a fantasy from a later time shows this to be so. The fantasy is said to reveal the tail as the male organ and the vulture's opening the child's mouth and beating of his tail inside it reveals an act of fellatio concealing a memory of the artist's being suckled at the breast by his mother. Freud then links the fantasy that is constructed from the core memory to an essential component of the artist's development: The absence of his father. Spending his early years with his mother alone provoked in the child an intense brooding and a concomitant need to understand how babies are made and the father's connection to their origin. Leonardo was later to suspect a connection between his scientific investigations and his childhood and he himself proclaimed that his treatise on the flight of birds, a study undertaken in the effort to build a mechanical flying machine, emanated from the vulture's visit to his cradle in infancy. As Freud demonstrates, these inquiries (which produced a detailed analysis of the mechanics of flight and the effects of wind on the flying of birds) derived even more directly from the sexual investigations of Leonardo's childhood.

Freud's interest, then, surpasses the sublimatory process as illustrated in the paintings of Leonardo, where "the smile of bliss and rapture which had once played on his mother's lips as she fondled him" reappears on the faces of Leda, John the Baptist, Bacchus, St. Anne, and, of course, the Mona Lisa on whose face "the promise of unbounded tenderness" is ambiguously coupled with the "sinister menace" of a woman deprived of the affections of her husband (pp. 117, 115). His preoccupation centers perhaps more closely even on the "fateful" compulsion, as Freud termed it, to create paintings and then care for them no longer, as his father had created and then abandoned him in the illegitimacy of his birth. For a second sublimation took control when the inhibitions in his sexual life were no longer sufficiently sublimated in his art, that is, when he lost a patron substitute for his father and a regression to his infantile past overtook the conditions of his present: "The development that turned him into an artist at puberty was overtaken by the process which led him to be an investigator … at first still in the service of his art, but later independently of it and away

1 See Harold Blum's (2001) excellent study of this paper.

from it." Important here is that what replaced the making of art, the search for knowledge and truth in scientific research, "seems to have contained some of the features which distinguish the activity of unconscious instincts—insatiability, unyielding rigidity and the lack of an ability to adapt to real circumstances" (pp. 121, 133).

Five years prior to this paper of 1910, Freud had written (in *Three Essays on the Theory of Sexuality*) of the "instinct for knowledge or research," an instinct aimed first, even before the question of the distinction between the sexes, at knowing where babies come from (p. 194). Others too have spoken of the "knowledge drive," as both Novalis and Ludwig Feuerbach called it, in terms of the primacy of drive. For Feuerbach, it is the certainty of the attainability of truth that motivates the search for knowing, itself a source of mental satisfaction and thereby happiness. Knowledge, moreover, is for him a means to agency. Feuerbach's linking of the drive to know (the search for truth) to both agency and happiness is strikingly close to Freud's conceptualization by virtue both of the pleasure inherent with it and the control and ownership it brings. For Freud as for Feuerbach, moreover, an essential component of the drive for knowledge is the derivative nature of the forms it assumes in reality: Psychoanalysis itself is first an exploration of the unconscious and only secondarily a therapeutic measure (see Blumenberg, 1983, pp. 446–447). But what does this tell us of the structure of fantasy?

The drive to know is a primitive need to represent what is absent, to fill in what is not there, and as a process of imagining it gives rise to many forms, one of which is fantasy. Dreams, ideas, concepts, and images are among the other forms the instinct for knowledge may take, but all exist not in opposition to reality (I will talk more about the unreal below), but as a means of adaptation to it (cf. Beres, 1960, p. 327). Indeed, fantasy—one form taken by "knowledge drive"—subsumes an awareness of reality and a desire to correct it. Its many functions, the innumerable dynamic services it renders, range from the reduction of anxiety and the maintenance of psychic stability to the guarantee of pleasure, the renewal of a damaged self-esteem, and a defense against conflict (see Abrams, 1984, p. 85). Its structure, however, is where the greater complexity of fantasy lies: It may be more or less developed along a narrative line and its cognitive (as distinct from affective) component may be difficult to disentangle from obsessive, stream of consciousness, or other kinds of mentation.

A close analysis of imagining as a process that gives rise to fantasy has been undertaken by Edward Casey. While the details of that study need not to be reiterated here, the broad parameters are worthy of mention, including the notion that, of the three modes of imagining studied by Casey in depth—imaging, imagining-that, and imagining-how—the first has sensory qualities (visualized and/or audialized); the second, which may or may not be sensory, may be particularly difficult to differentiate from intellection when not in sensory form; and the third (which also may be sensory or not) implies a notion of "personal agency" not implicated by the other two (1976a, pp. 40–48). Yet the features of fantasy as outlined elsewhere by Casey inform us even more comprehensively of its structure: Narrative, participatory, wayward, wish fulfilling, and thetic are those he astutely describes (1976b, pp. 19–25). The first is its storytelling aspect; the second, the engagement of the fantasist in the story; the next, the degree of control over the story exercised by the fantasist; the penultimate, the gratification the fantasy affords him; and, finally, the element of persuasion, the idea that while we know the scene not to be "empirically or externally real," we accord it a "*psychological* right" to exist within the mind.

But Casey goes further than this: He contrasts each of the structural features of fantasy with imagination and here is where I disagree. Fantasy "has a tendency to border on *hallucination* on the one hand and on *imagination* on the other," he tells us (1976b, p. 18). Yet hallucination is *not* to be conceived as fantasy gone astray, for hallucinatory experience *is* perceptual despite the absence of a stimulus. Similarly, fantasy does *not* convert to imagination as in daydreams or reveries, as Casey would have us believe, for it may be synonymous with daydream when fully localized in conscious awareness. While he is right to note the inherently non-narrative and episodic nature of imaginings, moreover (Freud distinguished the unstructuralized impulses from the more organized psychic content of fantasy; see Inderbitzin & Levy, 1990, p. 116), this is primarily a matter of semantics that, unlike the rest of his analysis, wears thin. Indeed, I would argue that fantasy, *as a kind of imagining* (and in this akin both to play and daydreaming), is always and already *an experience of the imagination*. This becomes more obvious when we consider fantasy as embodied within an individual's psychic structure.

In the clinical setting, the internal experience of a patient is invariably understood in accordance with the theoretical persuasion of the analyst. Consequently, fantasies—whose uniqueness is as particular to an individual as those with universal themes are common to all humankind are inevitably viewed as structured in a way that conforms to the language of that persuasion: The ego psychologist will emphasize body ego, defense, and compromise formations; the contemporary Kleinian will speak of internalized objects, projective identification, and the paranoid-schizoid and depressive positions; the self-psychologist will look to the vulnerabilities of self-experience; while the Lacanian will seek the linguistic-like symbolic underpinnings of the fantasy formation (see Rudden, 2008). Nonetheless, interpretation of the adaptive and/or defensive functions is the ultimate objective of the analytic work with fantasy, conscious or unconscious. Freud's demonstration of the family romance, for example, demonstrates how the child's imagination may aim to better what is critically perceived as an unsatisfactory reality with regard to the status of his parents, yet simultaneously express nostalgia for the lost paradise of the child's earliest years when his parents were overvalued and exalted. The aim, in other words, is to adapt to the changes that later phases of development impose on the maturing subject. Withdrawal into oneself by way of what has been called the "secret cocoon," the fantasy of a covert hiding place within the self, however, may serve the adaptive purpose of integration and enhancement of autonomy—the cocoon being a container for the self—or it may be a defensive strategy of protection against real or paranoiac threats, or overwhelming stimulation, from the environment. It may be dissociative and serve both defensively and adaptively in protecting the self from its own overwhelming affect. The content of the cocoon fantasy, as Roy Schafer (2008) has indicated, may be "a self-generating womb, that is, an instance of the omnipotent myth of auto-creation," "compensatory remnant of merger with an idealized mother's womb or her embracing arms and kisses," or an "anally conceived ... armed fortress or walled prison." The fantasy, in other words, has both bodily and relational themes that define its structure.

The structure of fantasy, however, is not to be confused with the structuralizing power of fantasy. Insofar as fantasies bear heavily upon the organization of psychic reality, influence experience, behavior, and perception, and are determinative of subsequent pathologies and adaptations, they serve a strongly structuralizing purpose. This is to say that however useful or not the concept may be considered for clinical work, we know that the unconscious fantasies of childhood play a strong and lasting role in adult mental life (Inderbitzin & Levy, 1990, pp. 126–127). In fact, fantasies are unique in both constituting and altering the organization of the psyche. At the same time, however, neither from the internal structure of fantasy, from its phenomenology, nor from the structuralizing force of fantasy, in other words, the effect of fantasy on psychic organization, is it a great leap to the very fantasy of structure itself.

Undoubtedly, the most significant and complex mental structure is the "self." If it is our personal agent, the experiencer of our subjectivity, it is also the one objectified in our discourse on the subjectivity of that inner experience. Thus the self is the beneficiary of wishful fantasy and the fantisizer bestowing the benefits. Psychoanalysis exemplifies this conflation of subject and object in the entity we term the "self" to the extent, on the one hand, that observer and subject of the observation are one and the same and, on the other, that the analyst himself is observer even as he enters the subjective field of the analysand. The analyst, the analysand, and the therapeutic process all display an inherent tension between subject and object that renders psychoanalysis dynamic. William Grossman (1982) believed this tension to be intrinsic to any theory of self and that theory of fantasy shows the structure of self to be but a fantasy: "As a fantasy, the details of the 'self' may be elaborated, distorted, re-represented, repressed, and otherwise defended against. In short, it may be conscious or unconscious. As the mental representation of the person as his own object, the 'self' includes some representation of the person's mind." It is a structure, a construct, that is a fantasized entity, Grossman maintains, with its own content as agent, as place, as the object of reference, and so forth. "Self depends on a person's view of himself, which from a psychoanalytic point of view means it is a fantasy" (Grossman, 1982, pp. 928, 929). Is one to conclude, then, that it is unreal?

Fantasy and reality

Fantasy may be characterized by its dynamic similarity to play: Like play, it expresses wishes, enacts their fulfillment, and is aware of its own unreality (Neubauer, 1987, p. 8). But what does it mean for fantasy to be unreal? Clearly, it is in existence and thereby real. Is its unreal aspect, then, the same as being untrue or something else? Robert Michaels has told of a situation in which a patient recounted a childhood dream that had recently recurred. Michaels' interpretation was greeted with rapid confirmation and all proceeded apace until the patient related that he had never had the dream. To this the analyst simply replied, "So what?" Whether the dream was fabricated at night or in the session was all the same to him; the interpretation of the content would remain the same (Colombo, 2008, p. 621). What changed with the revelation was that the dream was "in reality" a fantasy. The fantasy itself—that there has been a dream—was unreal for being untrue while what occurred *in* the dream was false for its lack of conformity to the external world.

Philosophers tend to rely on two opposing kinds of criterion with regard to truth, correspondence and coherence. Correspondence theory finds truth in the congruence between a proposition and external reality. Coherence theory locates it in the continuity of narrative explanations of that proposition. The first, which originated with certain of the classical Greek philosophers including Aristotle and Socrates and found favor in the medieval formula of truth as *adaequatio intellectus ad rem* (truth as the adequation of intellect to thing), is grounded in realism: Truth is determined by the accuracy of a statement as it relates to the world. The second, which does not presuppose the existence of an objectively knowable reality as does correspondence theory, is associated with metaphysical idealism of the sort espoused by Kant and Hegel.

Speaking of truth in relation to clinical psychoanalysis, Charles Hanly (2009) finds fault with coherence for requiring "that all the hypotheses of a given theory are mutually consistent one with the others." He rightly notes that "just as arguments can be valid without being sound because the truth of the conclusions depends upon the truth of the premises, so a theory can be logically consistent without being true." Moreover, while a theory must be coherent to be true, its coherence is not what renders it so: "If coherence were a sufficient and adequate criterion of truth, it would follow that the loss of reality in neurosis and psychosis would necessarily involve incoherence but it does not." Psychotic individuals, for example, may have severe perceptual impairments without impairment of "the logical functions of the mind required for coherent thinking" (pp. 364, 365). Thus Hanly subscribes to the criterion of correspondence which—unlike coherence, a necessary but insufficient condition for a belief or idea to be true—is both necessary and sufficient.

But correspondence theory, in Hanly's (1990) description, is based on a correlation of truth with objectivity as evidenced by a total absence of ambiguity:

> Even when a patient is filling the hour with reports of manifest dream contents to the exclusion of associations, the details of the material are clear and determinate. There is nothing indefinite or illusive about it. Of course, it is unintelligible and uninterpretable in the absence of associations; but this fact has itself an obvious interpretation. The patient is anxiously clinging to the manifest dream content.
>
> (p. 379)

And correspondence theory is based on the correlation of truth with objectivity as evidenced in stability: "Vagueness and uncertainty are themselves determinate states of affairs that have an explanation. They are not characteristic qualities of mental contents and states as such. The same is true of fantasies, memories, character traits, etc." (p. 379). Coherence theory, meanwhile—in assuming the possibility of multiple explanations of a given reality, in locating truth in cogency, in the simultaneous justifiability of varying accounts by virtue of their constancy of purpose and narrative consistency—gives credence to the subjective constitution of the real. Shifts in subjectivity, while they in no way alter material reality, do alter the psychic reality with which it is contrasted.

Astrophysicist Piet Hut (1999) has offered the following personal anecdote in which he describes such a shift in his "subjective" experience of the "objective" world:

> When I got my first camera, I noticed something very interesting. After an intensive period of picture taking, the streets of my familiar small town had somehow landed in a different world. I saw everything in a different light. More accurately, I saw the world as light, rather than as matter. My attention had shifted,

> first rather innocently from seeing a lit-up *building* to seeing a *lit-up* building.
>
> (p. 241)

Here, though, is another, albeit more complex, illustration of how Hut "plays" with external reality to illustrate just how perceptually (that is, subjectively) alterable it is, while in "truth" not being alterable at all: Hold a pen at a reasonable viewing distance, he advises, and move it closer and then further away. What will be observed is that the "perceived size" of the object, which gets smaller and larger, will differ from the "felt size" that will remain unchanged. Accordingly, we conclude with Hut that there are two types of pen: the apparent pen, whose size is relative to the distance from which it is viewed, and the "real" pen, assumed to be of stable size and equal in appearance to all who view it. But would it not be more accurate to conclude, Hut wonders, that there are truly three pens at hand? There is the pen of variable size according to the distance from which it is viewed, the "real" pen that is felt to be invariable in size, and then there is the "really real" pen, the only one that is objectively the same to all who come into contact with it, "the pen that that can be talked about, handed over, borrowed and forgotten-to-be-given-back; the pen that can be analyzed physically and chemically and described in scientific equations of various sorts." The first two pens are the pens of subjective experience; the third is not subject to interpretation of any sort. And yet, Hut finds even more pens that just those three: The pen we believe to be the "really real" pen when we close our eyes is also a pen to be reckoned with. Though we no longer see it, undeniably there is this pen that Hut calls the "convinced-to-be-there pen" and the pen of conviction is clearly not the same as the pen objectively known to exist. So now there are four: "the apparent pen, the seen-and-felt-as-real one, the assumed-to-be-there one which remains as a conviction when we close our eyes, and there is the objective pen, that others can agree upon." The first three are all subjectively experienced; only the fourth may be posited as objectively present. Hut, however, is not satisfied with four: Indeed, he goes further in distinguishing between the objective pen made of metal and plastic and the pen the scientist would see as an ensemble of atoms and molecules. Even the pen of the scientist can be divided into more:

> There is the pen of the solid-state physicist, describing its molecular structure. There is the pen of the nuclear physicist, describing the properties of the nuclei and the electrons that are the building blocks of the molecules. There is the pen of the particle physicist, who sees the nuclei as made up out of a bunch of quarks and gluons. And so on.
>
> (p. 243)

But here's the point: *Which pen is "real"? Or are they all real, but not in the same way? Or, maybe, as Hut asks, are some of them more real than others? Do the "less real" pens have some degree of imagination mixed into them?*

The question of greater or lesser amounts of reality in relation to fantasy is relevant to the question of truth in psychoanalysis on several fronts: the patient's revelations, the analyst's interpretations, and the relation of historical fact to psychic meaning in reconstruction, to name but the three most obvious. But there are alternative ways of thinking about truth in the psychoanalytic setting that do not rely on a concept of reality either as perceptually constituted or as a stable given. Two come immediately to mind, each of which weakens not only the subjectivity–objectivity schism, but the dichotomy of truth and falsity as well. Each allows for greater discernment of the complexity of the relation between fantasy and reality than such dichotomous thinking affords. I refer to the postmodern notion of truth as illusionary and the pre-Socratic concept truth as disclosedness (*aletheia*).

It has been suggested by philosopher Richard Rorty (1997) that the "term" postmodern be gotten rid of: "It's one of these terms that has been used so much that nobody has the foggiest idea what it means. It means one thing in philosophy, another thing in architecture and nothing in literature" (p. 2). And in psychoanalysis? For Jacques Derrida, the founder of the postmodern approach to the decoding of meaning known as deconstruction, psychoanalysis manifests the same resistance to that decoding evident in every field. But the resistance to the interpretation of meaning that is built into the therapeutic action of the psychoanalytic process itself is theoretically felicitous in its reflection of the illusoriness of meaning as singular and truthful: In other words, interpretation of resistance, a *sine qua non* of that process, is itself interpretable as is that interpretation and so on. Just as the unitary quality of meaning and its singularity of origin are the focus of the deconstructive effort whatever the realm of inquiry, in a postmodern view of psychoanalysis any search for *the* origin of meaning is dismantled in favor of the origin of an origin which originates in yet another to render analysis interminable. Psychoanalysis for the postmodernist involves, by definition, not only the complexity of origination, however, but the dissemination and engagement of meaning with other meanings in other spheres of investigation: "Resistance," for example, is a notion pregnant with political and historical implications (especially in France!). In short, the postmodern is defined in psychoanalysis, as it is elsewhere, by indeterminacy; it is the experience of undoing or decreating meaning as opposed to the totalizing endeavor of establishing it as fixed and unchanging. *It is a view of psychoanalytic process as a move away both from the absolute presence of objectivity that is assumed by the theory of correspondence and from the homogeneity of coherence.*

I have said that in resisting the fullness of meaning identified with the modernist project (Freud's own), deconstruction necessarily also resists the binary oppositions of subjective and objective and truth and falsity, byproducts of modern (Enlightenment) philosophy's emphasis on reason. How does it do this? One way is by taking reality for a social construction, the shared point of departure for the many and varied voices in contemporary relational psychoanalysis. If reality is not independent of us, an objective given that precedes and succeeds us, no essential truths are to be uncovered outside those we co-create by our interpersonal relations. Furthermore, as Donnel Stern (1997) has noted, "if there is no one thing to know, there can be no one way of knowing. Methods of knowing, too, are social constructions, and therefore imbued with unexamined assumptions and biases, so that no method or technique can be trusted as the road to truth" (p. 8). Glenn Larner (n.d.) concurs: "The spirit of reason ceaselessly analyses and leaves no space for the absence of meaning, for not-knowing, for a being with, a waiting for meaning to happen in dialogic encounter with the other." The spirit of reason and the authority it spawns leaves no room then for what is at the heart of relational psychoanalysis.

Stern's well-drawn argument regarding "unformulated experience"—that there is a kind of mentation "characterized by lack of clarity and differentiation" that lies in the unarticulated domain that awaits conceptualization, articulation, and understanding—would appear to be quintessentially postmodern. Yet there is this: The principle conclusion at which postmodernism arrives is that experience is fundamentally linguistic (while not necessarily verbal). After all, the premise of Lacan's contribution to the poststructuralist psychoanalytic enterprise, as we know, was the idea that the unconscious was structured like language. And the notion of "unformulated," which is to say chaotic, experience in no way conforms to the Lacanian paradigm. But Stern's interest is in the meaning of understanding itself, or hermeneutics, where what language stands for differs dramatically from the poststructuralist conception, however postmodern the two perspectives may be: "For poststructuralists, language is not a means of representation," he informs us, but "an arbitrary circuit of symbols that serve compelling impersonal and suprapersonal aims." For hermeneutists, however, language "maintains a representational function" and, moreover, "to take a linguistic perspective is to take one of the myriad valid (and sometimes contradictory) views that might be taken, so that no single person, and no historical epoch, can ever formulate anything like a full picture of reality" (p. 11). Therein lies Stern's distinctly postmodern perspective. It also resides in that "not-knowing" for which the spirit of reason has no tolerance. Relationalists even go so far as to speak of the pre-reflective experience of "sort-of-knowing," a state of implicit relational interaction that, when lacking for too long a cognitive formulation, may lead in the analytic setting to enactment. Sort-of-knowing differs from "knowing" and "not-knowing" in being at least partially dissociative (Bromberg, 2008c). Nonetheless, like the more explicit but not unambiguous experiences of "knowing" and "not-knowing," it bears the unmistakable mark of deconstructionist uncertainty. In so doing, it too evades the dualities entailed by the modernist truth-defining project.

Two additional concepts pertinent to a consideration of postmodernism and psychoanalysis deserve mention here: the *après-coup* and "decentered listening" (or "listening to listening") as they are discussed in the context of their interconnectedness by Haydée Faimberg (see, in particular, 2005, 1997; Faimberg & Corel, 1990). Unlike Stern, Faimberg is a conflict theorist, but one who nevertheless works, as does he, on the level of a deep dyadic intersubjectivity. Indeed, her perspective is no more based on the correspondence between psychic and material reality than his or that of any of his compatriots in the interpersonal or relational realms, any notion of objectivity deriving for them solely from within the intersubjective relation. But the Freudian concept of construction clearly informs her work in a way not relevant to relational praxis. That is to say that construction, which is never a reconstruction as the subject's past is not ever really known, is the frame within which Faimberg works, but it is also a frame with a non-classical edge: She makes a clear distinction between information and historicity to overcome the risk of solipsism that arises from the adherence to the reconstructive effort. And, arguing that construction is both retroactive and anticipatory (as indicated by the very structure of the *après-coup*, Freud's *Nachträglichkeit*, the allocation of new meaning subsequent to the fact), she shows that it is in the accession to psychic truths, as distinguished from the Truth as a singular and essential constituent of the materially and objectively real, that the solipsistic danger (the taking of the self as the only verifiable known) is deflated.

It is important to recognize the difference between a fantasy of *après-coup* and the actual operation of that phenomenon in the analytic session where it is not a matter of remembering or of filling in the gaps, but of creating links that have never previously existed. This is where the intersubjective "listening to listening" comes into play. It is in the kind of listening proposed by Faimberg—a new dimension of the evenly suspended attention and free association to which she calls attention—that the subject–object schism implicit in the "someone is speaking to someone" and the "someone is listening to someone" yields to something else: the sharing of an entity absent from the context of material reality. This sharing is the basis of the intersubjective exchange and the absent entity is the psychic object the account of which opens onto the historicity of the transference. It is not the dream itself, for instance, that is interpreted in analysis, to cite but one mode of construction, for the dream itself is but an absent object; rather it is the analysand's account of the dream. This putting of the psychic object *sous rature* or under erasure (where it remains present but only as a "trace," a mark of something anterior), as Derrida would have it, is the characteristic mode of undoing the dichotomies in question.

What Stern, Bromberg, and, in her way, Faimberg have described, then, is that space wherein objective versus subjective and true versus false are no longer meaningful. We have seen that Hanly disputes as relativistic the view of truth that lacks support for independent facts according to which theories can be examined. Moreover, he finds in the interpersonal or subjectivist construction of reality an ontological problem: "It is not possible to doubt the importance of relations between persons," he acknowledges, but "neither is it possible to doubt the patient's independent reality" (2009, p. 372). David Bell (2009) is another for whom psychoanalysis is "committed to a realist ontology" that defies the relativizing discourse of postmodernism. Previously, I cited the suggestion by Rorty that we rid ourselves of the term "postmodernism" for the uncertainty and ambiguity of its meaning. Bell would like to see postmodernism itself eliminated for the extreme relativism that causes it to dispense "with any conception of truth," provoking "its various counterparts, namely deceptions, lies, and misrepresentation also lose their foothold." Additionally, Bell argues:

> [T]he relativization of "truth" brings not a recognition that there are no ultimate truths, but a world in which the very terms "truth" or "reality" should themselves be abandoned as they have no meaning, only serving, so it is claimed, as a legitimation of power by those who claim to "know."
>
> (pp. 342)

But when Bromberg, for one, writes that "reality is shaped by the self-organizing configuration" (p. 352) of an individual's different self-states, is he actually denying the existence of an objectively real? Or is he saying, rather, that the "reality" posited by the philosopher differs from that of the psychoanalyst for whom psychic "truths" are reality's bedrock? And if it is so that there is a reality of the philosopher and another of the analyst, is this comparable to saying there is a pen of the nuclear physicist and another of the particle physicist, the point that Hut made while not denying, but on the contrary, offering evidence of the materially and objectively real? If Bromberg's claim is legitimate, would the reality of the philosopher and that of the analyst be equal in "truth" value or would the latter be less true than the former for being more fantasy bound? And to pose what is perhaps an even more harrowing a question, would less true as more imaginative ultimately mean less real?

One might define, as has Mark Solms (2003), a set of criteria for determining the real that begins with its being perceptible by means of our sensory modalities. Yet hallucinations are perceived (seen or heard), and we know them to be illusory as they cannot be seen or heard by everyone, so a second criterion comes immediately into play: To be real, a thing must be sensorially perceptible to all. But what are we to say of an emotion? Joy is certainly no less real for being internally perceived by a single individual and not available to others. Emotions, and similarly memories, are not hallucinatory, so one has again to refine the criteria by distinguishing between two kinds of reality—the reality of phenomena perceived in the external world and that of phenomena perceived in the internal world. Freud made the distinction between objectively and subjectively perceived reality by differentiating between those perceptions that are registered on one sensory surface of consciousness as opposed to the other.

But here's the rub: "[I]sn't it bodily processes, and specifically brain processes," Solms inquires, "that generate our internal perceptions? And doesn't that imply," he further inquires, "that the 'reality within us' is, in fact, the physical reality of the body and the brain?" Solms incisively justifies the psychoanalytic postulate of a "psychical reality" as distinguished from its physical correlate, however, by noting a fundamental aspect of reality and our means of perceiving it—namely, that the very ways in which we perceive the world are limited by the very modalities of perception themselves. The modality of vision, for example, is limited to the perception of what is external to the perceiving subject while the modality we call emotion can perceive only those processes that are internal. Furthermore, as Solms explains, "[I]t is in the nature of the modality called vision that it can only represent the things it perceives ... in the form of light, color, orientation and so on. No matter what the actual properties might be of the thing that exists out there in the world, the visual modality can only represent that thing in a visual form, in the form of visual images." The same is said of the modality we call emotion, that:

> [I]t can only represent the things that it perceives ... within the qualitative range that is appropriate to the emotional apparatus. In other words, it can only represent things in the form of pleasure and unpleasure and so on. No matter what the actual properties might be of the things that exist deep within us, the emotional modality can only represent them in an emotional form, in the form of emotional states.
>
> (p. 94)

The conclusion to be drawn from this is that all we can know of something is its perceptual representation. And this causes Solms to revise once more his initial criterion for the determination of the reality of something by saying that it is not that we actually perceive what is real, for we do not perceive what lies behind the perception; rather, *we infer it*.

Citing the example of depression, Solms derives two significant implications from this reasoning: First, that the feeling of depression and its neurochemical correlates are "two different perceptual representations of *the same underlying thing*." And, second, that "the unitary underlying thing that generates both of these perceptual realizations is in fact neither an emotional feeling nor a visual image. Behind both the emotional feeling of depression and the visual image of the chemical process that corresponds to it, there lies something else, something which is independent of our perceptual modalities, and which can, in itself, never be perceived directly." This leads Solms to conclude that, if our conscious perceptions of what we take to be reality are truly only "indirect representations of it," then "the actual stuff of reality" is "non-perceptual, and therefore unconscious" (p. 97).[2] And mental processes—of which fantasy is one—are both real and unreal: I have said they are real for being in existence and for describing or projecting our inner thoughts and feelings; they are unreal for being inferences as opposed to direct perceptions, for being representations or retranscriptions—figurations, in short, which allow the unthinkable to be rendered thinkable (p. 104).

What Solms' reasoning has done is brought us closer to Bromberg's (2009) own assessment that, in its relation to the workings of the imagination (the enactment of fantasy), the entire question of "objective versus subjective, and thereby 'true' versus 'false' loses its meaning" (p. 352). The same may be said of fantasy in aesthetic form. Hut empirically illustrates the existence of multiple realities that are each dependent upon the subjective–objective and true–false dichotomies. But in doing so he also reminds us through his "play" with the pen that imagination is ultimately nonperceptual or, rather, it is perceptual but in the sense that it is distorted, altered, refigured perception. In explicating the co-construction of a transitional space wherein analyst and analysand negotiate their relational experience, Solms and Bromberg have shown (the first intrapsychically, the second interpsychically) that the most we can say, and say with legitimacy, about external reality is that it is that from which the imagination, for all its unreality, forms its very real images. Images are not formed *ex nihilo*, but are generated from other images and, in this sense, reality is not fixed but expansive in measure relative to one's capacity for openness, receptivity, and responsivity. Neither, then, is it in opposition to fantasy the very structure of which now becomes clearer.

An analogy between music and these alternative ways of thinking about truth and reality with regard to psychoanalysis may help to summarize: Truth on the order of both correspondence and coherence is comparable to the musical tradition of consonance, while modernist, whether high or post, truth theory is analogous to dissonance. Emanating as it does from

2 I would have used the term *nonconscious* here as opposed to *unconscious*. See Oppenheim (2012).

within the analytic dyad, from within the sphere of transferential and countertransferential enactments, moreover, truth for the postmodernist is contrapuntal: It is an open-ended deconstruction in being deconstructed by yet another deconstruction ad infinitum. This is the postmodernist's way out of the closure of truth as knowledge of reality. And it is the postmodernist's way out of the closure of truth in solipsism.

I am reminded by the variations in truth theory of the preface by Albert Camus to his novel *The Stranger* in which the author explains that the protagonist, Meursault, is a man who, without any heroic aspirations, accepts to die for truth. It is for not having cried at the funeral of his mother, which would have been to conform to the rules of society, that he is condemned to death (although the pretext for his trial is a murder). Lying, Camus (1992) reasons, is not only saying what is not so, it is also saying more than what is and more than what one feels. Had Meursault cried as the jury deemed appropriate, this man driven by a passion for the truth would have been lying. Instead, by refusing to conform, and by the omission of an act of feeling that did not exist for him, he revealed what was true. Similarly, untruth in the form of omission in the analytic setting (whether by silence or even by those memories that serve to "screen" repressed material) is not a question of falsity. And not revealing all that is present in the associating mind is a revealing of truths, unconscious and conscious, that are thereby uncovered. (As Freud put it, "it is the 'distraction' which allows impulses that are otherwise hidden to be revealed"; 1910, p. 119). This brings me to the Greek notion of truth as unconcealedness or disclosure. The Greek word for truth—*aletheia* (αλήθεια)—as revelation or unveiling is a wholly different way of conceiving the constitution of meaning in psychoanalysis. It is a concept much ignored throughout the history of philosophy prior to Heidegger's resurrection of it early in the last century. But as we will see in the following chapter, it is the basis for the act of "insighting," the very act that renders plausible the analogy of psychoanalysis to art.

3

"INSIGHTING" IN PSYCHOANALYSIS AND ART

Thus far we have considered imagination, as it relates to the self as agent, from the perspective of the inherent connection between perception, expectation, and affective valence as they, in turn, relate to fantasy. We have seen how, as in the extreme case of anosognosia, sensory input is mediated by the attribution of meaning. And we have seen how, as evidenced in the aesthetics of psychoanalysis and of art, representation is partly determined by its function—the managing of identity and the preservation and enhancement of self. Ernst Kris (1952) developed the notion of the centrality of ambiguity in art. His interest lay in the process whereby art is both communication and recreation and in the multiplicity of meanings to which the artistic endeavor and the reader/viewer's response gives rise. Ambiguity calls forth, he noted, "the problem of the standards of interpretation" (p. 259), standards, I would argue, that extend from art to psychoanalysis in the comparability of insight attainable in each.

> The painful part of my reality is that all those horrible experiences really happened to me! After years of psychiatrists telling me that I made it all up in my mind—"Do you have memories? Well, they're false; don't believe them!"—I've learned to keep these realities to myself. I remember staying up all night meditating on my predicament (my inability to reclassify my experiences as FALSE) and I came up with a solution which was a compromise. I would continue to believe what happened to me as true but LIVE as though it were false. This compromise saved my life and continues to do so today, but at an emotional cost. I suppose this is called "insight."

"Insight" is defined by psychiatry as an individual's awareness that what was felt to be outside oneself is, in fact, within. It implies acceptance of illness and psychic disorder. In psychoanalysis, it is used to mean something quite different, to which I will return later. For the moment, suffice it to say that what this patient's words describe is neither the kind of understanding traditionally sought by psychiatrists in their treatment of the severely ill nor that sought by psychoanalysts who tend to work with less ill patients considered to have greater capacity for self-observation. Rather, what this citation attests to is a realization on the part of the patient that to function in society *feigning* awareness, *appearing* to have changed how he thinks about his past, was necessary and would be sufficient. Here is how this individual concluded his explanation:

> I'm referring to experiences I had leading to my first break and during my illness. All my psychiatrists told me those things didn't happen in reality. After failing to re-characterize those events as false, I was presented with a mortal problem: "How can I trust my mind and survive in an environment that is completely hostile to my truths?" I was completely alone, stressed and suicidal. Having been failed by psychiatry, I sought to resolve my problems myself; therefore the compromise I have described saved me and this would not have been possible without this "insight."
>
> (anonymous, personal communication)

What this patient takes to be "insight" is a rational *deal* he has made with himself—a deal that, interestingly enough, albeit not truly insightful, works! His inability to give up the incongruence between what he believes and what was declared by others as *untrue*, and to achieve the conformity in behavior and thought demanded of him, necessitated a rational compromise meant to fool his psychiatrists into thinking he had achieved understanding and acceptance of his plight. In choosing to believe one thing and act another—in short, by virtue of a ruse—he shows not "insight" but the ability *to play at* having the deeper understanding he lacks; he shows *imagination* and a meta-awareness that *does* have a certain usefulness: It allows him to outwit not only those treating him, but others as well, so that he can function in accordance with his own beliefs.

Joanne Greenberg (author of *I Never Promised You a Rose Garden* and numerous other books) has described her recovery in astonishingly similar terms: She discovered that to do something she liked doing she too had to make a lucid agreement with herself. "I made a deal with my brain to help me to do it (though I didn't think I was listening): 'If you think *this*; you can't think *that*.' Others didn't make that deal; they would walk down the corridor and see that every door was open; which door do you go through?" (personal communication). The objective of Greenberg's deal making was entirely different from that of the patient just quoted: Balancing her cognition as she did was solely in the effort to gain control over her irrational thoughts, while his compromise with himself was primarily to survive the demands of others. Yet for both, it was imaginative thinking in the form of a *willed* and cogently conceived compromise that was imposed on their inner worlds. To put it otherwise, thinking *about* what it was not deemed alright to be thinking led to bargaining, a strategy by which they were able to manage their illness (eventually even overcome it) and achieve an improved relation with the external world.

At the 2007 annual meeting of the American Psychiatric Association, mathematician John Nash spoke globally of a compromised adaptation to the environment and suggested that "[H]umans are notably subject to mental illness because there was a need for diversity in the patterns of human mental functions." Evolutionary biologists know full well, he noted, that "the natural phenomenon of mutations serves to prepare a species for adaptation to changing conditions or for improved adaptation to an existing level of environmental circumstances" (p. 2). The idea of biological compromise in the diversification of the species through mental illness grew out of Nash's thinking on bargaining more generally. So too the game theory for which he became known, a schema of decision making and strategizing upon which a larger theory of rational behavior is based. In fact, his very first paper that dates to his second semester of graduate study at Princeton University when he was only 22 is entitled "The bargaining problem" and treats the subject of the interaction between rational bargainers in the context of economic exchange. It was for the development of his thinking on bargaining, its connection to game theory and extension to the political and social sciences and more, that he became a Nobel Laureate almost a half century later, in 1994.

"The idea of exchange, the basis of economics, is nearly as old as man," observes Syliva Nasar (1998) in her biography of Nash, *A Beautiful Mind*; but for centuries the meaning of bargaining power, the way to predict how bargainers will interrelate, eluded those in the field. It was not until Nash sought to define not a solution per se but the conditions that a solution would have to satisfy that such a theory came into view. "Nash's theory assumes that both sides' expectations about each other's behavior are based on the intrinsic features of the bargaining situation itself," Nasar explains. Indeed, it was *how* rational bargainers interact that interested Nash from the start. In the only course in economics he ever took, and that was as an undergraduate, Nash arrived at the notion that "the bargain depended on a combination of the negotiators' back-up alternatives and the potential benefits of striking a deal" (pp. 88, 90). This was the crux of "The bargaining problem" that appeared in 1950 in *Econometrica*, the preeminent journal of mathematical economics.

The originality of Nash's thinking is striking: He developed his theory *prior* to entering graduate school (he was an undergraduate at Carnegie Institute of Technology, as it was then called, where he had gone to study electrical engineering), which means *prior* to his involvement with those in game theory whom he would later encounter at Princeton, and *prior* to reading the leading work (*The Theory of Games and Economic Behavior* by

John von Neumann and Oskar Morgenstern) in the field. This is significant because Nash's early fascination with the possibilities of formulating a model of two-person bargaining, with what Nasar terms "the dynamics of human rivalry," a preoccupation that would lead to his "theory of rational conflict and cooperation" (p. 13), among the greatest intellectual achievements of the 20th century), speaks to something in the psychology (or more accurately, the neuropsychology) of the man. Indeed, we know from Nasar that Nash's commitment to rationality, his dedication to the purity of thought, was extreme: He considered computers or what he called "thinking machines" in some aspects superior to humans and "was beguiled by the idea of alien races of hyper-rational beings who had taught themselves to disregard all emotion. Compulsively rational, he wished to turn life's decisions—whether to take the first elevator or wait for the next one, where to bank his money, what job to accept, whether to marry—into calculations of advantage and disadvantage, algorithms or mathematical rules divorced from emotion, convention, and tradition" (p. 13). Moreover, as a fellow graduate student remembers Nash: "He was always buried in thought. He'd sit in the common room by himself. He could easily walk by you and not see you ... Nash was always thinking ... If he was lying on a table, it was because he was thinking. Just thinking. You could see he was thinking" (p. 69). Nash, however, was found eccentric—lacking in affect, excessively introspective, and isolated—not just by his peers as a young adult but by his own family as a child. He was a daydreamer who very early exhibited features of a schizoid personality. Inclined to be solitary, secretive even, Nash was generally emotionally cold and his little interest in social relationships very much concerned his attention-giving and loving parents who persistently sought ways to help their son develop more normally.

Donnel Stern (2009) has written eloquently of the need for the other through whose ears we learn about ourselves. We need the other to bear witness to how and what we experience, to help us order our experience as a narrative, and to become a cohesive self (see, in particular, Chapter 4). The isolated child (whatever the etiology of that isolation) must find alternatives for the visceral feedback that he is unable to absorb. New ways of creating a sense of agency need to be found; an imaginary other (the stuff of fantasy) may help. In the adult, where a fragile sense of self has been jeopardized (perhaps by some form of extreme stress), delusional thinking may serve the same purpose: Heightened efficacy in what is perceived as an unsafe world. Delusion, in other words, may be useful, not only deleterious; but, of course, like hallucination and other such symptoms, it is also an overwhelming disruption of one's life.

In itself, theorizing is an active way of giving shape to the world. It is not an acquiring of knowledge so much as a giving of form. Nash's game theory is a way of understanding social behavior. His so-called "solution concept," a theory of restrictions in games, is a way of predicting the strategies to be used by players and, thereby, the results of the game. I would submit that theorizing, and theorizing about game strategy in particular, was a way Nash found to help himself: It allowed him to structure his own subjective experience of difficulty in relating to others and to understand on a more sophisticated level of cognition what he could not comprehend on a more primitive emotional level. In fact, it was a *scientifically* rational thinking that became substituted for the more ordinary rational thought of a healthier psyche. Nash (1995) has himself written of his "change from scientific rationality of thinking into the delusional thinking characteristic of persons who are psychiatrically diagnosed as 'schizophrenic' or 'paranoid schizophrenic,'" confirming that the dichotomy for him was not between the rational and the irrational but the *scientifically* rational and the irrational. Over time, then, Nash experienced the world as increasingly incomprehensible and hostile and he was diagnosed with paranoid schizophrenia in the late 1950s. Almost a decade had passed from the time he wrote his first paper on bargaining until his diagnosis, giving credence to the idea that his theorizing helped him to manage the difficulties wrought by a schizoid personality and those of the prodromal period of schizophrenia, a phase that can last for several years.

It was, however, Nash's spontaneous recovery (that is to say, his improved capacity to function professionally and socially achieved without medication or other treatment), a recovery that came about gradually after 1970 (when he abandoned neuroleptics) and continued into the 1980s, that appears to harbor an even more profound connection with the focus of his work. After numerous hospitalizations, Nash imposed upon himself the means to ignore the hallucinatory voices to which he was prone and to adjust the irrationality of his thought processes in conformity with the normative standards of rational thought: He has said that he gradually began *intellectually* to "reject some of the delusionally influenced lines of thinking" characteristic of what he calls his "orientation" and it is precisely this "intellectual" rejection, this *willed* reversion to the rational, that is reminiscent of the compromises noted earlier (see Nash, 1995).

That branch of applied mathematics known as game theory explicates success based upon the strategic determination of one's choices in accordance with the choices of others. What are these "games," be they economic, political, or other, if not about managing perceptions and ensuring that one's anticipations are congruent with the anticipations of others? Moreover, Nash introduced the concept of game equilibrium—"non-cooperative games"—in his 1950 doctoral dissertation of the same name. I would argue that title and theory are less ironic than they appear: While in the "cooperative game" groups of players compete by the exercise of mutually accommodating behaviors, in a "non-cooperative game" players' decisions are made independently of each other and any cooperation between them is meant to enforce the individual player's position alone. My contention is that Nash's thinking on "non-cooperative games" and, furthermore, on behaviors that can more generally be modeled like a game, as well as on the restrictions that lie therein, assisted him by giving form to his own limited social relatedness and to some extent satisfied a need to intellectualize the deficit to make sense of his world. This is to say that he found a means of increasing his sensitivity to the behavior of others through the strategy of games and particularly that of the "non-cooperative" game. But in a way remarkably similar to that of the first two individuals we have just encountered, he also found his way back to better functioning from a life derailed by irrational thinking; when shaping his world in this way no longer sufficed and conversion to full-blown illness took place, he found his way back by compromise and navigating rationally. Like them, he used *thought-as-action*, *creative thinking*—which bears no relation to "insight," to the acceptance and submissiveness required by psychiatry today.

From early childhood Nash helped himself by negotiating: His superior intellect, obsessive thinking, and endless reasoning determined the *active* direction his genius would take. Recovery from illness entailed more than awareness of his disorder; it was a rational decision to assert his will *actively* against it that brought relief. Charles Rycroft (1968) has elegantly described the compromise the patient caught in a web of irrational thinking is obliged to make. Speaking of a case in which withdrawal from reality, the massive decathexis typically experienced by those with schizophrenia, resulted in the patient's having "become a nonentity in his own eyes, a person with no roots either within or without," Rycroft explains how "spontaneous attempts at recovery" are defensive attempts to escape that state. They are "designed to protect the patient from either re-experiencing despair or recognizing the strength and nature of his impulses" (p. 101).

This defense "involves denial of psychical reality and omnipotent reversal of the true psychical situation; the thoughts that in psychical truth have become bereft of significance come to be regarded as precisely the only objects to have any significance." As Rycroft further elucidates:

> The sole survivors of the psychic catastrophe of repression come to be regarded as the only inhabitants the world has ever had. The stones which the builder rejected become the foundations of a self-fabricated world. Once this omnipotent reversal has occurred, the cursorily improvised becomes the magically conjured-up, and the way is open to creating a new world in which a new significance and a new identity can be found—or rather could be, were it not for the presence of other human beings in the external world which the patient must perforce continue to inhabit.
>
> (p. 100)

The omnipotent defense is exposed as such just when, in this ill-fated attempt at "recovery," the grandiose self-assessment is perceived as made in vain. If the extravagant self-estimation is not shared by all others then clearly it cannot serve its intended purpose. It is then that the individual perceives compromise as his only choice:

> He must either live such a secluded life that his omnipotent fantasies never clash with the reality-conceptions of others, or he must modify his ideas so that they gain him disciples; or must ... keep his private fantasies to himself and learn to behave towards others "as a reasonable man is used to behave towards his fellows." (p. 101)

"I'm in a contest of will with the world" is how one person with schizophrenia has described his situation (cited in Davidson, 2003, p. 197). It is this contest that led the patient whose remarks introduced this chapter, as it did Greenberg and Nash, to choose the third option Rycroft describes. What I am getting at here is the meaning of "insight" and what it may imply.

Psychiatry uses the term *insight* to denote a breakthrough in the apperception of a mental disorder; one is said to have insight when one simply acknowledges one's psychic illness. Poor insight may be attributed to defensive mechanisms (emotional strategies for coping), or to the disorder itself, to a neurocognitive deficit (such as frontal lobe pathology) impeding awareness. But just how necessary is insight to recovery? From the three examples above, we see that the mind has other means of effecting compromise. And "normalizing" psychotic thinking may, in fact, prove far more helpful to patients than insight thus conceived. Indeed, the entire notion of adjustment may need to be rethought, for thought style differences deserve, after all, the same respect as differences in skin color, sexual preference, and so on.

Psychoanalysts tend to speak of insight as discovery of another kind and the primary goal of analytic treatment is to increase the detection of *meanings* and the *functions* they serve in the interest, precisely, of *agency*, the ability to control and alter one's life. Psychoanalytic technique is focused on how best to make the patient cognizant of the impediments to freeing the agent within. Unlike insight pure and simple, something passively acquired and accepted, "insighting," the term Samuel Abrams (1996) has adopted for the capacity to actively seek those impediments and understand their neurosogenic influence, retains the operational feature by which it is defined. Abrams explicates "insighting" as "a non-existent transitive verb meaning discovering, integrating, or knowing in a new way" (p. 77). Far more than awareness, it involves a coming to know the *nature*, not the fact, of something not previously known.

Quantitative research is of unquestionable value for augmenting the scientific understanding of recovery. But it is exploration of what is going on in the minds (and brains) of individuals through qualitative study that explains the consistency in the stories we have just heard. Among the leaders in the qualitative research on recovery from schizophrenia, Larry Davidson (2003) has been most impressive in demonstrating that regaining a sense of ownership of one's own experiences is the single most important tool in combating the illness. Indeed, loss of agency—as a result of "cognitive intrusions and disruptions," the "decline in functioning" they bring on, and the "delusional and other idiosyncratic ways" in which the person attempts to give meaning to that decline—is one of the most significant reasons why people with schizophrenia refuse the diagnosis and are thereby considered to be lacking in awareness (pp. 152, 156). As we have seen, however, and perhaps most visibly in Nash, there is a very keen awareness on the part those experiencing psychic changes and an active effort to make sense of them. Greenberg has related just how acutely aware she was from the start that something was very wrong. In fact, being told she had schizophrenia was very "liberating" for her. While most people given the diagnosis are not so ready to embrace it precisely for the loss of agency and the stigma associated with the illness, there was a "wonderful paradox" for her in her experiences being given a name, for she felt she could then "trust her instinct that things were not okay" (personal communication). She found self-confirmation in the diagnosis, ironically, and that helped her in her struggle toward reconciliation with the irrational, in the active process of bargaining, deal making, and negotiating known to those in recovery from the illness who learn to live "outside" it. What makes the enhancement of self the very tool for success is the *thought-as-action* strategy the self employs. This is precisely what Nash's story makes so clear: *Rather than the acceptance of illness awareness implies ("insight")—in other words, the passive absorption of knowledge—it is the active role assumed by the individual in the process of discovering and knowing in new ways ("insighting") that matters.* It was the transformation of knowledge into new meanings that made the difference for him. *Both before his ultimate conversion to schizophrenia and in the recovery phase, it was discovery in the form of game theory and mathematical research that led him to new ways of knowing the world.* The process he employed was highly creative: It was the unfolding of a new adaptive capacity not entirely unlike that of the "insighting," as Abrams calls it, that takes place in psychoanalysis and in the making of art as well.

"Insighting" in psychoanalysis

For the individuals just encountered, compromise has been the strategy for achieving awareness, although awareness of *difference* not of illness per se, and avoidance of difference, conformity through rational thinking, is what they have endeavored to maintain. But compromise is not "insight" either in psychiatry or psychoanalysis where emotional metabolization of understanding is the means to relief from psychic pain. In classical psychoanalysis, "insight" is a matter of bringing into consciousness what has been rendered unconscious through repression. This involves some degree of reconstruction of the patient's past. Relational analysts do not seek understanding through reconstruction so much as the clarification of the interpersonal field, but change in relational patterns is the result of the active unfolding of meaning just as it is for the classical analyst. Whether the analyst resists the fantasy to which that meaning gives rise in the transference so as to adapt it to reality or enters the fantasy to effect change from within it, understanding as act, not fact, is what reveals meaning as subjective "truth."

Stern (1997) writes eloquently of "formulation as the attribution of meaning," but the implication is not that the previously unformulated (sensory) experience is changed by its articulation. Rather, by its formulation meaning is revealed as truth in the very sense of *aletheia* to which I referred at the end of the last chapter: The disclosure of meaning by way of its formulation is the uncovering of truth not as a preexisting entity but continued creation. New formulations occur, new images are rendered, as one develops the capacity to discover meaning. Resistance to formulation and its concomitant meaning is for Stern a resistance to new ways of understanding as opposed to the familiar ways one had unconsciously maintained when the experience remained unformulated or unsymbolized. Stern rightfully notes that the defense is not against a thought as no such form has as yet been given. Instead, it is against thinking as a process in itself; a state of "creative disorder"—the unformulated experience—is more comfortable (in a sense) for its familiarity than the ambiguity and uncertainty of the new meanings that emerge with formulation. Indeed, "autistic certainty" is resistant to unfamiliarity: "Some of the experiences that emerge when resistance is resolved are no more predetermined than the daubs and streams of color in a Pollock painting" (pp. 47–48, 39, 76).

This, in fact, is precisely where the gap between the classical and relational perspectives narrows: The potential for their bridging lies in the recognition that what goes on in the mind of the patient is of greater import than the intent of the analyst (whether or not one views the patient's mind inter- or intrapersonally); it lies in the greater regard for the analyst's own experience as a participant in the ongoing creation or, more accurately, co-creation (irrespective of how the thorny matter of self-disclosure on the part of the analyst is treated); and it lies in the awareness that there are ways of not-knowing and ways of knowing and that (whatever we choose to call them, however we think about their inherent structure) it is the movement between them that is liberating. This is to say that the bridge between the perspectives lies *within the mode of passage rather than at the point of arrival*, which is precisely what I take Samuel Abrams' non-existent transitive gerund "insighting" to mean. Treatment is not about cure, but about developing in the patient the capacity to discover, to adapt and assimilate, to know in new ways.

Unformulated experience—unarticulated meaning—exists for Stern as a fixed state of dissociation, an interpersonal field from which our actions are dictated. Not dissimilarly, Abrams (1996) cites "the most commonly recognized neurosogens" as having "become embedded in the unconscious as fantasies or transformed into pathological structures" (p. 77) that diminish the self as agent of its own motives. As I said earlier, Abrams sees analysis not in terms of "resultants" but "emergents," in terms of "the forward pull" of the patient's creative, as re-organizational, capacity. Stern, as well, does not dwell on the embedded fantasies in the aim of uncovering hidden truths; psychoanalysis for him, as for Abrams, is "the emergence, through curiosity and the acceptance of uncertainty, of constructions that may never have been thought before." Furthermore, as Stern (1997) explains it, "these constructions are part and parcel of the new world patient and analyst are creating between them" (p. 78). Whether the analyst thinks more in terms of the inter- or the intrapsychic, just how he integrates these components is what the non-hierarchical relationship is ultimately all about: The interpersonal relation is what is operative in the analysis; how that operation is experienced by analysand and analyst constitutes the intrapsychic dimension. Conceptually speaking, then, the co-creation of a new relation between self and world is the yield of the capacity for "insighting." Indeed, the "offering" (also Abrams' term) not of interpretation by way of inequality in the relationship (one who knows, one who does not), but of "new ways of knowing" (p. 83) by means of a non-hierarchical partnership is the essence of psychoanalysis as Abrams sees it.

Empirically speaking, "new ways of knowing" are not solely the province of the psychoanalytic alliance. Consider an image of a material object, any object. Where does its meaning reside? For most of us, meaning of the objective world is constituted by our many and diverse contextualizations and subjective valorizations. For some, however, the ability to constitute in relative conformity with the generic contextualizations and valorizations of others is lost. At the time of this writing Gavin McCabe is a 46-year-old man who was working toward a doctoral degree in biochemistry in England when, in 1986, he had a psychotic episode. Schizophrenia was diagnosed a few months later and his hopes of a career in scientific research were dashed. "It's an automatic thing that [people] know what things mean, like a clock, or how to speak with people, but you can lose all these very important skills," McCabe told me. Ultimately, however, he returned to reasonably good psychic health and he attributes much of this to gardening:

> My psychiatric nurse thought gardening would be good for me because there's something about connecting with the earth and the environment and the seasons. I think gardening works on many levels. There is the idea of experiencing the seasons and accepting change as a natural progression rather than it being something to fear, or feeling it's something you can't control.
>
> (personal communication)

Fear of change and ambiguity, fear of lack of agency, fear of internal chaos—these are regulated for McCabe by gardening, by a rendering comprehensible nature at large. They are regulated by the unfolding of meaning (change as progression) on a level of emotional as well as cognitive comprehension, which is to say by formulation, by shaping. This is also a revelation of the process itself, much as it is in both psychoanalysis and art.

"Insighting" in visual art: Oskar Kokoschka

Joanne Greenberg has said that "mental illness is a rupture of the metaphors that make our lives coherent" (personal communication). As game theory was for Nash, art may be transformative through the restoration of metaphoric coherence. It may also be transformative, however, in destabilizing the absolute quality of the self—world relation and creating new, less familiar modes of relating. Not representational, art is rather a defunctionalizing, as Duchamp so aptly demonstrated with his "readymades," and a reconstitution in accordance with, but not reproductive of, the spatiotemporal structures of the world as we know them. "Surrealism" was the name given a certain artistic (verbal and visual) avant-garde, but all art is "sur-real" in the sense that it offers a new reality founded upon, if not congruent with, the old. In this sense, art truly is a metaphorical achievement: It is like—but not one with—the world and, as such, an active discovery, an unveiling or disclosing of truth (that of our subjective experience of "world") understood as *aletheia*. So, too, is the "insighting" of psychoanalysis.

Neither in psychoanalysis nor in art is the meaning of truth juxtaposed to error. Yet in their relation to truth insight and "insighting" differ fundamentally: The former, fixed as it is within the time of its occurrence, is shrouded by a vision of accuracy while the latter, atemporal and active, displays its revelation by revealing itself as a revelatory process. Truth as *aletheia*, the truth of art and the truth of psychoanalysis, is thus not verifiable but inherent within the at-work quality of the transaction. In his remarkable essay "The origin of the work of art," Heidegger (1971) locates that origin in art itself, naming art the source of both the work and the artist (p. 17). To read that "art is present in the artwork" is a far thornier idea than one might assume insofar as it begs the question of the very nature of art. But more perplexing still is the notion that *art is the origin of the artist* and it is this that allows for the comparison to the idea articulated by Abrams; namely, that the integrity of the analyst's offering derives from his position of equality and his non-confirmative stance with regard to the patient. It is by virtue of the capacity for self-discovery that the origin of the analysand as agent lies with psychoanalysis and not the analyst.

Heidegger offers the example of the peasant shoes painted on several occasions by Van Gogh: What is revealed by the artist is the "equipmental being" of the shoes, their usefulness, which is not in any manner *described* by the artist (there is no allegorical or otherwise narrative informing of the viewer). Rather, it is *shown* to be "at work in the work." What occurs in the painting in question, in other words, is the emergence of the shoes into the unconcealedness, the "occurring," the "happening of truth at work" (pp. 34, 36). What occurs in the painting is not the reproduction of the shoes, but a setting to work of truth. And it is through this happening of truth—this making of a space into which the work can unfold to bring forth art—that the making of the artist *takes place* as well. This is to say that never before was the artist in the world as he is now. Such is the force of art that it promotes the artist's emergence, *through his own creative process*, anew. This transformational quality is thus owed to art's truthful essence wherein its aesthetic resides. Like the *taking place* of truth in art, truth *happens* in psychoanalysis: That is, psychoanalysis and art are the *process of truth originating*. Accustomed ways of thinking and being are transformed by both in an *original knowing*, but knowing does not consist for Heidegger in a formulation *about* something any more than it does for Abrams in insight. Rather, it consists in remaining within the openness that preserves *the work at work*; it consists in preserving the active nature of the work as *truth at work*.

It is with this congruence of truth as *aletheia* in art and psychoanalysis in mind that I turn to the Viennese artist Oskar Kokoschka (1886–1980). For both his thinking on and practice of visual imaging illustrate the deep connection between the origination of the artist in his art and the individual's discovery of himself within the non-hierarchical and jointly investigative venture of analysis. In his 1971 autobiography *My life*, Kokoschka described an early realization: "I must not pursue routines or theories, but must find through my painting a basis for self-knowledge" (p. 37). Looking at some of the many portraits that date to the pre-First World War period, a span of about six or seven years preceding his call for military duty in 1915 during which the evocation of his subjects' psychic reality was his major preoccupation, we see that there is unity in the pursuit of self-knowledge.

Despite the great diversity of his subjects—many of whom he hardly knew (particularly those whose portraits he painted on the recommendation of his patron, the architect Adolf Loos; Natter, 2002, p. 90)—and his well-deserved reputation for brilliance in depicting their own unique psychology, these works are vividly transparent. There is little new about the idea that the search for the self is a motivating force in creative activity; what is noteworthy in Kokoschka's case is the degree of awareness of it and the psychodynamic response it provoked in his work.

In his 1912 lecture "On the nature of visions," Kokoschka considers with precision the special form of knowing that comes from seeing and notes that "the state of awareness of visions is … a level of consciousness at which we experience visions within ourselves." What he describes is an interconnectedness of subjective and objective experience: in-sighting, *an envisioning of self within the seeing of other*. The act of seeing is the visual source of self-knowledge insofar as envisioning is a *knowing-in-vision*. This is the very process of discovery and coming to know in new ways for which Abrams substitutes the non-existent transitive form of the word *insight*: "insighting." The form of visions, their patterns and also their significance, modify consciousness, the artist explains, such that there is "change in oneself." It is a process that "imparts[s] a power to the mind," that is, an "adding of something to ourselves." Denying from the start any prospect of delimiting the shaping of the image in the mind, or even the ensuing alteration of self (the enhancement of agency through self-awareness), Kokoschka nevertheless articulates the metamorphosis of impression into vision and image with conviction. Art's dynamism, the unnamed process of "insighting" as in-sighting, is elegantly expressed as follows: "My mind is the tomb of all those things which have ceased to be the true Hereafter into which they enter. So that at last nothing remains; all that is essential of them is their image within myself. The life goes out of them into that image as in the lamp the oil is drawn up through the wick for nourishing the flame." Perhaps more to the point, he continues:

> And with what sudden eagerness must the lamp-wick seek its nourishment, for the flame leaps before my eyes as the oil feeds it. *It is all my imagination, certainly, what I see there in the blaze … Without intent I draw from the outside world the semblance of things; but in this way I myself become part of the world's imaginings.*
>
> (pp. 285–287; emphasis added)

Kokoschka explicates vision, moreover, in terms of movement, that inherent in the growth of an impression into a vision, that innate within the transmission of that vision to canvas or paper. And, as if in support of the analogy between psychoanalysis and art that I am contextualizing in terms of Abrams' notion of "insighting," he defends art as "the constantly active, living material of thought" (1971, p. 32). But this is less abstract than it might seem: Kokoschka often literally kept his subjects moving while he created their likeness. When asked in 1954 by Pablo Casals if he might practice his cello as Kokoschka painted him, the artist replied that he could *only* paint the portrait if he did so. ("A person is not a still life," he wrote, "not even a dead person"; pp. 182, 33). Egon Wellesz, a composer and musicologist, described his experience of being painted by Kokoschka thus:

> Kokoschka started work while I played the piano, worked at my desk, or paced up and down the room ... On the first day I asked him if I was allowed to move while he was painting me. "Do you think I'm such a bad painter," he said, "that you have to sit still for me to be able to paint you? You can do what you want."
>
> (Natter, 2002, p. 90)

Others have reported similar experiences of "sitting" for this portraitist. When working with young people—Kokoschka's effort was not to teach art, but to teach *seeing*—he encouraged painting models who were not posing but in motion. Visual experience is by nature transitory and it was precisely to this evanescence that his students were meant to give form (Kokoschka, 1971, p. 176). If I have linked truth as *aletheia* to that of "insighting" and claimed the active status of inquiry and discovery the basis for the connection, it is that knowledge by virtue of being revelatory is fluid and it is in no small measure to its movement that the magnificence of the portraits that marked Kokoschka's early career is owed.

Kokoschka claimed the "truth" of his portraits to be found not in the "externals of a person—the signs of his clerical or secular eminence, or his social origins," in the socially signifying details of attire and so on, but in the light cast upon the dynamic of a person's psyche by the pictorial image: "In a face I look for the flash of the eye, the tiny shift of expression which betrays an inner movement," he wrote. But how was this search for the inner reality of his subjects and his depiction of it transformative for the artist? How did it enrich his own self-knowledge and bear upon his sense of agency? We can answer that by means of the theoretical discussion of vision in the essay just cited. For it displays how imagination is revelatory of truth in the subjectivity of meaning, in the interpretative process of seeing, and how by the act of imagining the artist creates reality. Indeed, do not the wise "teach us," he subsequently inquired in his autobiography, "that man is simply a product of his material environment? But I wonder, where does reality reside? Where are the frontiers of the real, when a great mathematician in his theory of relativity can call in question even the traditional concepts of time and mass?" In accordance with what he had set out to prove in his essay on vision, he related that he believed, "on the contrary, that a world in which we can feel at home exists only by virtue of our experiencing it as we do ... Only the human mind, thanks to its forming power, makes us capable of grasping the immense possibilities of creation" (1971, p. 14). Among the greatest of those possibilities was for him to encounter reality as the shaper of his own experience.

We can also respond to the question of the transformative nature of portraiture for Kokoschka, though, by considering what lay behind his notion of vision as the origin of awareness and behind his idea as expressed in that essay, that feeling pours into the image to render it the plastic embodiment of the soul. Manifested in his preoccupation with locating the inner truth of his sitters was the need to locate himself within them and seeing himself there was in itself empowering. He said as much at the close of another essay where he wrote, "I content myself with painting portraits because I can, regarding this as my way to humanity, a mirror that shows me when and where and who and what I am."[1] A clue to how this was so is found in the following: The "inner movement" Kokoschka detected in his subjects was frequently one of distress, madness even, or at least he thought it so. "It's odd that throughout my life I've known so many suicides and people who were mentally ill," Kokoschka mused in *My Life* (pp. 33, 42). Yet perhaps it is not as "odd" as he thought. In fact, if his fascination with the "inner face" of his subjects and his uncanny ability to render visible what was hidden behind it served to reflect for him who and what he was, one wonders how much was a perception of sharing with those he painted something of their inner world and how much was attributable to his imagination, to projection and thus to fantasy. Just how "true," in other words, is the inner truth of his subjects that he is renowned for having captured? (In this regard, his writing to the wife of a Viennese jeweler "Madam ... I'd like to do a nervously disordered portrait" is telling; cited by Natter, 2002, p. 90.) Clearly the psychologically informed portrait was his domain, and of this he was a master, but how much did his seeing of himself in his seeing of them and his objectification of his own affective states in theirs belie their truth in favor of his own?

In many of his portraits, there is little, if anything, to situate his sitter in space or time and, more significant, sometimes there is hardly a resemblance borne to the individual so dynamic is the undercurrent, so privileged the emotional content over the actuality of representation. Furthermore, that so much of the portraits' energy derives, and consistently so, from the depiction of the sitters' hands and arms, more so even than their faces, and from their powerfully executed gestures already reduces the individualization. Even when his subjects are more clearly

1 This is the last line of the artist's essay "I paint portraits because I can, 1961," reproduced in Natter (2002, pp. 236–238).

particularized and identification seemingly evident, it may still be more slippery than one might suspect. The identities of those in his celebrated painting *The Tempest*, for example, are commonly attributed to the artist himself and his lover Alma Mahler and still there are doubts; there is the distinct possibility of conflation as we learn from Peter A. Knize (2002):

> For many years my mother had a steel box in which, she told me, she kept correspondence between Kokoschka and herself. She made me promise that upon her death I would destroy this correspondence without looking at any part of it. Later she announced that she had changed her mind and (through the offices of the psychoanalyst Dr. Kurt Eissler) they would be kept safely at the Freud Archives until fifty years after my death. This led me to suspect that there had been very strong feelings between my mother and Kokoschka. Also, looking at the famous *Windsbraut* (*The Tempest*; 1913), which supposedly portrays the artist with Alma Mahler (1879–1964), there seems to one a striking resemblance between her and my mother (1905–1979). Yet in real life, when I visited Alma Mahler with my mother in the 1960s, I did not see any resemblance whatsoever.
>
> (p. 70)

The result of the predominance of the psychological over the physical reality in a large number of instances was that the paintings were refused by the sitter as being either unflattering (the painter had the good fortune of usually being compensated nonetheless by Loos) or, more important, simply unrecognizable. But the point is not merely the degree of psychological interpretation in the early work (with its tropes of misery and disintegration rendered in an agitated brushstroke or a deliberate use of line that would later yield to far greater subtlety), but that there is something essentially *disturbing* in this dynamism. There is an emotional tension, an emergence and resistance, revealed through the physical presence that, in begging the question of the origin of the "panorama of hypersensitive characters, or rather, people depicted as such," to cite Patrick Werkner (2002, p. 34), is worthy of contemplation.

An early subject, the Dutch scholar Dr. Emma Veronika Sanders was described by Kokoschka as one who "always seemed strangely distracted" while he was painting her: "Although on the surface calm and composed, her thoughts were obviously far away, and her great, sad eyes, gazing into nothingness, made me think of a madwoman. It was this that I expressed in my picture, as if I had had a premonition that she would be in an asylum a few years later" (1971, p. 42). And apparently she did become ill ("the young lady became mentally deranged—something none of us had anticipated" is how the Danish writer Karin Michaelis put it; Natter, 2002, p. 132).

Remarkable in this 1909 portrait is the terrible aloneness and despair that Sanders exudes both from within the calm of her face and from her hands, the right one strangely hidden, the left one open, as though holding something, but curiously empty. As previously noted, Kokoschka often expressed through hands and arms some psychological profundity. In the Sanders work, it is an inner void. The opposition between the calm of her demeanor, the tranquility of her presence, and the distinctly lost look she has about her tells us she is there but not entirely. And the slightly outstretched hand is poignant in its symbolic emptiness. Lotte Franzos, in a portrait variously dated to 1908 or 1909, is shown with a striking left hand that lies in her lap, before her pudenda, "curled inward," as one critic has observed, "like a claw" (Werkner, 2002, p. 34). But she too has an open hand, her right, grasping at nothing while perched ambiguously against her left arm. (Curiously, the same gesture is repeated in the portrait of Rudolf Blümner, painted in 1910.) As in the Sanders painting, Franzos' face has an absent, if dreamy quality to it. She too is present while elsewhere. Are we to suspect, by virtue of the consistently enlarged but also empty hands, the projection into the sitter of some sort of masturbatory fantasy and/or one related to the anxiety of castration? The symbolism is certainly suggested, but we have no significant basis on which to make such a determination. What interests me, rather, is the troubling nature of the oppositions, another of which appears in the portrait of Auguste Forel, the Swiss myrmecologist, neuroanatomist, and psychiatrist whom Kokoschka painted in 1909–1910: Dark eyes juxtaposed in their intensity against pales greens and white overlaying an able-bodied torso portray incomprehension, a puzzlement that appears directed at the sitter's own helplessness as indicated by the raised pose of arthritic bony hands. The hands, like the eyes, stand out against the muted tones of rest of the work depicted as they are in the high relief of a sharp black outline. Thus are other sitters similarly revealed in an air of incongruity and disparity: Sometimes absent in their presence, sometimes incapacitated in their robustness, they often betray a dynamic tension underscored by the contradiction of a hand, either enlarged (so as to render the rest of the body strangely small) or fully or partially hidden, that ambiguously offsets the gesture of the other.

Another with the pain of madness in his face, a man who was interned in the Steinhof mental hospital in Vienna at the time Kokoschka painted him (1909), was Ludwig Ritter von Janikowski. Arresting in this painting is the way in which mental dysfunction is revealed not only despite the quasi neutrality of his facial expression, or even the vapidity and strangeness of his eyes, as in the portrait of Sanders, but in the angular structure of his gaunt visage and, also, the way in which color in the face is informed by the torrent of colors behind the head. Swirls of color above that yield to blackness below are picked up in the recesses beneath the eyes and on the nose, lips, and ears so that deep muted reds, greens, and blues are viewed as hollows in the yellowed flesh. Crevasses in the brow and between the nose and mouth accentuate the weariness and isolation. It, too, is as troubling to the viewer (in its play on his or her emotional responsiveness) as the artist's skill at capturing the psychological veracity is appealing.

It has been said that "Empathy is the method of expressionism" (Hodin, 1948, p. 213). Certainly Kokoschka was empathically in tune with those who sat for him and he conveyed by the motion and rhythm of his brushstroke their spiritual and emotional lives in such a way as to stimulate empathic attunement in the viewer. Disregarding the aesthetic of beauty for that of psychological truth (or, more accurately, locating the one within the other), he never strove for harmony but for the dignity of the individual qua individual. My point, however, is that his fascination with what constituted that individuality was motivated by more than artistic concerns. The vision of his "inner eye" of which he wrote in his autobiography reflected a focus as inward directed as outward. With his frequent depiction of isolation, despair, the degradation of both physical and mental illness, the need for self-identification through his work bestows upon his claim that "Art never lies!" a singular meaning (1971, pp. 33, 199).

Yet we can understand both *how* the urgency of Kokoschka's search for self-knowledge was expressed in his unique capacity for uncovering the psychology of the sitter and *why* it found its way to so many with physical or mental illness only when we consider the tension between intimacy and anxiety evident in so many of these portraits. Even the complete detachment or indifference seen in some of the work from this period (the portraits of Adolf Loos, 1909, and Joseph de Montesquiou-Fezensac, 1910, to name but two), portraits that provide such a striking contrast with those that are exceedingly expressive, can be understood in terms of this dialectic.

Kokoschka was a poet and playwright as well as a visual artist, and in one of the poems included in an illustrated book for children, *Die träumenden Knaben* (*The Dreaming Youths*), a work of poems and lithographs commissioned just a year before the portraits of Sanders and Janikowski, we read:

> … next to you, seeing your arm,
> Bending, a story so fragile it ceases to be
> As soon as anyone touches it.
> I see behind all words and signs
> (Oh, how joyful I am!)
> That you resemble me,
> How you resemble me.
>
> Do not come closer.
>
> (cited by Berland, 2008, p. 27)

Although descriptive of the poet's awakening sexuality, this evocative passage may be said to be emblematic of precisely of what would appear soon thereafter in the portraits: the simultaneous need and fear of closeness produced by the recognition of self in the other. To put it differently, when identification brought not individuation but the threat of fusion, when influence (such as that of the archetypal Woman)[2] was overwhelming, what was already a remarkable linkage between his life experience and his art became all that more visible. Of this, *The Tempest*, with its two lovers engulfed in deep-toned swirls of torrent, is particularly illustrative: The female, only quasi individualized, is seen asleep with a most serene look upon her face and a gentleness that is reflected in her stilled arms and torso, while her lover, clearly particularized in the portrait of the artist, is both awake and utterly expressionless. The dialectic plays out formally in the enveloping storm and the couple's unresponsiveness to this metaphorical tension and in the lines of the bodies that lay near one another in intimacy though without any interconnection between them. Already it appeared in the tentativeness (hers) and trepidation (his) of the faces of Prof. Gans Tietze and Mrs. Erika Tietze-Conrat in the 1909 double portrait of the art historians, a painting where outstretched hands deliberately seeking one another belie the adverse indifference of the visages. Overt passion is again absent from the 1912 double portrait of the painter and his lover Alma Mahler in which vacant faces accompany hands just slightly apart, but whose nearness is strongly suggestive of the near embrace of their posed bodies. One year later Kokoschka would paint the extraordinarily rich in movement and similarly dialectical *Two Nudes: The Lovers*. As much here as in any other of his depictions of concomitant apprehension and longing, the image is memorable for the drama of discordant emotion and conflict. Writing of its dreamlike quality, Tobias Natter terms the painting an "uneasy fantasy" (2002, p. 164). In an exterior flowered landscape, the couple is lovingly embraced in a dance. Their naked bodies, however, face opposite directions and the two faces, hers stark white and expressionless, his tense and preoccupied, are once again dialectically out of tune as much with the loveliness of the nature surrounding them as with their lovers' embrace.

In a 1953 letter he wrote to the Museum of Modern Art in New York, Kokoschka testified to self-knowledge as the objective of the many portraits he made of himself: "All my self-portraits had been painted in the sense of stock-taking, in the view of estimating individuality." For him, "the self becomes a constant in a self-portrait, that does not vary even after

2 With regard to what Remigius Netzer terms Kokoschka's "fear and awe of Woman," see his "Postscript" to *My life* (1971/1974, p. 215).

years when age, life, ambitions changed the person of the creator."[3] This constancy of self is what Kokoschka was after in his portraits of the other and it was what he was after in the portraits he made of himself. In the former, he sought his own individuality as much as the sitter's; that is, he sought their uniqueness but also found himself in his models. In the latter, he often did the same by creating dramatic fantasies in which he appeared as a mythological or religious figure. Adopting the persona of biblical or mythological subjects (Christ, Adam, and Achilles, among others), he more dramatically merged his self with the self of the other as he had done in his early pictures. But he also staved off the fear of merger by moving into the far safer zone of the unreality of the dramatic fantasy.

An analysis of Kokoschka's handwriting by a graphologist revealed an agony of creation, a "confidence alternating with despair," a creation that was "self-torture" not because he was "in the grip of strong irrational forces," but because he was unable to "abandon himself to his unconscious" (see Hodin, 1948, p. 218). That, I believe, is what the dialectical tension of his work attests to: an extreme self-consciousness and a persistent need to control the impulse toward fusion or merger. We look at the deep anger set in the large dark eyes of Frau Hirsch, the sitter for *Woman with the Large Eyes* (c. 1908) or at the "great false teeth" of Father Hirsch the artist liked to see bared in rage in *Portrait of an Old Man* (probable date 1907)[4] and are struck by the seething. Yet the neutrality, the passivity, and detachment of Tilla Durieux, the actress the painter was commissioned to paint in 1910, intrigues us with its indifference. That Kokoschka was disposed to capturing psychic turmoil, expressed both within the dialectical interplay of a single work and that between his paintings, confirms Edith Hoffmann's observation that "The fascination of Kokoschka's life—and of his work—consists to a great extent in the phantasy which he brings to play on mundane realities" (n.d., pp. 9, 116). But the absolute interpenetration of his psychic life with his work is also striking. It is in this regard, in the way he transposed to the canvas the tensions that plagued him, evident in the dialectic between profuse expressivity and, at its antipode, the emotional vapidity of certain of his early subjects, that art may be seen as having served a transformative purpose, one to be understood as something more than the sublimation of drives and their derivatives.

The oppositions so notable in the work, the interplay of contrary modes of being either perceived in or projected onto his subjects by the artist, and visible too in the portraits he made of himself, may be viewed as stemming from a need to master the forces of mental or physical degeneration to

3 Letter from the artist to Dorothy Miller, October 4, 1953, The Museum of Modern Art, New York, Department of Registration: Oskar Kokoschka (cited in Natter, 2002, p. 164).

4 Date given by Wingler (1958, p. 293).

which he was drawn. What is more certain, however, is that through recognition of self in other (whether an effusive or a disinterested other), by both capturing the inner face of his subject and projecting his own onto it, Kokoschka was able to externalize, to render visible to his own eye, and thereby take in or assume aspects of a self-identity that, for whatever reason, eluded him. Stern (2004) has noted that "Dissociated states, because they are unsymbolized, do not and cannot bear a conflictual relationship to the states of mind safe enough for us to identify as 'me' and inhabit in a consciously appreciable way" (p. 213). I would not want to speculate on the eluded self-states that Kokoschka was seeking to integrate. Nevertheless, as he made very clear in his writings, making art allowed him to draw from without to install within. Transformation took place in the painter's "representation" of others in both senses of the word, for he not only created their likeness but took their place, as he himself put it in "On the nature of visions," and "put on their semblance through [his] visions." Through their psyches, it is his "psyche which speaks" (p. 287).

The singular motivation behind the portraits of others and those of himself as well—in a word, self-knowledge—may have been served, therefore, by the effort to tolerate, if not overcome, the oppositions he suffered. Rather than emphasizing in the act of creation as experienced by Kokoschka sublimatory aims that cannot be legitimately articulated without the psyche of the artist at hand, my aim is to stress another means of transformation in this art. Indeed, psychobiography tends to put the artist on the couch and offer a diagnosis. While not without interest, it runs the risk of neglecting the virtuosity and aesthetic intelligence of the art. That is not my interest here. What I am suggesting is that painting for Kokoschka was an ongoing process of investigation, one focused on self-discovery, and that what was tapped by the portraits of this prewar period and the self-portraits of his entire career were "new ways of knowing." Painting was a means of objectifying the conflict between intimacy and anxiety of closeness that remains a constant in the early work—whether expressed in the interplay of presence and absence, fusion and separation, or effusive affect and emotional withdrawal. What Bromberg calls "standing in the spaces" is the awareness of conflict that allows for its negotiation and this, one might argue, is precisely what Kokoschka was after in taking stock.

Construed thus, the analogy between psychoanalysis and art becomes clear. Patients resist the "offerings" of new ways of relating just as the painter struggles with the interactive process at work between him and his art. Here is Abrams (1996) on analysis: "The psychoanalytic process unfolds as each of the inevitable resistances to the new capacities for relating and adapting is engaged and overcome" (p. 85). Here, as earlier, is Bromberg on art: "Each painting … must be allowed to possess a changing identity of its own as it is being painted, and this identity must be free to instruct and inform the painter as to how it is to be painted in an evolving rather than a preconceived way." Ongoing self-inquiry ("insighting") in a feed-back feed-forward context is the crux of the matter and wherein "truth"—both psychoanalytic and aesthetic—resides.

Part II

MONKEY SEE, MONKEY DO

{L}e temps qui change les êtres ne modifie pas l'image que nous avons gardée d'eux. {[T]ime, which changes people, does not alter the image we have retained of them.}

Marcel Proust

For when all is said and done, it is impossible to destroy anyone *in absentia* or *in effigie.*

Sigmund Freud

4

THE TRANSGENERATIONAL TRANSMISSION OF FANTASY

Jane is the artist daughter of a well-known artist father with whom she claims to share a work-obsessed lifestyle. She describes this as stemming from "an addictive personality" and notes that her father's grandfather, also a much-known figure, had "an obsessive personality" that caused him to do "things in the extreme." If Jane likens herself to her father and to his paternal grandfather in turn, it is that she sees in the lineage genetically transferred traits. As if to illustrate the point, she notes that her great-grandfather was exceedingly preoccupied with family while her father, appearing to have no such interest at all, was defensively on the other side of the same family-intensive coin. The result, she explains, has been equivalent: "a worshipping and controlled family" that has revolved around the "'absent him'" (Freud, 2006).

We will learn more about Jane, who shares with her father Lucian and great-grandfather Sigmund the surname Freud, in the following chapter where the focus is on imagination and artistic influence, specifically that of artist parents on artist offspring. There we will see how the dependence of feed-forward on feed-back, creation on re-creation, is not only perceptual but relational in essence. Indeed, artist offspring of artist parents reveal the "revisional intensity," as Christopher Bollas (1999) has termed it, which "reflects the dense overdetermination of psychic life" (p. 169). They allow us to see how art, like psychoanalysis, evokes the experiencing self that, when "objectified in a different and challenging way" (p. 176), is transformed by a furthering of agency.

Here, however, Jane's story serves to introduce the concept of transgenerational transmission as a means of understanding the development and evolution of fantasy. Genetic memory, ego development, attachment patterns—all aid in explaining the origins of that mechanism whereby imagination functions in the service of agency. The source of fantasy as a defensive or protective measure and as a means of securing and even furthering the sense of self is a complex area of investigation. From the perspective of transgenerational transmission, the evolution of fantasy takes the meaning of "truth" to new levels, as growing up in a family as celebrated as hers—particularly one centered on the "absent him"—renders so clear. For it brings to the fore not only questions of child development, ego function, character traits and the like, but questions of private versus public myth, family secrets, and transhistorical memories, and provokes consideration of the power of imagination, singular or collective.

Additionally and importantly, it brings to the fore relational patterns. In so doing, the transgenerational transmission of fantasy returns us to an earlier debate, one that occurred when what is known as attachment theory was first formulated by John Bowlby after the Second World War. New research on attachment and trauma, so significant in recent years, has enriched our understanding of relational patterns in child development and their transmission across generations, although we are seemingly no closer today than a half century ago to integrating relational patterns with the dynamics of unconscious fantasy that are the foundation of classical psychoanalytic theory. Such integration, however, would appear to lie in recognition of the following: Insofar as a primary function of the brain is the acquisition of knowledge, imagination exists to attain it. Limitations imposed upon the investigative functioning of the brain produce imaginative thinking and fantasy, as does the urge to replace what is perceived as not fully satisfying. In its intimate link with the neural organization of the brain, imagination has much to do with inheritance, with the readiness—innate or learned—of an individual to construct meaning in a particular way. More precisely, the construction of meaning results from events in the world and from the actuality of relationships. Yet it also consists in the shaping of their representation in the mind. Representation is not independent of fantasy, itself based in memory, and is thereby derivative of the very principle of gratification outlined by Freud. However much we find ourselves once again where early attachment theory and psychoanalysis once parted ways (a rupture to which I will return later), the point is that integration of views on attachment and on the inner representational world is to be found in *how* knowledge is acquired—the theoretical and neurobiological principles of knowledge acquisition—and in the *functional gratification* it provides.

In asserting that a primary function of the brain is the acquisition of knowledge, I take my inspiration from Jaak Panksepp, Mark Solms, and others who have outlined the homeostatic objective of knowing. Solms and Oliver Turnbull (2002) remind us that the search for knowledge is the means by which human regulation occurs: Knowing is consciousness of how we feel and awareness of feeling (whether "good," "bad," or in between) is precisely what allows us to survive (p. 91). Nobel Laureate Gerald Edelman calls it "neural Darwinism." Panksepp (1998) attributes the investigative instinct of the mammalian brain to what he calls the "SEEKING system," the system that "responds unconditionally to homeostatic imbalances" and notes that arousal of this system is invigorating, akin to the anticipatory feeling we experience "when actively seeking thrills and other rewards" (p. 145). Before turning to ways in which imagination confers gratification through the transformation of perceptual data into knowledge, we need to address a series of questions requisite to this exploration: As Semir Zeki (1999) has articulated them, "What is the 'organizing principle' that is necessary for acquiring all knowledge; to what extent does it 'preexist' within us; and to what extent does it depend on, or [is it] nourished by, experience?" (p. 2058).

The concept of human inheritance

Human beings, observes Mervyn Peskin (1997), "are a biological phenomenon 'uncomfortably' close genetically to species which are not human" (p. 386). The discomfort of this genetic closeness stems, of course, from the likeness to lessness. Despite being genetically similar to other species, however, we are unique, and we are so not only in our cognitive, linguistic, and other human capacities, but in our defensive modes of adaptability to the environment. In fact, it is the defensive organizations to which we are inclined—those best suited to our innate disposition as individuals—that make, in large part, for the differences in feeling and behavior that distinguish us not only from other animals but from each other. One need not review how individuals differ in the mediation of their inner world to that outside them. But we would do well to remember the significance of constitutional factors and that these inclinations toward particular coping mechanisms and defensive organizations are themselves susceptible to genetic influence (see Neubauer & Neubauer, 1996, pp. 98, 106–107, 117).

Genetic influence is easily if erroneously associated with genetic determinism. Yet the notion that hereditary transmission plays an important role in our mental as well as physical lives, and thus in the fantasies to which psychic organization gives rise, fascinates not only for the programming potential of genes (a fascination inseparable from the need to remain steadfastly alert to the ways in which genetics may serve non-humanitarian purposes). It fascinates as well for the potential of genetic reversal by the environment. It is not, however, so much at the level of the genes themselves as at the level of the chemical compounds acting upon them that researchers are now finding support for the effects of nurture upon nature. This is to say that in the molecular action that impacts the expression of genes (without modification of an individual's DNA), in the epigenetic changes that determine how genes behave, answers to a number of questions are increasingly thought to reside: How, for instance, might an event occurring in the first years of life, or even prenatally, affect what happens genetically over the long term? How might defensive responses to the perception of threat be transmitted from mother to child and even across multiple generations? How are psychodynamically meaningful constructs—perceptual (hallucinations), ideational (delusions), or other (however adaptive or maladaptive)—epigenetically induced? More specifically, how does stress reactivity vary among individuals and how are these differences transmitted across generations (see Meaney, 2001)? And what might be the implications of such findings with regard to the faculty of imagination?

Paradoxically, given its now highly discredited status, the Lamarckian concept of the heritable transmission of acquired characteristics is echoed in the idea that the environment induces (and possibly even reverses) physiological adaptations that bear on psychic function. Against Darwin's concept of natural selection, Lamarck's hypothesis of the mechanism of adaptation—whereby traits may be acquired and genetically embedded, and thus made heritable—has lacked plausibility. But epigenetics appears to restore credibility to Lamarckian theory as it begins to uncover how the process of expression occurs in genes determining not only physical features, but also psychological traits and behavior. Indeed, Lamarck believed not in a passive evolutionary mechanism, as it is often negatively described, but in changes in the environment that result in changes in the *needs* of those inhabiting that environment. It is the changes in need that engender the alterations in behavior. Epigenetics, as the mechanism of such changes, helps to explain vulnerabilities to certain mental disorders and why some pathologies (the schizophrenias, for instance) do not manifest until environmental stressors challenge the tenuous sense of self associated with young adulthood. It also helps to account for why the effects of childhood trauma are often not evident before the hormonal and other stressors of adolescence come into play. Consider the following statement by Regina Sullivan and Elizabeth Norton Lasley (2010):

> Traumatic experiences such as abuse can work their way into a child's genes. This fact may come as a surprise, since most of us think of genes as something we are born with. Of course, the genetic material we receive from our parents is important, and lays the foundation for who we are and what we become. But how our parents treat us as we grow can greatly influence the way the genetic material is "read" and "used."

Once this "reading" and "using" have occurred, might they not (as Lamarck hypothesized) be transmitted across future generations?

Interestingly, Freud himself was taken with Lamarckian thought as evidenced by his writing on phylogenetics. Unlike those (Hartmann, Kris, Erikson, and Jones) who considered psychological mechanisms (primarily identification) sufficient explanation of the transmission of acquired characteristics, Freud turned to a Lamarckian phylogenetics around the time of the First World War (Ritvo, 1965) and even proposed to undertake a collaborative text on Larmarckian theory and psychoanalysis with Sandor Ferenczi, although this never came to fruition. The idea that "memory-traces of the experience of our ancestors" are heritable, as Freud (1939, p. 99) wrote of the Jews in *Moses and Monotheism*, is seen in totemic symbol inheritance, the Oedipus complex with its concomitant fear of castration, and elsewhere. In fact, Freud's Lamarckian thinking extends to his belief that war, all through history, has a phylogenetic component, and he went so far as to claim an archaic feature also for dreams, proposing that "symbolic connections, which the individual has never acquired by learning, may justly claim to be regarded as a phylogenetic heritage" (1915–1916 [1916], p. 199).

But it is the notion that fantasy itself may have a phylogenetic basis that is of interest to us here. "It seems to me quite possible," Freud wrote in 1917, "that all the things that are told to us to-day in analysis as phantasy ... were once real occurrences in the primaeval times of the human family, and that children in their phantasies are simply filling in the gaps in individual truth with prehistoric truth" (p. 371). He says much the same in a text published the following year with regard to what he terms "the prehistory of neuroses":

> All that we find in the prehistory of neuroses is that a child catches hold of this phylogenetic experience where his own experience fails him. He fills in the gaps in individual truth with prehistoric truth; he replaces occurrences in his own life by occurrences in the life of his ancestors.
>
> (1918, p. 97)

Even more to the point is this: "I cannot feel surprised that what was originally produced by certain circumstances in prehistoric times and was then transmitted in the shape of a predisposition to its re-acquirement should, since the same circumstances persist, emerge once more as a concrete event in the experience of the individual" (p. 97). Indeed, he concludes a propos of fantasy thus: "Wherever experiences fail to fit in with the hereditary schema, they become remodeled in the imagination" (p. 119), allowing us to see how fantasy is formed of inherited residues of memory, acquired characteristics to which one is predisposed across generations. How pertinent is Freud's Larmarkian thinking on fantasy today? Does the notion that the environment bears upon epigenetic regulation, by transgenerational programming and even, potentially, by its reversal, find support in contemporary psychoanalytic theory? Lastly, does it bring us closer to the "organizing principle," as Zeki (1999) calls it, necessary for the acquisition of knowledge defining a primary function of the brain?

Memory as fantasy/fantasy as memory

"Is the memory of something having happened the same as it having happened?" asks the principal character in Edward Albee's celebrated 1965 play *Tiny Alice* (p. 64). The question is apt, for as neuroscience focuses today on what is known as "top-down" processing (the impact of psychosocial experience on genetic expression) in addition to "bottom-up" processing (the effect of neurobiology on subjective experience), the meaning of historical reconstruction becomes more complex. Studies by infant researchers attest to the existence of nonverbal memory, memory antecedent to secondary process mentation. Psychoanalyst Jenny Kaufmann (2009), in a moving paper entitled "In the shadow of suicide: Lessons from mental health professionals who have been there," describes her own childhood nonverbal memory of her mother, who committed suicide when Kaufmann was 26 months old: "While I could not conjure up specific memories of my mother *per se*, I did have a memory and a sense of my mother's presence—i.e., what it felt like to be with her, and I did have a sense of what it felt like to be without her,.which I experienced as her absence." How this experience of presence and absence was felt subjectively is, indeed, a kind of memory, albeit not a remembrance of actuality. It is what we might call an immaterial memory, a memory constituted of an internalized parent–child interaction and of loss; it is a memory that has been encoded, neurobiologically and psychologically, as the memory of an ever present while absent object. Like actual memories that come to light in treatment via association, non-actual memories reveal themselves in transference repetitions—with psychoanalytic process demonstrating that memory, material or immaterial, is never an autonomous (i.e., uniquely historical) phenomenon, devoid of a fantasy component.

Kaufmann tells of the conscious fantasies that were part of that nonverbal memory as she relates her father's disavowal of the life he left behind to adapt to a new reality. He remarried a woman with two children of her own and moved his young daughter to another city. As he did so, he strove "to obliterate the previous reality [she] had experienced with him and [her] mother," not only by "living in opposition to it" but by "opposing it": "'You don't remember your mother, do you?,'" he repeatedly asked her in such a way that the question was experienced by the child as a mandate rather than an inquiry. Restricted to that, never acknowledging the impact of the child's horrific loss of her mother, the exchange never deepened. Having been told that her mother had been hospitalized, and that she had fooled by escaping those who were meant to protect her there, Kaufmann ceaselessly fantasized about the woman she remembered without being able to image her. She fantasized about the escape from Chestnut Lodge, about her mother's route upon escaping, the "moment between her jumping and landing", and "the fate of her body." Inherent within the conscious fantasies was the nonverbal memory of a mother whose implicit if not explicit objectification occurred only within the subjectivity of the child's felt experience. Would the memory of her mother have been otherwise had her father not imposed upon his daughter what she took to be a directive not to remember the life he disavowed? How much was her need to know about her mother, a need at the origin of her conscious fantasies, encouraged by the experience of her father's denial?

Determining the narrative course of her adult life were the unconscious fantasies Kaufmann continues to ponder. As she elsewhere reveals, her mother "was 25 years old when she married, 29 years old when [her child] was born and 31 years old when she died." Kaufmann repeated the first part of that scenario by marrying, not coincidentally, at 25 years of age and having her first child at 29. Did she unconsciously harbor the fantasy that she would come to "know" her mother more profoundly by trying in this way to "become" her? Was she unconsciously informing her mother and, more importantly, proving to herself that *she* would live by not dying when her own daughter reached the age of two (2011, p. 180)?

Trauma lies not in a real life event, but in one's response to it. However passed from one generation to the next (biologically and/or psychosocially), traumatic response and defensive measures against it manifest in the next generation to the degree that such events have not been metabolized and or worked through. One might expect the silence maintained by Kaufmann's father with regard to the family tragedy to have in some way impacted her own caretaking of any children she may have had. Furthermore, had she harbored feelings of being betrayed by her father when he remarried upon the death of her mother and took new children into his life or, alternatively, feelings that it was not she herself who was betrayed but her mother, such feelings might have contributed to conflictual feelings about childbearing itself, and to a sense of culpability at playing into that betrayal by having children of her own. Yet, how much she, as the child of a father who disowned his suffering and could not overtly acknowledge that of his daughter, reflected as an adult that disavowal is information Kaufmann has not made available to her reader. Besides, we are obliged always to remain aware that difficulties in children may have more to do with their own constitution than with the relationship they have with their caregivers, with the ways childhood traumas are relived by parents as they care for their children (cf. Shapiro, 2011). Moreover, my interest here extends beyond the question of transmission through a single generation to the transmission, of fantasy and the defensive mechanisms it may stimulate, across multiple generations.

While there is little in the literature on the transmission of fantasy and defense as such (the concept of universal fantasies being of another order), the intersubjective transmission of trauma across several generations is extensive. The interface between the "big history," or larger sociocultural frame of catastrophe, and the "little history," an individual's personal story, has been closely studied, for instance, by Françoise Davoine and Jean-Max Gaudillière whose writings are informed by the intergenerational effects of the Holocaust, specifically, and war, more generally, as well as other forms of massive trauma. Many years of clinical experience and reflection on the therapeutic relationship have led to their understanding of how severe psychic damage results from the dialogic—yet silent—carry-forward of horrific experience from one generation to the next.

We are reminded by Vamik Volkan (1998) of the 1942 study by Anna Freud and Dorothy Burlingham, *War and Children*, and their reflections on the "unconscious 'messages' passed between mothers and children" during the bombing of London in the Second World War (paragraph 17). Volkan, who has significantly contributed to our understanding of large-scale ethnic conflict, has himself had much to say on the fluidity of psychic borders of mother and child and how unconscious fantasies, as well as anxieties, perceptions, and expectations, are transmitted from one to the other. The adolescent who remains overweight to assuage the silently transmitted anxiety of her mother that she has not the resources to feed her children illustrates the first of two kinds of intergenerational transmission Volkan has studied. The second involves "the depositing of an already formed self or object image into the developing self-representation of a child under the premise that there it can be kept safe and the resolution of the conflict with which it is associated can be postponed until a future time." As he explains it, the "deposited image" is then something like a "psychological gene" that bears upon the child's identity. So-called "replacement children," whose self and object representations include that of the deceased sibling as transmitted by their caregiver, carry within them a "'foreign' psychological gene [that] influences or modifies the child's identity" (paragraph 22).

The work of Haydée Faimberg also comes to mind for her exploration of what she calls the "telescoping of generations," a process of identification in which "the object of identification is in itself a historical object" (1988, p. 104). Essential to her theoretical perspective is that the identification structurally includes "fundamental elements of the internal history of this object" (p. 107). That is, the identification is comprehensible only in terms of a "condensed" history, one that does not fully belong to the generation that experienced the trauma or to that of the offspring who, having absorbed a particular manner of parental functioning, repeat coping mechanisms in their own successive familial object relations. The identification described by Faimberg always involves a "telescoping" through, at a minimum, three generations.

Citing Freud's "On narcissism: An introduction" (1914), Faimberg considers how identification with parental narcissism, for instance, imprisons the child and impacts her own intergenerational object relations. Here the mechanism of transmission is itself made clear: Loving the ego narcissistically, which is to say like an object, a narcissistic individual maintains the fantasy of autonomy while requiring constant appropriation and confirmation by the other. In her identification with her "internal parents," the child's narcissistic regulation entails "an alienated or split identification of the ego, insofar as its origin is found in the history of the other" (p. 106). As Faimberg explains, there is a defining moment of narcissistic love, which she calls "the appropriation function," and a defining moment of narcissistic hatred, "the intrusion function," both of which are characteristic of narcissistic function with respect to object regulation. In the former, the 'internal parents' appropriate the child's positive identity while, in the latter, they "actively [expel] into the child all that they reject," thereby defining the child by her negative identity. Thus the child is paradoxically rejected for having a history congruent with that of her parents and "with all that is not accepted by them in their narcissistic regulation." The child's split ego produces both a "feeling of estrangement and also the estranged organization that belongs to another person." Once again, it is three generations that we are looking at for, clinically speaking, "the parents themselves are not the only protagonists of the relationship" (p. 107). Rather, by way of the fantasy that one's own objectified ego is loved as "the centre and the owner of the world" (p. 105) and by way of the alienation of the individual by his introjection of *the entirety of the parents' own history*, the family system is enlarged and perpetuated, as is also seen in the transgenerational impact of sibling relationships (cf. Coles, 2007).

What all these studies show us is that transgenerational transmission is not reducible to the child's imitation of parental behavior or to ideas passed through the generations: Rather, it is the consequence of psychological mechanisms, for the most part unconscious, that bear on the child's identity, mechanisms of which memory is a key component insofar as it is implicit within all behavioral patterns. In its relation to fantasy, unconscious memory provides the individual with an organizing structure by taking, in the developing ego, the form of identification with selected aspects of internalized objects. It is beyond the scope of our present purposes to consider in depth how identification, with its encrypting in memory of relational paradigms, may be transmitted across generations. Suffice it to say that the infant–caregiver dyad, as viewed by many today, is not a starting point of ego development, but a nodal point of fantasy continuance, the means whereby object and self-representation are incorporated into memory and behavioral patterns repeated on the basis of that incorporation.

Consider the mother who tends to be dissociative: Disconfirming in her child the existence of any subjective experience whose expression destabilizes her, her consistent non-recognition of aspects of her child's experience will force those aspects to be subjectively felt not as who she *is* but who she is *not*. Non-recognition that is unrelenting is fearsome, traumatizing even, as we saw in the story shared by Jenny Kaufmann; when this child becomes an adult with children of her own, it is likely that she will repeat the attachment behavior for identification through attachment—identification always harboring an element of fantasy—is a shaper of the child's core identity. And that repetition, or some variation of it, may be passed on to subsequent generations.

Consider also the child who rids herself of what is experienced as intolerable by emptying it into the parental object representation and then identifies with that fantasized perception of its location in the other so as to exert control over it within her own self. Projective identification is a powerful mechanism of transmission of relational patterns, one that is common both to parents and children, transmitters and receptors. Robin Silverman and Alicia Lieberman (1999) have explored its function in the context of violent behavioral patterns whose mutual influence extends both forward and backward across generational barriers. Delineating "both the processes by which parents transmit traumatically based internal representations to their children and the child's assumption of the parent's experience, which is then secured at the level of fantasy and manifested in costly cognitive, affective, and behavioral patterns," Silverman and Lieberman describe the child's interaction with the parent such that "each influences and modifies the other" (pp. 162, 172). Here, again, one sees ample evidence of the manifestations of such transmission across multiple generations.

Consider, finally, in the context of the permeability of psychic borders between adult children and their parents, the matter of estrangement. Estrangement may constitute, among other things, a defensive maneuver against dependence that manifests in the grown child's own parental caretaking. Parental anxieties about separation that impede individuation and autonomy in their children may be such that the next generation similarly wages battle against the perceived threat of independence beyond adolescence, the period to which such struggle is normally restricted. And from that generation it proceeds to the next. Defense, as we see from each of these examples, is indeed a powerful tool, one that protects against the imagination—yet it is also a powerful legacy, one not infrequently ripe for continual transmission.

But when such examples occur throughout multiple generations of a family, is it always that attachment patterns are repeated ad infinitum? Is the memory in which fantasy is grounded, in other words, always a relational a priori? What are we to say when such behavioral patterns skip a generation? Do we then determine that such unconsciously motivated behaviors are not necessarily restricted to aspects of dyadic bonding (or its disruption), that is, to experience? Are we not also obliged to recognize that neurobiology and interpersonal relations constitute a complementary inheritance?

Twin studies suggest that genetics play a role in certain sensitivities (affect regulation and impulsivity, for example) demonstrating that behavior itself is not inherited but that alterations in neurotransmitter systems are transmittable. And structural changes in the brain (such as in the region involved in emotional memory, the hippocampus), thought to occur as the result of trauma, add to the biology of vulnerability (see Siever, 1997).

I have argued (in agreement with Zeki, Solms, and others) that a primary function of the brain is the seeking of knowledge. As information conveyed transgenerationally, knowledge genetically proscribed is also experience driven: "Human beings do adapt to their environments by means of transmitting from generation to generation an acquired 'record' of the experience of the group," as Henry Edelheit (1978, p. 65) has put it, confirming the Lamarckism to which Freud himself subscribed.[1] (Epigenetics, as I claimed earlier, would appear to prove Lamarck right, just as Darwin is proven right by genetic encoding in DNA.) Yet Zeki's initial question concerning the "organizing principle" necessary for the acquisition of knowledge has not been addressed.

What is required for the absorption of data as knowledge? Zeki (1998) locates it in the brain's capacity to abstract, which he defines in physiological terms as the ability of different areas of the cerebral cortex (the visual, auditory, somato-sensory, and so on) to emphasize the general over the particular. Abstraction is not the domain of sensory regions of the brain alone. Cognition and judgment, of course, play important roles, as do other activities and physiological properties of the brain. Neither is abstraction independent of the capacity for specification; the latter being a derivative of the former. But it is the capacity to recognize or identify, and this through perceptual constancy, that permits the brain to acquire knowledge in an efficient way. Zeki's experimentation has focused of late primarily on vision, which he deems the most efficient of the knowledge-acquiring senses. (Indeed, some kinds of knowledge are limited to that sense alone—color, for example, or facial expression.) Examples from visual art, in fact, are most often used to support his thesis that "color or object constancy," "situational constancy" (when the brain categorizes, over and above the particularities of a given event or situation, its being festive, sad, or otherwise), and "narrative constancy" (identification of a scene in a painting, say, despite variations in detail or style) are what allow the brain to

1 "When Ernest Jones begged Freud to omit from *Moses and Monotheism* a passage promulgating the Lamarckian view of inheritance (the inheritance of acquired characteristics), Freud simply refused. Jones argued that no responsible biologist any longer regarded Lamarckian theory as tenable. Freud replied that they were all wrong and that the passage must stay" (Edelheit, 1978, p. 62).

extract from the persistent variability in information it accesses those elements necessary for identification of the characteristic features of what is viewed. This extraction of constant and distinctive properties is the principal requirement of knowledge acquisition, much information being discarded as a result of comparison with what is already stored as known. Memory, then, is the *sine qua non* of knowledge as a primary function of the brain.

Yet it is the association of memory with fantasy—"two classes of knowledge" as Solms and Turnbull remind us (2002, p. 139)—that I wish to underscore here, for it is in their overlap that transmission across generations occurs. And relational patterns between self and other, such as they are transmitted across generations, become psychic knowledge precisely through the kind of abstraction that Zeki defines in terms of visual knowledge and knowledge derived from the other senses as well. To cite J. M. Knox (2001), relational patterns are "stored in implicit memory in the form of internal working models, which can be considered to be *both a form of memory and a form of fantasy* because the wishes, fears, dreams which we bring to an experience become incorporated into the memory of that experience" (p. 631; emphasis added).

The writings of the late French novelist Nathalie Sarraute dramatize the point, particularly the autobiographical *Enfance* (Childhood), in which she demonstrates how the data of sense perception (even that which is preverbal) are transcribed (in the present or later on) into knowledge precisely via word and image. Sarraute also powerfully illustrates the potential damage caused by not giving voice to pain that has been silenced and how subjective is the constitution of meaning ultimately sought by the mind/brain through memory. "'It isn't your home,'" the author remembers her stepmother replying to the question of whether they would soon be going home. So painful is the remembrance that Sarraute fears "losing touch with reality, of taking off into fiction" as she relives the experience in articulating it. Yet, informed that she might not have "received" the phrase as she did, she comes to reflect on other options: She might, for example, "to keep within the bounds of reality, try to imagine that [her step-mother] used those words because it was still understood [her biological] mother was going to take [her] back." Or she might, this time, consider that the responsibility of making a permanent home for the child was more than the young stepmother had anticipated and that her response was not the cruel rejection it appeared to be, but an effort to unload a weight too burdensome for her to carry. In this way she comes to "know" the words as retainers of sensations. She comes to "know" that phrases that run throughout the book—"*Nein, das tust du nicht*" ("No, you're not to do that"); "What a tragedy, though, to have no mother"; "How can anyone hate a child?"—are as traps "which pounce on you and hold you captive" (1984, p. 107). She comes to the knowledge that the meaning of words is not innate within them, but determined by her reception and memory of them, by the force of her fear that shut out any ambiguity to fix within them the meaning *she* gave them: "Even at that moment, there was nothing in them, nothing around them that was invisible, nothing to be discovered, to be examined ... the way I received them, they were closed on all sides, completely clear and naked" (pp. 115–116). As she so wonderfully illustrates in *Enfance*, this knowledge is liberating and empowering; it is precisely what allows her to utilize words creatively as a writer thereby increasing her sense of mastery over her anxieties, increasing her sense of efficacy, and increasing her sense of self as executor—what Joan Raphael-Leff (2009) calls "generative agency."

Imagination, knowledge, reward

Sarraute came to the knowledge of herself as owner of the meaning ascribed to words she remembered by imagining other meanings they might have had. She released herself from the terrifying captivity of words and phrases by fantasizing and she did so in much the same way as the child who uses play in the aim of negotiating separation and fear (cf. Raphael-Leff, 2009, p. 40). This play with fantasy came from the memory of the words themselves—"'It isn't your home'"—that enabled her to depict the process on the larger scale of the literary work (necessarily part reality part fiction). "Generative agency," the enabling of creativity (generativity) through knowledge born of fantasizing, returns us to the notion that feed-forward in the making of art is feed-back dependent. Added to the formula now, however, is the pleasure of enhanced agency the ownership of meaning affords. It is the reward, in a word, of knowledge whose perceptual object is knowledge itself, the gratification of input that stimulates, in turn, further imaginative output in a process of renewal.

How is Zeki's notion of abstraction as requisite to the acquisition of knowledge relevant to the interplay of memory and fantasy Sarraute's writing evokes? I would argue that what is abstracted from the flow of information, from the variability in what she relates as perceived both externally and internally, is a glimmer of the constancy and even potency of self. Erik Erikson (1956) famously wrote of identity as "a persistent sameness within oneself" (p. 57). I would suggest that the "generative agency" Sarraute illustrates so finely in her work (and which exemplifies the case of the artist more generally) is an augmented capacity to create that derives from an increased awareness of that sameness, a constancy obtained through the diminution of excessive fear and anxiety (and its disintegrating consequences) and strengthened by the finding, through the fantasized meanings of words and phrases, of her place within a complex system of familial relations and exquisitely articulated modes of attachment. Sarraute's often riveting determination to situate herself historically brings to mind one objective among others of the family romance fantasy—knowledge of the self through knowledge of one's history (Freud, 1909 [1908]).

Not uncommonly, it is the fantasy of the child who has suffered early object loss (either through death or disappearance of another sort) that the absent object will return. As in the family romance, in which fantasy parents of superior lineage are imagined as replacements for the child's birth parents, the fantasized relationship with the absent parental figure is idealized. As noted earlier, silence on the part of a remaining or substitute parent makes metabolization of loss that much more difficult; in the case of very early loss before the child herself is able to put words to feelings, idealized mythmaking is intimately connected to the developing sense of who one is. This was certainly true of Kaufmann, for she lost her mother when she was not yet of an age when she would have been verbally proficient. Despite her inability to articulate her loss and the inaccessibility of material memories of her mother, and despite her having "a sense of strength and determination" suggestive of her having achieved "a core sense of self" prior to her loss, her fantasies were meant to supply her with a sense of identity through the *story* of the life she was meant to have had. One significant feature of the narrative she creates lies in her modeling of herself as a writer (in addition to being an analyst) after the writer–mother she never really knew (2011, p. 180). The need for idealization and identification with a mother lost to her at a later age than Kaufmann's (and not through death), an age when words that would ultimately serve her therapeutically were available to her and became the objects of intense scrutiny, are eventually obliterated for Sarraute, however, by the persistent replaying of phrases that progressively bring forth the true meaning of the absence, the rejection it signified.

In an illuminating paper that merits renewed attention today, Anna Freud (1960) took issue with John Bowlby's biological theory of the inborn urge of the infant to bond with its mother and the attachment behavior deriving from this bonding or its disruption. Not that the biological and behavioral considerations themselves were found lacking by Freud (or by Melanie Klein who, as Bowlby's supervisor during his training, had already stressed the importance of a child's fantasies about her mother over the real world events of greater interest to her supervisee). But the data derived from them, Freud maintained, were insufficient without regard for the metapsychological thinking at the core of psychoanalytic theory:

> As analysts we do not deal with drive activity as such but with *the mental representations of the drives*. In the case of the biological tie of the infant to the mother this representation has to be recognized, I believe, in the infant's inborn readiness to cathect objects with libido. Equally, we do not deal with happenings in the external world as such but with their repercussions in the mind,

> i.e., with *the form in which they are registered by the child.* In the case of the activating events, it seems to me that they are experiences as events in *the pleasure-pain series.*
>
> (p. 54; emphasis added)

Mental life, she explained—built as it is "on the drive derivatives and the dynamic interplay between them; on the sensations and perceptions arriving from the internal and external world; on the pleasure-pain experiences; on mental imagery and fantasies" (p. 54)—implicates complexities not accounted for in Bowlby's theorizing on attachment. If, as I have ventured, the schism today between relational and classical thinking in psychoanalysis need not be viewed as an irreconcilable dichotomy of paradigms, it is that the "new" research in attachment theory is essentially a return to the bend in a road we have been down before. What takes us *beyond* it are precisely the points made by Anna Freud (and highlighted in the citation) regarding constructs in the mind as *derivatives* and *registrations*—abstractions as opposed to actualities—and the primacy of pleasure as the basis for psychodynamic (and, I would add, aesthetic) exploration and change. Therein, in fact, is to be found the "organizing principle" behind the transformation of perceptual data into the psychically "known": Gratification obtained by the knowledge-seeking brain.

When Anna Freud was writing, and more to the point, when her father was developing his thinking on the "pleasure-pain series" to which she refers, the neurobiology of the brain was little understood. Today we know that the brain does indeed have reward centers, assemblages of cortical and sub-cortical pathways whose "physiological profile depends upon the sustained and controlled release of neuro-modulators such as dopamine, oxytocin, vasopressin and serotonin" and that mediate patterns of cell firing "strongly related to satisfaction and satiety" (Zeki, 2009, p. 204). (For its involvement in sexual arousal and modulation of neuronal activity by increases in levels of dopamine, the nucleus accumbens, in each hemisphere of the brain, is commonly cited as one such center in the multi-nodal system of brain regions constituting the pleasure center.) Chief among the impediments to the gratification of the pleasure and reward centers that constitute the neurological basis of Freud's pleasure principle is variability (innate or acquired) in the brain, for its being a source of constant conflict with the uniformity imposed on humankind by society. Also at odds, however, with the satisfaction of the reward centers, and for Zeki of the utmost importance, is the knowledge-seeking function of the brain, the knowledge-acquiring role of that organ, with its "capacity to form synthetic concepts that are commonly left unsatisfied" (p. 206).

Thus fantasizing, the storytelling of creative writing, even the narrative of visual art, all serve a psychobiological function in as much as pleasure resides in the lessening of that unsatisfied need, in the reduction of variability (which is to say, the increase of synthesis) attained through the granting of aesthetic form. Unconscious identification, as summarily discussed already in the context of early object loss, is one mode through which the synthesizing story aimed at reducing the pain of "not knowing," the unpleasure of the infinite variability of unlived experience, may be told. Memory as fantasy and fantasy as memory, in other words, render the virtual real.

The reduction of variability and the increase of synthesis are served as well, however, by the servicing of ego function in relation to the self. "The self is always divided into many dimensions ('actual self,' 'ideal self,' 'social self'); into levels of maturation ('infantile self,' 'mature self'); and into foci of identification (object representations)," as Pinchas Noy (1979, p. 244) writes, and the ego must exert significant and persistent effort to maintain the integrity of the self. Ordering and organizing by the perfecting of aesthetic form is yet another mode through which the ego may do so:

> The search for "perfect form" in art, including its elements of order, symmetry, harmony, and balance, is a part of the organizational effort, and it reflects the activities of the ego in ordering the disparate parts of the self, in reconciling the opposites that may threaten to tear the self apart, and in enabling the maintenance of a stable self-image.
>
> (pp. 244–245)

Pleasure in the capacity of the imagination derives from the reduction in variability and the protection of the self against divisive forces, to be sure, but it also ensues from the increase in agency that Raphael-Leff (2009) defines as deriving "from ownership of achievement and the power of one's own ideas" (p. 40). Margaret Mahler's (1967) description of the driving force behind early child development, behind the earliest "self-feeling" that originates out of the pleasurable state of symbiosis with mother, comes to mind. The child's development of self and even her personality depend for Mahler upon her response to her mother's own responsiveness to the progressing individuation. Like the child who responds to mother's mirroring by increasingly becoming aware of her self as autonomous, the artist responds to her work with the enhanced sense of agency that, in turn, generates further creative activity. Raphael-Leff adds to the idea of artistic expression as promoter of "generative agency" the additional component of gender identity and the idea that awareness of anatomical difference, with its acceptance and transcendence in play, "entails a momentous shift from being someone else's creation to becoming a potential (pro-) creator" (p. 15). This shift involves changes in affect brought on by feelings of inadequacy and powerlessness accompanied by the desire and need for competence and control. As omnipotence and grandiosity yield to greater awareness of reality, the quality of play becomes noticeably different and, at around three years of age, "generative identity" extends to "generative agency." What child development teaches us about creativity, in sum, is precisely what Raphael-Leff has observed in her clinical work: That "creative mental activity and fantasy production are in themselves enlivening," "that production of symbolic imagery provides empowerment," and that "endorphins aside, part of the exhilaration of imaginative play is a developing sense of *creative agency*" (p. 40). Using one's own capacity to metabolize experience through its aesthetic depiction or to aesthetically portray some form of experience in its originality is exhilarating precisely because it implies competence and the ability of the imaginative artist, like the playful child, to mine one's inner resources (cf. p. 40).

Jenny Kaufmann has said that the preverbal (immaterial or non-objectified) memory of her mother is what has sustained her through a lifetime of trauma (personal communication). That memory, like the verbal memories of Sarraute, is deeply invested with emotion and, therefore, embodied by the biology of the self (that is, the libidinal energy of the child), while also informed by patterns of attachment (inclusive of rupture) and the fantasies to which they give rise. The continued dichotomizing of drive and relational theories is not in the best interest of understanding the mind/brain, indeed, human functioning generally speaking. Rather, greater recognition of the role played by object relations in drive theory (already prominent in Freud) and, in attachment theory, of biological imprinting and child development should allow our attention to turn to the now most critical matter of agency—agency as an affirmation and enhancement of identity and self and as generator of creative capacities in the individual, as the interviews with artist children of artist parents in the following chapter are meant to show.

5

THE ANXIETY OF INFLUENCE REVISITED

Artists of artist parents

Some years ago, critic Harold Bloom (1973) wrote a short book in which he described a theory of poetic influence. His argument was that intra-poetic relationships are indistinguishable from the history of poetry and that "strong poets make that history by misreading one another, so as to clear imaginative space for themselves" (p. 5). Poetic influence, Bloom reasoned, does not render poets any less original, although it is feared that it does, and this is the anxiety of which he writes: the anxiety of influence, the title of his book.

By "poetic influence," Bloom does not mean the ideas and images that are transmitted from earlier to later poets or anything else that might be located in source studies or even in the biographies of poets. Rather, he refers to profundities found only in "the study of the life-cycle of the poet-as-poet" (p. 7). Poetic influence or "poetic misprision," as Bloom prefers to call it, may consist in *correction* of the precursor's work or in *completion* of it; that is, a reading of the parent work in a sense other than that in which it was written. It may take the form of deflation of self in the younger poet or of a "flooded apprenticeship" (whose uncanny effect is not that the new work appears as if written by the precursor, but that work characteristic of the master appears now to have been written by the apprentice). Bloom's thesis is best summed up as follows:

> [A] poet's stance, his Word, his imaginative identity, his whole being, must be unique to him, and remain unique, or he will perish, as a poet, if ever even he has managed his re-birth into poetic incarnation. But this fundamental stance is as much also his precursor's as any man's fundamental nature is also his father's however transformed, however turned about.
>
> (p. 71)

I cite Bloom here because his theory of poetry may be broadened to the discussion of imagination with regard to all the arts, but also and, more important, because the anxiety of influence subsumes internalization the various forms of which reveal the many functions of fantasy. In the current section of this volume, I look at the imaginative expression of fantasy as a product of internalization, of self and object representation (in some measure unconsciously imposed by the parent upon the developing child), and at the transgenerational transmission of fantasy (and the defenses it may evoke). Reserving for later discussion of the construct of self with regard to the imaginative expression of fantasy, I explore in this chapter the experience of several artists working in the same artistic modality as an artist parent and I do so for much the same reason that led Bloom to his theory of poetry: The belief that what is unique to the artist (literary or visual) is not unique in the sense of entirely new. In broadening the scope of the "anxiety of influence," however, I am extending the concept of "misprision" to the internalized objects and object relations with which our deepest fantasies are concerned.

Investigation of the intellectual milieu that gave rise to an artistic movement or to the creative expression of an individual is the work of cultural historians. But what that creative process *feels* like subjectively has not yet found its place in the literature. What we mean by imagination and the fantasy in which it is articulated was the focus of the earliest chapters of this study, but *how* and *what* that expression *gratifies* remains to be explored. Looking at, listening to the art of those born of artist parents, particularly those whose artistic practice is of the same genre as their parents', tells us much that is significant about whence their work emerges. It tells us much about the playing out of internalized interpersonal configurations in art and how this adds to the conceptualization of art as an active process of expressing, resisting, and reconstituting desire and instinctual need. Art made by artists who are the offspring of other artists, furthermore, should also tell us much about the diminution of the "anxiety of influence" that accompanies the increase in agency, the growth and self-awareness, and the satisfaction inherent within the granting of new meanings to what has already been encoded within.

I make the point throughout this book that imagination (and what I mean by "creativity") is not the making of images *ex nihilo*, but the association to images and percepts encoded in memory and the generative capacity of that association. How encoding occurs is not only a matter of higher level cognitive function and the impact of visual perception on thought, but of one's inner representational world as determined by emotional development and growth. Object and object relation representations structure personality and they do so in ways that have been outlined by Freud and by numerous psychoanalysts since. Although there is considerable variation in its definition, the concept of internalization has remained central to the storing of objects (in the psychoanalytic sense) and relational patterns in the mind. Indeed, it is the process around that representations, as informational content (or "ideas," as Roy Schafer calls them), coalesce.

In his now classic work *Aspects of internalization*, Schafer (1968) considers how the triad of incorporation, introjection, and identification reveals fantasies associated with internalization and, without entering into detail, we can summarize with David Olds (2006) the distinctions Schafer makes between them: "*Incorporation* involves a kind of fantasy of taking in the object in a way that resembles eating it"; "*Introjection* is the taking in of the object as a kind of fantasy and retaining that object in a virtual inner space such that one can have a dialogue with it. This may more accurately be described as internalizing the object *relationship*, in the form of a virtual dyad"; and "*Identification* is the modification of the self to resemble the other" (pp. 20–21). Unlike the fantasies of incorporation and introjection, identification involves the wish (conscious or unconscious) to become like the internalized other, though the emotional valence of the relation of self to that other is not to be assumed by the mere fact of the wish: While that valence may indeed be positive, negative emotions or aggressive impulses may, of course, foster such a wish defensively.

Contextualized internal representations of objects and object relations are the substance of the narrative psychoanalysis progressively creates. So, too, they are the substance of the artistic corpus, the "life-cycle of the poet-as-poet." Therein resides the "anxiety of influence," but also the uniqueness of the artist's imaginative being. Bromberg (2006) contends that:

> [I]n clinical work emotional experience must be generated in a way that allows the self as agent to be present simultaneously with the self who experienced the event. It is the analyst's job to facilitate this process and thereby allow the patient to be fully present in all his particularity.
>
> (p. 199)

Making art is comparable in that, while the work cannot be reduced to the psychobiography of the artist and should not be used to analyze (or worse, pathologize) the artist, the psychohistorical perspective—especially when offered by the artist him or herself—can shed light on how the sense of self as agent is enhanced by the creative act in much the same way as it is in psychoanalysis, that is, *by the coexistence of the artist's self in the present with the self of his or her past*. It is the artist with an artist parent who puts this point very much in high relief.

Kiki Smith

Kiki Smith is a New York City-based artist born in 1954 to opera singer Jane Smith and architect/sculptor Tony Smith. Considered among the most revolutionary artists of our time, her work is enormously varied in subject, size, and material. Religion, mythology, cosmology, folk tales, and feminism have all left their thematic mark on her powerfully rendered drawings, prints, sculptures, room-sized installations, photographs, and miniatures. Smith works in plaster, clay, paper, glass, bronze, beeswax, papier mâché and whatever other materials suit her extraordinarily innovative and ever expanding investigation of human and non-human experience of being in the world. As has been noted, her art is "by turns intimate, universal, visceral, and fragile" and it continually provokes us "to think in new ways about the physical, philosophical, and social issues of our time" (Grynsztejn, 2005).

Raised in New Jersey with twin sisters, Smith was as a child apprentice to her father. Tony Smith worked center stage in the family home and he regularly had his young daughters make cardboard models for his modernist sculptures. Although in her youth Kiki Smith resented the discipline involved, as an adult she is "endlessly appreciative" of having learned, and in that way, what it is to work. Indeed, her father put his art before all else, and whatever the emotional consequences of that for his daughter, and whatever the psychological reasons for her doing so, she clearly took in her father's regulating of life by art, his need to prioritize as he did, and it has served her well: She has said she creates "messes" in her personal and daily life, and that her labor-intensive art making requires her to be pragmatic and affords her a sense of control.

Following a year at Hartford Art School, Kiki Smith moved to New York in 1976 setting up shop in her own home. Interestingly, like their father, neither she nor her photographer sister, Seton, has ever had a studio. In her interview with me, Smith spoke of always having worked in a house: "I never had a studio. When I have attempted it—because, you know, it's like a prize in art school—it was like being ripped from familial life. It's just depressing to me." I wondered how this need to work in a domestic environment (her current "studio" is the living room of her large house on the Lower East Side of Manhattan) might relate to her father's also having worked at home, and not in an attic or annex but in a very centralized space. Might it provide a means of emotional connection to him? After all, most artists retire to the spatial elsewhere a studio provides to stave off intrusion from the outside. Smith sees her working, just as he did, in the midst of all else as a matter of that having been her "model." But what was it that made that model so meaningful to her, indeed so emotionally necessary to her, that it remains determinative to this day? Smith situates it in "The idea that there was integration, no separation between the life and work space physically and mentally." The spatial integration of life and work as emblematic of, or at least a dimension of, the mental integration is telling: It would seem to say much about a shared (internalized) relation to external reality. Roy Shafer (1968) has noted that daydreaming renders the environment passive with respect to the daydreamer's wishes. The Smiths' integration of life and work seemingly serves an analogous purpose.

I inquired further about Smith's relationship as an artist (often making sculpture) to her sculptor father. Asked specifically about any competitive feelings she may have had, she replied:

> I realized I was competitive with my father when I realized how much I felt like a failure. I always felt like a failure. When I was young I would see friends of my father and cross the street because I was felt so ashamed as though I was presumptuous to put myself in the same arena as them. My father was immensely intelligent, and knowledgeable, and he had a lot of information. The idea of putting myself in that pantheon was really mortifyingly embarrassing or humiliating or putting myself in a position to be embarrassed and humiliated. I remember that the first review I had somewhere said I should leave art making to my father. What I was making was ridiculous, but I felt like I was healthy enough or I needed it enough [to go on doing it]. That was the place where I felt most comfortable, the most myself, the most able; it's the place where I get to feel the most evident or share myself the best. Twice I had boyfriends who said, "You're going to be more famous than your father." It scared me! It scared me and made me ashamed to be taking my father's space. But as I get older, I get to enjoy my father's work. I love my father's work. I grew up loving it and taking it as a reality, as a possible. I believe in the possibility of his work and I like that I can be beneficial to his work as an adult and to my sister Seton's.

In the winter of 2002–2003, the Palm Beach Institute of Contemporary Art ran a group show, "The Smiths," with the work of Tony, Kiki, and Seton. Critics differed on the degree of congruence, despite differences in medium, some seeing a very apparent connection between the three, others seeing none. I asked this Smith how she sees her work in relation to the other Smiths:

> My father's work and my sister's work are completely familiar. I *know* their work in a visceral, emotional, spiritual way that is common to me in the sense that it is *of the same*, even though we were very different; we had very different ideas. I admire both of them and I have been lucky in a lot of ways that they weren't.
>
> I was 26 when my father died and I was so very young emotionally. My father was supportive of me making things, but I was also happy that he died because I don't think I would have become me. I would have been too self-conscious to be me with him there; I would have been too ashamed to show him what I was doing, to be judged. You don't want to have to murder your family to have autonomy but sometimes it doesn't hurt when they disappear. Half of my family is alive

> and half is dead. I really don't mean it; I would prefer that they were all here and that I had grown up. But I think there are ways in which people gain autonomy and freedom. I always thought we were like a string with sugar crystals growing around it, that we had all decided to stick together in a family constellation, and when people leave you can turn to other people and project people into those roles if you need to, but you can also be free of that kind of relationship. I like that idea. It wasn't like genesis or that we were from one another but that we were in a constellation for a given period of time. It's more that there are certain profound interior activities that you've recognized and that because of that you were together as a family, that we were able to recognize one another in some way. Rothko's children talk about their father in a way that I really couldn't talk about my father. My father's work to me is extremely subjective: I have a visceral, emotional response to it.

Smith's idealized cosmology of the family is curiously juxtaposed to the "visceral, emotional" responsiveness of which she speaks. And the dichotomy is clearly reflected in her work where the celestial and the earthly meet.

Also of particular interest, particularly in view of the preceding comments, is that the artist has repeatedly said she does not think she is good at sculpting:

> I'm not good at making things, but it doesn't stop me. Some people are stopped by things that are perceived as hindrances, that they aren't good at. That's the part I really enjoy, that I have to work at it! I'm not good at it; I have to struggle, but that's the part I like. *I like the struggle. I like that I have to work at it*. I like the *discovery* involved in it. Not having aptitude is not a reason not to do something. I am essentially a self-taught person. I had to teach myself the conventions; in art school you learn about perspective—I certainly never used it in my work! Not having aptitude is not a reason for not doing things. I've had many students and many friends who had enormous aptitude for doing anything but what they were peripherally doing had no real necessity in it, whereas art is completely about necessity. It's an investigation, it's exploratory. You have to have a very deep payoff in it, in your identity.
>
> I remember a friend of mine, older than me, who used to say that you have to have a very deep connection to it so that people can see that you care. But it can't be so idiosyncratic that it is incomprehensible. It has to be able to have its own life, separate from me. I am not making things to reveal myself, or to be perceived as autobiographical. I am not interested in trying to show myself. Winnicott said artists wish to

> reveal themselves and to remain hidden. I think it's like an army; you get to put out all your soldiers so they can't get to you; it's like there is this moat between your work and you. So in one way it does represent you, but in another way it doesn't, it's separate from you. In a way there is this risk taking when you put it in public. It's like showing a little too much flesh, but at the same time; it gives them space to have their lives, people get to have an authentic experience of their own, not your experience. If I talk about why I make certain things, it can have a narrative, but that's very different from the work itself. It has to have enough space for other people to enter into. My work is not didactic. I'm not trying to make ideological stamps on the universe, how I think people should be or how my life is. It's like a buoy on the sea, a Flying Dutchman. It moves and shifts. You have to have a very deep personal and emotional connection to what you are doing, that somehow makes your life better, but also it's just interesting how things are put together. We live in visual world, in a tactile, visual three-dimensional world. Lots of things have a developed history, a developed social, economic, emotional language that we have inherited. We know language, we know object language. We know pattern recognition; we know the material of culture. What one is doing is playing in those possibilities.

Describing more about her subjective experience of making art, what being an artist feels like to her, Smith continued:

> You can have an initial impetus, but what happens is different. Present making is a very big part of making art to me. People please. That you can generate something that is generative, that you get to show interconnections, citations to other artists' work. It just feels good. There are just so many different reasons and ways for why one would do something.
>
> Often it is just tremendous fear and despair: "What will I do? Life will fall apart." Then I remember that I am not on *my* time, on *my* schedule, but that I have been given part of creativity, that each person has their splinter. Sometimes I want to be *their* splinter. Sometimes I am jealous: How come they have been given more creativity? How come things in their lives seem more bountiful? How come they are more able to do things in a more organized way? It's just a stupid sibling way. Or sometimes I can have feelings of terror when there is no particular apparent thing to be doing, or I can't feel it.
>
> A lot of times you are making the future and you don't know it; you don't have a visceral or conscious awareness; you can't taste how it is

connected so you just have to have faith; I have to trust my work and follow it. And then five or ten years later you see it, you see it as a link past to future. You have to take a chance on doing it. It's a collaboration between you and the world. You're given one bit of information, then there is a distraction, you have to do something. Everything in its own time. Without time you wouldn't have had the knowledge, you wouldn't have had the realization. You wouldn't have had that six months earlier or two years earlier. It's not on our time. It's something that is going through you. You have to have a good reason to participate in it. People don't participate if they don't have good enough payoff in it ... It always is a collaboration.

When I was younger, I was frightened to finish things. I couldn't see the difference between having an idea and doing it. Doing it beat the crap out of you! You may have initial idea; but then you have to have the real *experience*. That's where things come out very different, in a way you never have imagined it. You can have presumptions about what you want it to be. A lot of it is about giving up your daily life personal agenda and seeing what happens. In hindsight, I can see that a lot of my work is incredibly biographical, sometimes in a very psychological way and sometimes in a very literal way. And also my interests as I get older change—how I want to be an artist, what I think it means to be an artist, what I want to do with that privilege of being a public artist and also what subjects are engaging to me. And sometimes you have to go back, you have to go back and deal with what you left unfinished, what is incomplete; sometimes it is like you are catching up; you are going over old turf that you're not satisfied with. Also, art is a job. Somebody wants something; you get on a train and go do it. There is a lot to being a career artist that is different from being a "pure" artist because it's a job. I spend half my time in airports flying about here and there. But that enables me to have the times when I just get to work. Then there's also that making art gives you an excuse to learn about things. It's a way of getting an education; it's a self-education in all different kinds of ways—physical, emotional, spiritual, domestic.

Asked more about the *pleasure* involved for her in making art, Smith revealed that there is a way in which making art "saves [her] life." By that she meant that it occupies her time, gives her something to do. Having an art career has many kinds of psychological implications, she mused, in the kind of attention it beings to the self, but there is also this: "It has a repetitive aspect to it and a cumulative aspect to it. It calms one down, physiologically. You get free of yourself by the activity; you get less self-conscious."

Alluding further to her feeling that she is "someone who has no inherent talent for making things," she spoke more of the *pleasure* she derives from the creative act:

> I am not somebody who has a lot of ability to render things in a classical European mode. I have gotten better at it. But there is a pleasure in that struggle, being on a journey, not in terms of the content but, in terms of process. In etching, you start out with nothing and keep going back and back and back. You reiterate your commitment to something and you keep going back in your relationship to inanimate objects, with their physical properties. Your work is a collaboration between you and the universe.

"What about the collaboration between you and the artwork?" I inquired:

> You are in a dialogue. I don't think about it in terms of the specifics of the artwork, but in terms of the physical quality, the material qualities of what I am working with. Often, you have an initial intention, but I am not an imaginative person; I don't have a lot of imaginary interior life going on.

This was astonishing to hear, and not once but several times, from one with so uncanny an ability to transform the commonplace into the captivating, from a so truly innovative and, indeed, imaginative artist. Smith not only transforms unusual (blood, milk, semen) and sometimes banal (glitter, body casts, glass beads) matter into aesthetic material, but relates the human body with nature and the cosmos in such a way that her work is simultaneously both exceedingly physical and deeply spiritual. The print *Untitled* (1985), for instance, links an entangled intestinal form with insects and leaves that play off one another. *For All Souls* (1988) compares human with artistic reproduction through the repetition of images of fetuses. As has been noted:

> The artist made *All Souls* at a time when she was creating a body of work about birth. Her title, however, alludes to All Souls' Day, a Catholic feast day celebrated on November 2, when the faithful pray for the souls of the dead who have not yet fully atoned for their sins. This day also coincides with *Día de los Muertos* or Day of the Dead, a festival which Smith observed in Mexico in 1985. The spirits of the deceased return to their loved ones on the Day of the Dead, which is observed on November 1 and 2. Celebrants honor deceased infants on the first day and adults on the second. *All Souls* is infused with a spirit of birth; the work's title, however, implies

> a spiritual presence in death, and the connotations of that title further animate the work.
>
> (Whitney Museum of American Art, 2006)

"So you're not aware of fantasy motivating your work?" I probed:

> Not so much. Things just occur to me, they seem apparent to me to pay attention to, some vision in my head to pay attention to. Some of it comes directly from looking at the world, paying attention to it: Islamic culture put copper and silver together in an inlay as something to pay attention to. I'm very visually oriented and I can see the greatness of historical forms a lot, but often I have no particular personal contact that belongs to that form. It's as though I want to utilize a particular experience, but I don't have any particular reason to be doing it. It's like when you walk down a certain street for no reason. You have no reason to be going there; you just walk down that street.
>
> A lot of the time art is a way of organizing and making a manifestation of one's present condition; it's synthesizing the information that you have been given, that you are paying attention to, and organizing it into physical form. It's like modeling. You're asking, "Is this what reality looks like? Is this a possible model for reality?" A lot in sculpture is also mimicry. It's wanting to include yourself in the continuum and put your feet down. I like that you can just take what occurs to you. A lot of things occur to people but not necessarily in that way, in a visual form. But artists for some reason or other just *do* it; just suspend their disbelief and see what happens. Part of it is like a proof, you can prove your existence and your ability, your power to do things.

Smith's art is often autobiographical: The four-part linocut *How I Know I'm Here* (1985–2000) includes complex images of the artist taken from photographs of her in various poses. *Pietà* (1999) is a moving drawing that shows the artist holding her dead cat. But what comes through most in the autobiographical references is not life narrative, but what is suggested by Bromberg earlier—the bringing together of past and present self-states: Smith has made several photographs of herself in a black, hooded cloak with a basket of apples attesting to her continued and highly motivated interest in fairytales as well as legend and folklore. In *Sleeping Witch* (2000), we see the artist's own hand on a bed of leaves holding a black apple. *Banshee Pearls* (1991) is a self-portrait comprised of 12 lithographs containing multiple images of the artist. Carrie Springer of the Whitney Museum of American Art in New York (which has acquired a substantial collection of Smith's work in a variety of media) explains that "In Irish folklore, a banshee is a female spirit that foretells a death in the family by wailing outside their home. Smith's title also has a personal reference. Her father, who was ill throughout her childhood, used to say that she was 'like a banshee.'" Smith was not a reader as a child; rather, she was very visually oriented and always preoccupied with understanding the appearance of things: "*Looking* was my way," she told me, of taking in the world, a world in which there was much thinking about death:

> My father was sick the whole time. And depressed. I grew up with an abnormal concern about mortality. He thought about death and was very morbid. He was concerned about dying; he planned to die not just once but multiple times. I would say he was a hypochondriac, but he had real diseases, real diseases from his life style. His personality brought on real diseases. Then there was the Catholic thing—the physical manifestation of spirit. We never went to church and we didn't talk about anything in my family, but my father did talk about the body. So that was a barometer, a way to read the landscape: how the body was doing. And it led to how I thought about things in a very physical way.

A constant in the autobiographical depictions is the rejoining of present adult self-states with the self-states of the child of that death-infused environment.

Smith once told an interviewer:

> Skin is the surface or the boundary line of the body's limit. The skin is actually this very porous membrane so on a microscopic level you get into the questions of what's inside and what's outside. Things are going through you all the time. You really are very penetrable on the surface; you just have the illusion of a wall between your insides and your outside.

This is one of the things that interested her around the time that she made the poignantly gestural *Virgin Mary*, a 1993 sculpture of wax, cheesecloth, and wood. Having seen cadavers for the first time, she felt the difference in "working from reality," the difference between "imagining one's body or the insides of the body" and "looking at the insides of a body." But the interest of that piece goes beyond the skin, bodily boundaries, and physicality. The gesture of Virgin Mary is itself truly captivating with its delicacy and grace. Smith (2006) has said she made the piece "in one of the traditional positions of the Virgin Mary," that is, standing with her arms just slightly opened outward. I asked her about a relevant observation she previously made; namely, that "Making those gestures also changes your relationship to your environment." Citing a friend talking about his lover, she explained:

> He would say he wanted someone who could greet him with open arms. And I thought, "I can't do that"; I thought, "I don't have it in me to do that physically," maybe at that moment in my life. He wanted that you could open your body, your soul, your psychic being. And I thought, "I can't do that; that feels too scary." Then I thought that the Virgin Mary—opening her arms just slightly, that lower inclusiveness of her arms—is less threatening than if she had them way up open. When you do that, it physiologically opens up your being. You see that in Tutankhamen's tomb with those women with the scorpion, those sculptures. It's like that. When you do those postures, it's like a mudra, or like a form. Some of those are coded effects in different cultures. But they also have physical effects.
>
> And I had another friend, Margaret Dewys. We practiced posture meditations based on architectural, archetypal types of gesture. By placing your body in specific circumstances or poses it changes your consciousness. I think that's why you can read other people's bodies, other people's gestures. You can hold your body or the body holds you and it happens simultaneously with the physicality ... your mind. When you're making figurative sculpture, you're making gestures and the reading has to come through those gestures. And you can respond to sculpture and read the gesture from two, three, five thousand years ago because you recognize and can read the gesture and put yourself in that situation. When I watch dance, "I know what that feels like." When I was younger I often took on attributes of other people's stance, just the form of the human in our brain is why people can like looking at pictures of flowers as much as the flower, or the image of the person, and not just the person—it sometimes can be preferable to the person. We read the *form* in the picture. It's different from our *idea* of form. Sculpture is about reading form.

Kiki Smith does not perceive her work—with its somewhat scandalous display of body parts, its somewhat disturbing depiction of beasts and monsters, its somewhat repugnant excretions, all of which are highly seductive in their inventiveness if, at times, bordering on the vulgar or repulsive while also uniformly wonderful to behold—as a reaction against the abstract, cool lines of her father's minimalist sculpture. This is an interesting perception in view of the radically different aesthetics that define their work and one might be tempted to see in the difference a defensive maneuver on the part of an artist daughter who felt shame, embarrassment, and failure even—who felt not worthwhile—in the shadow of her great artist father. Yet moving in this interview from humiliation before the greatness of her father to the sense of "power" that making art gives her, and that via the pleasure of the struggle to do what she feels she is not good at, is suggestive of something more fundamental: Making art is her way of avoiding "tremendous fear and despair," while in the making there is such struggle that one takes from the interview the more compelling idea that underlying her art is a fantasy of achieving closeness. Struggling to make what she feels she is not good at is a source of pleasure, as Kiki Smith so clearly states, perhaps because it is an entry into her father's world. He suffered throughout her childhood with physical illness and depression. Her identification with that suffering and her internalization of his "fear and despair" appear to be precisely what allows her to feel validated and good as she makes art. The fantasy of connectedness with father, whether organized around shame (the forbidden desire for closeness), failure (in not being good enough), or object loss (her father's work came before all else), reveals how identification as a means of preserving the object may find expression in a process (however painful) that yields deep gratification.

Jane McAdam Freud

The daughter of Britain's most celebrated 20th century painter, Lucian Freud, Jane McAdam Freud has not only an extraordinary visual, but cultural legacy with which to grapple in her own work as an artist: The great-granddaughter of Sigmund Freud, she has referred to her legacy as "both a blessing and a curse." McAdam Freud is a multidisciplinary artist whose work, comprising drawing, sculpture, and film, is represented widely in collections in Britain, Germany, and Greece as well as the United States. The following interview, conducted prior to her father's death in 2011, further illustrates the subjective meaning of the "pleasure" of making art—the experiential "knowledge" obtained through the generative association that is creativity—as it relates to aspects of identification and internalization of an artist parent:

> *In 2005–2006 you were artist-in-residence at the Freud Museum in London which culminated in an exhibition of a series of prints and in the art book* Relative Relations. *You were interested then in the commonalities between your own art and your great-grandfather's famous collection of antiquities. And you also did some prints of him as well. In those prints there seems to be a special concentration on vision, a preoccupation, perhaps, with eyes and with seeing versus not seeing. In one portrait of Freud, for example, there is an absent right eye (no. 5) and another (no. 12) has an eye that is accentuated by being enclosed within a square. What can you tell me about that? Why the eye? What are you saying about vision, his vision? And had you been in residence*

elsewhere than at the Freud Museum do you think the portraits might have been different in this respect?

In September 2006 my residency culminated in an exhibition of my sculpture and installation works. It did include the two drawings of Sigmund Freud that you mention. In these drawings I wanted to focus my attention on the visual acuity, both conceptual and perceptual of Sigmund Freud; the way in which, as Lesley Chamberlain points out in her book of the following title, he was "The Secret Artist." Chamberlain looks at Freud as a literary artist, but the title inspired me to look at him as a visual artist through his collection of antique sculpture!

Regarding my focus on Freud's eye (or its absence), it is significant that my attention is on his *right* eye in both drawings. The right eye sits on the right side of the brain making reference to lateral cerebral activities. It considers Freud's own creativity. From being an inspiration to the surrealists, I see Freud also as a forerunner to conceptual art practice with his "feel" for ambivalence and for making meaning out of concepts using the material of ideas and associations. As an artist with an inclination towards the conceptual I can connect with him on this level.

It is also interesting that even though Freud built up a large classical sculpture collection and wrote about both Michelangelo and Leonardo he was in denial about his art appreciation. It remained his secret from himself.

In my first drawing, the shape of the square spiral substituting the right eye suits two purposes: Firstly, it is based on the old Freud Museum logo (which I have always liked) and, secondly, the spiral substituting the eye evokes a looking inward for information, both neurologically and psychologically speaking. This image makes references both to the literal interpretation and a conceptual one. The words "Eye Mind" appear along Freud's shirt collar. These words can be read in a literal and separate way as "Eye" and "Mind," drawing attention to the eye (or its location) in the same position we consider the mind to reside—the higher portion of the head. "Eye Mind" can also be interpreted phonetically as "I Mind." Freud did after all mind about the mind—he had his eye on the mind and its workings in as much as psychoanalysis is the understanding of mental processes—the activity of the mind was his greatest concern. Of course, as in all art, it is self-referential—"I Mind."

Freud's eye is lost completely in the second drawing. It is replaced by the words "An Eye Out For Freud" meaning one has to keep a close watch—"An Eye Out" for the point Freud is illustrating while inevitably being inspired by his mass of associated illustrations. One can have so many ideas when reading Freud as his writing is full of associative/conceptual references.

One eye in and one eye out of the drawing with its motto "an eye out for Freud," also shows that dualistic idea of extremes meeting. I was thinking of him being such a visionary and that to see so clearly may also mean to be blind. I wonder what he may have been blind to? So much I can imagine! Is it possible to be so perceptive and have nothing lacking to balance this acute sense of insight? One blind spot was his smoking. His unbreakable addiction may have been part of the other side of his clarity of vision.

The fact that I was Artist in Residence at the Freud Museum explains both why I focused in on Freud the man/relation and why I used the square spiral logo. Had I been Artist in Residence at another venue and had I chosen to make a portrait of Freud then perhaps I wouldn't have focused on the eyes in the same way.

You are an accomplished artist who works in a number of mediums. Like your father, you make sculpture and drawings. Drawing, in fact, was your father's first medium and it continues to be an important part of your work. Do you think you have been consciously or unconsciously influenced in your drawings by his work? Are there images of his work in your mind as you work? Would you agree that there are perhaps memories of his work imprinted within your brain of which you are not consciously aware, but which impact your own work nevertheless?

I do agree that there must be memories of my father's works imprinted within my brain. When working I am not at all conscious of his work. However, I have noticed that sometimes images come through. I do not think that it is necessarily medium related though. One example was an image of a zebra. The piece I carved, "Moments and Memories," was ultimately reproduced as a bronze medal in reward for winning the Italian State Mint prize in 1991. It was years later that I found the early work by my father featuring a zebra's head which I must have seen many times and forgotten.

Another example might be in the use of the couch which I find features heavily in some of my life drawings. Lucian and Sigmund both used this prop. Perhaps my father's way of scrutinizing people while they lie on the couch which features so avidly in his paintings was unconsciously gleaned from my great-grandfather who scrutinized people on his famous psychoanalyst's couch.

There are differences in the way we work, though. My father focuses on painting from life, exploiting paint which is his medium. He does draw too but he is medium led.

I work in the postmodern tradition and my art education took place in a different artistic climate. My work is concept driven. I like to use the medium and dimension according to the concept. That is why

I prefer to work under the title of multidisciplinary artist or conceptual sculptor.

You have made a great many portraits in sculpture. Lucian Freud puts portraits on the canvas. Is there any connection to be made on any level—aesthetic, psychodynamic, neuroscientific—between his portraits and your own?

With the family portraits I can sometimes see an aesthetic connection—we both seem to make the eyes larger than in reality. There is perhaps more of an aesthetic connection with Jacob Epstein's work. As well as Epstein being a sculptor there is another reason. Lucian's early portraits often depict Kitty, who is my half-sister Annabel's mother and Jacob Epstein's daughter. I have made sculpture and drawings of my half-sister Annabel and the drawings have some resonances with Lucian's early images of Kitty (though there is the familial resemblance to consider). In Epstein's portrait sculptures of his wife (Kitty's mother), I can see an uncanny correspondence.

I look at people in the same way as both my father and great-grandfather. The person/effigy is endlessly fascinating and disturbing, but always full of information. I think there is a connection to "analyzing" (whether through image or symbol) that goes back on my father's side to Sigmund. My best portrait so far is coincidently (or perhaps not) my portrait bronze of Annabel; it is truly charged.

Psychodynamically perhaps portraiture is a way of linking to my father however in a medium in which I am able to reinforce my own identity. Otherwise, it may simply be part of my biological programming.

Did you watch your father work as you were growing up?

I do not recall watching him work in childhood but I do have memories of him watching me work. My mother always said that he watched us in fascination but did not interact much. As a child I painted endlessly with poster paints on board and I do remember feeling I was doing something important when I was drawing or painting, as this was the one thing that seemed to capture his attention. I continue to have this feeling as an adult.

How do you think your relationship to your father has revealed itself in your work on levels other than that of the imprinting of visual images in memory? Affectively speaking, for example?

I always want to make images larger than life in every sense which I think I get from an early impression of Lucian's work as demanding attention. This may have been an unconscious instruction and so early on that is what I wanted for my images or objects.

Affectively, having such a famous artist as a father is perhaps the opposite of what a psychoanalyst may surmise. I am neither rebelling nor wanting to emulate as I am not an oil painter and therefore do not feel in competition or overshadowed. My relationship to him on one level is analogous to his with Sigmund. Sigmund presented a great shadow over Lucian, yet Lucian chose a comparable path, albeit using a different medium—similarly scrutinizing the other/the human / human condition. I take the fact that Lucian succeeded against the odds as an inspiration and furthermore as an instruction. I understand that I must forge my own path in my own way while accepting that I am unconsciously doing some things in a similar way.

Aesthetically speaking, your father makes extraordinarily beautiful art while explicitly ignoring the notion of beauty on the canvas. His work is extremely intense and sensual. Your prints appear to me to have a very "fine" quality about them, as though you were trying to distinguish yourself from both the voluptuousness of his work and his aesthetic.

Your first point about the quality of the craft of painting being important in my father's work is well observed and I agree. I do think, however, that his work is also very fine. The considered brush strokes and the quality of the paint involve concentrated, meticulous and measured application. I have studied images containing my father's works in progress and have seen that although the completed paintings look very loose, the canvases are covered methodically from one end to the other. They do not seem to be treated in a broad overall fashion. Early in his education, Lucian was trained at the Central School of Art in what was then the "craft" department. It encompassed engraving seals, metalwork and such skills. The Dutch painters were trained in this way as the training involved understanding the microcosm which can serve in examining the broader brush strokes of the overall. Coincidentally, I was later to do the same course as part of my early training, sitting in the same studios and having the same early instruction.

I have no desire for my work in drawing to be like my father's. It is what it is. My work in drawing objects, for example, makes use of cross-hatching which you can find in the drawing of most artists who have had any classical training. My training included a three-year scholarship in Rome, which had an influence on my drawing technique. However, as I said earlier, my medium and dimension depend on what my concept is—for example, my latest drawings are done on the computer.

Your father is known to work day and night, seven days a week. Can you talk about this dedication to his art in terms of his parenting and the consequences for you as an artist?

I understand that this behavior means he cannot parent conventionally. I have not known anything else. With my relationship to children I have done things a little differently by default. I became stepmother to our two boys aged eight and nine (they lost their biological mother). In this way, I was able to have children in my life without taking time out. I taught them to cook so that they were able to take care of that practicality when need be. I am there for them emotionally and although I am always working, my studios are at home and I have learnt to work with them around. I find it easy to do two things at once, an example being we could all be watching a film and I could be doing a drawing or some wax modeling at the same time.

With my father putting his work first, I feel programmed to do the same, even though I do not necessarily believe it is the right thing to do. However, as well as the desire to work all the time, I have a need to.

I have romanticized my father as a figure, less so as I get older—and he gets older. Now I accept that he is who he is and he behaves as he does. I get on with my own life. The positive I can take from my father's dedication to art and not family is that I feel confident in the knowledge that I have achieved on my own and have never been dependent on his help, which brings a feeling of confidence and independent ability that I might not necessarily have had. Before I began using my full name, Jane McAdam Freud, I used only my mother's surname. As Jane McAdam, aged 33, I was awarded the Freedom of the City of London on merit for my works collected on behalf of the City. It was only publicly revealed that I am Lucian Freud's daughter when I had to present my documents.

Did you sit for him? If so, what was that like for you?

We sat for each other and made sculpture. Although very intense it felt like a great privilege for me to be working with my father. I loved the fact that he was so delightfully modest—he asked me to teach him about modeling in wax. Over a period we regularly sat for each other while simultaneously working. I knew that my father had made some sculpture early on. Both my father and my mother have told me at different times that they would have liked to have done sculpture. Perhaps I feel I am making sculpture on their behalves!

I do feel very inspired by my family ties and went on to examine my perceptions around this legacy through my residency and exhibition Relative Relations at the Freud Museum. My accompanying film "Dead or Alive" uses the psychoanalytic idea of "Condensing" by merging my sculpture with objects from my great-grandfather Sigmund Freud's collection.

Do you think identification with your father, an internalization of him as an artist, had something to do with your becoming an artist yourself?

I did internalize Lucian as an artist as much as a father as I knew him so well through his works. His catalogues were always lying around our home. An identification with my father definitely contributed to my aspirations of becoming an artist, but I also identified with my mother who I saw as a great natural talent. She was very modest and sacrificial. All of her schooling took place in posh boarding schools. They (and later I) recognized her talent for painting and drawing and, unheard of for her conservative schools, who waved aside their prejudices, she was encouraged to go on to study at Saint Martin's Art School in London. Her painting and drawing was quite different from my father's early work; his works seemed to me more childlike and naive. I can however see the unflinching concentration in his early drawing and can understand the long hours he commits to mastering his passion.

My mother had four children with Lucian and put all of her creativity into bringing us up and managing her life. She was always able to draw in a way that looked effortless. My mother's pedestal was highest in one way but she was not necessarily more influential as I always felt sorry and regretful for her that she did not fulfill her artistic potential.

From a distance, I watched my father put all his time and creativity into his work. I saw his life and his works unfolding on the public stage and transforming into the magnificent creations that they are today. I decided very early on that making art was a good choice for a life and decided he was my example.

Did your father instruct you, teach you about making art? Was there any sense of seeing through his eyes as you became an artist in your own right?

When I was in my early 30s, my father looked at the work I had produced during my scholarship in Rome as well as subsequent pieces and showed great interest. He pointed out parts he particularly liked. I remember a piece called "Fish and Form," a small two-sided bronze where he really liked the way I had modeled the hand. He did not like it if I explained anything about meaning, though. His comments concerned the form and aesthetic, but not the content.

I would not say he instructed or taught me in the formal sense at all. That is not his way. I have always made my own decisions and choices. He once asked me if I wanted him to arrange a studio for me, an offer which I declined explaining that I like to get things for myself. I get the impression that he admires my independence of spirit, which I inherit from my mother, who maintained this independence throughout her life.

I was, however, given invaluable advice from my father during the period we spent working together. A memorable and useful piece of advice was with regard to scale. He suggested I work in various scales, rather than sticking to one; at the time I was very keen on intimate bronzes that could be held in the hand. I took this advice and have since also embraced multiple disciplines and dimensions. For example, my practice now spans drawing, sculpture and digital media.

I do not think I have a sense of seeing through my father's eyes now in the way I do my great-grandfather's. This may be because my relationship with Sigmund is objective, as it is further removed than the more subjective one with my father.

Do you think, genetically speaking, there is something to make of the fact that you are a visual artist, as is your father, as was his father, the architect Ernst Freud?

I think there is something to be made further back. Visual art is not so separate from other disciplines. Art uses the same process as psychoanalysis but with a different name. Objectivity is part of the art process just as analyzing is part of the analyst's process which brings Sigmund in (also explaining his view that artists don't need analysis).

Progress in genetic science has proved that there is a gene for most things, so we now know that we inherit much more than the color of our eyes. The fact that my mother was an artist too makes a difference in that if there is a gene for having a predisposition for ability in the visual arts I stood a very high chance of inheriting it.

I feel passionately about the big questions that evoke most art—about life's meaning, such as our relationships to time, nature, each other and religion. People rather than buildings drive my work, though, and that is the one area where perhaps I do see some common ground with Freud and Freud—Sigmund in the way he analyzed their behavior and perhaps my father in the way he *is* able to objectify people in his work. My aim is to relate to people through making art—making art is a way of life for me.

What can you say about the transmission of feeling into art? What does that mean to you as an artist to think about how what you feel is transmitted into a work of art?

I enjoy making art to work through my feelings, although it is far from therapeutic. It is part of my practice to make my unconscious conscious, perhaps picking up on Freud's pursuit "where id was ego shall be." My art informs me about myself after its inception by showing me manifestations that reflect my life's stories. Underneath the forms and representations is all the information that has driven the pieces into being.

I remember an early work I did while an art student at the Central School of Art. It was a wax carving—a portrait of Picasso to commemorate the centenary of his birth. It took every inch of my concentration. Every mark mattered. Everything of me went into it. That sense of intensity seems to me to be embodied in the piece and comes back every time I look at a completed work. In fact, I find it extremely difficult to part with certain works. For this reason I like the casting and printing processes where I can keep a copy.

Can you talk about the "pleasure" that making art has for you? What does that pleasure consist in?

I interpret "pleasure" as meaning homeostasis and of course Sigmund Freud saw the human psyche as striving towards a peaceful state.

I see my reality as a series of divergent emotional, intellectual and social needs jostling for position and demanding consolidation. Equilibrium comes from that. Art gives me that outlet.

Making art is where I feel at one with the world, where my equilibrium centers. It is where I know who I am and what I think, where I feel safe and confident. When I am working on a piece, building up layer upon layer, I feel as though I am bringing it to life. It feels spiritual in a secular sense to bring life into an image or an object. It lies between excitement and feeling sated as though one has quenched a great thirst. This description sounds quite sexual and so it appears Freud was quite right when he talked of sublimation. The works take on their own diktat and it seems that often I hand over to a work at a certain point, directing its course and outcome. This may seem odd but a relationship develops between me and each work. I get to know a piece and it leads me.

Does making art have any bearing on your sense of self?

From the very beginning my sense of self was inextricably linked to art. I was always treated as though I had a special talent. As a result, I understood the power of art.

The way our sense of self appears is not necessarily how we are. I agree with Freud in that I believe perhaps dreams give us our greatest insights. As an illustration of this, I would like to cite an experience from a few years ago. I went to Mexico City to deliver a paper to art students from three colleges. The audience was far greater than any I had presented to previously. The projection screen was so enormous that I was dwarfed by my own images. I was so overwhelmed that I had no control over my voice. I began by speaking in a very high pitch rather like a young child. However, as the talk went on my confidence increased and my voice became stronger. It was as though I grew up on that stage.

That night I had a dream. In the dream I returned home to the UK at the end of the symposium. I opened the door and was excited to see my little girl (I have no daughter in reality). She ran towards me, a toddler, and I put my arms out to her. She stood rigid, angry and said in a very cold, adult voice—FUCK OFF. It was shocking, a nightmare. I told one of the other participants about the dream and he agreed that I had seemed to reenact the growing up process on stage.

My interpretation of the dream is that the child who greeted me with such a harsh adult rejection was *me* as an internalized child. In her adult voice, she told my inner child to leave me alone and not to interfere. Perhaps if the frightened child loosened her grip, I could be more confident.

My confidence comes through making art. Art is a sort of "play," perhaps child's play. Maybe the child is integral to my sense of self and also my art practice.

You had a show in London entitled "Reflections on Subject as Object." Can you tell me about the work for that exhibit, how it came to be titled as such and whether the philosophical implications of the title have psychodynamic implications for you as well?

This show focused only on my portrait work. The title alluded to one of the pairings in the show involving two self-portraits. In this pairing, I wanted to differentiate my effigy from my person. I wanted to explore the confusing "language" in use when making a self-portrait: Is *it* like *me?*—is clear. Is *my* face longer?—is not. Without understanding whether the question is directed at the object or the person, the question is ambiguous in that one is not clear as to the owner of the "my" and whether "my" refers to the object or the person? The sculpture is quite clearly not the person. It is "it," an inanimate object. This piece later informed me about the psychodynamic implications.

By deconstructing the process of making art and playing with the resultant analogies I reflect the psychodynamic meaning. The subject matter is a moving target in terms of perceptual experience but I try to decode my unconscious processes. I will use the "self-portrait" experience to explain.

On the back across the shoulders of one self-portrait I carved the word "Objective" in reverse which then contains the word "it." This I paired with the "shoulder" part of a second self-portrait where, by accident, the head had become severed from the shoulders. In this dramatic unplanned action (the severing), I was intrigued at my own objectivity—*its* head (the head of the sculpture) had become separated from *its* body.

To these shoulders I added a collar and tie. The necktie looked quite phallic. On the back of the work with the collar and tie, this time I inscribed the word "subjective" written in reverse which also contained the word "it." The original "subject" for observation was my reflection, an image in reverse. The splitting in two had become the subjective interpretation of objectifying me. Hence the word "subjective" carved on the reverse.

The psychological component driving this process, I think goes back to childhood and can be expressed in the dream of the angry child cited earlier. Both my parents being artists, it was normal for them to look objectively at people or objects. (I have learnt to do it too.)

I realize from the dream that I didn't like being objectified. I remember clearly being confused and annoyed at my mother for her long periods of staring and her objective comments. It is possible that the child in the dream is also rejecting this!

In making a self-portrait, the subject and object seem sometimes fused and otherwise interchangeable. In my life I have been fortunate enough to experience making art with both parents but I think that the severing of the head manifests the process of objectification in terms of symbolically separating the emotional from the intellectual, i.e., the head from the heart. Also the tie brings in the male element perhaps making a subjective comment on my father's ability to objectify.

Eric Ernst

This interview is perhaps less obvious in attesting to the psychological complexities of having artist parents (and grandparents) than the previous interviews, for neither the need to secure an identity through difference nor the potential for creative impotence caused by competitiveness appears, on the surface, significant. Yet having painter Jimmy Ernst for a father and the internationally known Max Ernst for a grandfather did, as we shall hear, play a considerable role in Eric Ernst's becoming an artist himself. And the belief that one's identity is truly independent of family history brings to mind the origin of what Freud called the fantasy of the "family romance": The need to place oneself outside the lineage whether in avoidance of rivalry, to separate from idealized objects, or any other such aim

You have spoken elsewhere about your gratuitous beginning as an artist. Do you really think it was all that gratuitous; or do you think you would eventually have found your way into art as a means of defining yourself in relation to your father and grandfather—either as a continuation of a certain aesthetic lineage or as a way of distinguishing your own identity?

Actually, I wouldn't describe it so much as gratuitous as compelling evidence of environment being as important as genetics in determining these things. As to whether I would have inevitably found my way into art, I sincerely believe it would have had nothing to do with either the continuation of a family legacy or a way of distinguishing my own identity. Instead, while extremely proud of the accomplishments of my family in the realms of art and culture as well as cognizant of the deep impact they have had on me, I nevertheless believe my own persona and identity exists quite independently of the influence of those from whom I draw inspiration.

But you also said "Children of lawyers become lawyers; children of artists tend to become artists."

I think, once again, that there is a profound impact of environment in this regard. Having said that, however, I would also have to admit that I have never done any legitimate empirical research to justify this observation and that it is probably a bit of a blanket statement that is probably difficult to prove. Nevertheless, it seems to me that from an admittedly experiential perspective, that most of the people that I knew and grew up with as children of artists, ended up involved in one form or another in creative endeavors when it came to choosing careers.

Did you grow up with your father's art surrounding you? How do you think you might have been (consciously or unconsciously) influenced in your art by his, perhaps in your use of color?

My father's work has been a constant physical presence throughout my life, especially as a youth as I would come home from school every afternoon and simply hang out in the studio, watching my father paint, listening to news or baseball on the radio, and leafing through the nudie magazines he would use to make collages.

I kind of viewed my father's studio as my own personal sanctuary. Perhaps the most interesting thing about watching him work, aside from his maniacally intense and delicate process, was in my constantly badgering him that whatever he was working on looked great and he should simply sign it. He would usually fix me with a rather jaded look that said "You just don't get it" and turn back to the canvas.

Interestingly enough, my sensibilities about these things weren't unique in that Jimmy had an exhibition of unfinished works at the Aldrich Museum in Ridgefield, Connecticut, at which he had the opportunity to sell a number of the paintings but stubbornly refused because, in his mind, they weren't done yet, even if just about everyone else thought they were.

As to how I may have been influenced by him in my work, while I share an affinity for the interaction of linear and geometric elements that are hallmarks of my father's works, his particular approach was so unique in its labor-intensive layering of imagery and flattening of the distinctions between foreground and background, that it was rather easy to initially work away from any overt pictorial repetition of his style.

Having said that, and while I can't recall any instance when his imagery imposed itself physically within my mind as I worked, there were any number of moments when, upon completing a painting, I would step back and see his impact and influence in very subtle ways.

As to color, while my father once said "If you want to sell, use a lot of red and blue," I prefer to believe that these are dominant colors in my work due more to the impact of my period in Japan studying wood block printing than the influence of whimsical marketing advice from my father.

Did your father instruct you at all, teach you about making art?

We worked together on a number of small paintings over the years where he would show me a certain technique and then we would take turns improvising until, usually, we would decide we'd gone too far and the painting sucked.

Once, I believe when the Hirschorn was doing a show of collaboration works and the curators were coming to the house to borrow a couple of paintings (a Max and Magritte collaboration as well as one where Max had painted over part of one of his father's still lifes), Jimmy and I figured if we did one they might take that as well so we did a mixed media double self-portrait. They didn't take it but it was later exhibited at Guild Hall in East Hampton, New York, for a collage exhibition.

Perhaps the most entertaining aspect of the endeavor was in the degree of contention over the common areas of the canvas; horizon line or empty space, impasto or wash, textured or smooth. Eventually we finished but not before a match of wills over whether in the sun shape in the center of the canvas we would collage a photo of a nude woman (my choice) or a photograph of Adlai Stevenson (Jimmy's patron saint of politics). I won.

Can you talk about the "pleasure" that making art has for you? What does that pleasure consist in?

Process is less important to me than the sheer measure of satisfaction I feel when I finish something and sit there pondering it. Perhaps the best description would be to borrow a phrase from the Dean of Students at my boarding school who, when describing the scourge of recreational drug use that semester, referred to it as "cerebral masturbation." That pretty much describes my own intellectual sensations after I finish a piece.

You said elsewhere that the pressure of having Max Ernst as your grandfather is no different from the pressure every artist feels to live up to a certain standard, that set by one's predecessors. Are you really able to separate out the fact that he was your grandfather, that Jimmy Ernst was your father, and that you might have felt or feel now in some way competitive with either or both?

Strangely enough, I feel neither a measure of competition nor any sense of pressure derived from any genetic connection to these people. I do feel an immeasurable sense of pride in their accomplishments but have always been cognizant that their achievements are not mine and that to stand on the shoulders of a giant doesn't make one a goliath as well.

Instead, as an artist, I view Jimmy and Max in much the same way I do other icons who have influenced me and whose work I hold up as a standard by which I judge my own evolution as an artist.

Does making art ever feel like a way of gaining—or regaining—emotional closeness to your father? To your grandfather?

My father was always a significant presence in my life and I believe my emotional proximity to him, which continues to this day, would have been a constant factor in my existence regardless of what career or path I chose.

As to Max, he was a rather distant figure, both geographically and psychologically, so whatever emotional connection I have to him is a bit more complicated.

Can you tell me about the process: You make a mark; as you do, you take it in perceptually, and then you alter it, either directly or by making other marks around it. What is going on in you as you do that?

I haven't the faintest idea. I do find as I draw on the surface that the interaction between geometric images and negative space somewhat organically develops, but even this remains something of a mystery until the colors are added later. I really haven't the foggiest notion how these things will turn out until the work themselves tell me I'm done.

Alina Rubinstein

A psychiatrist/psychoanalyst in private practice in New York City, Dr. Rubinstein, the daughter of pianist Arthur Rubinstein, is on the faculty of The Institute for Psychoanalytic Education affiliated with New York University Medical Center, where she trained in psychoanalysis, and on the voluntary staff in psychiatry at the Mount Sinai Medical Center. Having grown up in a musical family and studied piano from age 6 to 17, Dr. Rubinstein has continued playing for pleasure ever since, performing chamber music for the first time in medical school, but then not again until shortly after 9/11/2001. In recent years she has also performed several times alone and with others in public settings and she has begun studying the cello, satisfying a longstanding dream

When did you first learn to play the piano? Did you want to learn play or was it expected of you?

It's almost embarrassing, as a psychoanalyst, to admit that I have no specific memory of my first or early piano lessons, although I know that I was between 5½ and 6 years old when I began. I doubt that I asked for them, because I was very shy. I think it was just taken for granted because I was clearly musically inclined. It feels as if I've always played.

My earliest musical memories are of sitting under my father's grand piano (with my 22-months younger brother, my constant childhood companion) trying to manipulate the pedals while my father played. I do have fragmented visual images of my teacher, an older woman named Mrs. Gold, at the piano testing my pitch, and of being rewarded with those little brown-and-yellow stamps of composers when I did well.

Was your talent at the piano apparent early? Did your father feel you were talented and make that known to you?

My father thought I was talented for the piano, and did communicate that to me, both directly and through my piano teachers; however, the message he conveyed was quite conflicted. When I was a young, he was always pleased to hear me play and encouraged me. He would even insist that I (and my brother) play for his friends—who were, not surprisingly, often eminent musicians themselves. But he was away concertizing most of the time and paid scarce attention to the particulars of my musical education. As a result, the fact that I never learned to sight-read well as a child, relying instead on absolute pitch and a very quick musical memory to learn new music escaped my father's notice, until one day when I was already in my late teens. He was astonished to discover this flaw, but by then, the skill was much harder to acquire.

My father would tell me in those days that I should be a pianist, and yet never suggested my learning music theory. Through self-study as an adult I have built somewhat upon the intuitive understanding I gained from being surrounded by music. I have been trying to make up for my deficiencies over the last seven years, just for my own satisfaction and pleasure. Growing up, I was unaware of the existence of pre-college conservatory training where many musically talented children learn some theory and get experience playing in chamber music ensembles and youth orchestras. Such programs existed even when I was young, and although I imagine that if I had been a real musical *prodigy*, someone would have seen to it that I got more focused training. I assumed that the children of other musicians of my father's stature who had benefited from that kind of training were just more worthy. So in spite of my father's apparent positive attitude towards my innate talent, there was no real follow-through.

Did/do any of your siblings play? Did they want to play and was it expected of any or all of them to learn to play as well—or are you the only piano-playing offspring of Arthur Rubinstein?

I think that it was just assumed that all of us would learn to play, given two prior generations of musicians in the family (my mother's father was a violinist, composer and conductor and founder of the Warsaw Opera and Philharmonic). My two older siblings who were

10 and 11½ when I was born, both took piano lessons but gave them up after a year or so, though they are both very musical. (They were born in Argentina and Poland, respectively, while my father was on tour, but then they all had to flee France in 1939 as tiny children to emigrate to the US. My younger brother and I, on the other hand, were born in "paradise"—southern California—and had much less upheaval in our external lives as young children, which surely played a role.) My sister has told me that she wanted desperately to play but had no facility for the piano: She became a professional ballet-trained dancer (as was my mother), actress, and later a photographer. My older brother rejected classical music, preferring the swing music of the 1950s. My 22-months younger brother showed musical talent very early, and I believe started lessons around the same time I did. My brother became an actor and director, but also a (primarily self-taught) composer of many film and television scores.

Did your father teach you to play himself? Were there the normal issues children have around practicing or was practicing a very different experience for you? Was he a harsh critic of your playing or encouraging and how was the father–daughter interaction affected (solidified, jeopardized, etc.) by your playing?

My father was rarely home, and had no patience for beginners (probably especially his own children), so he never taught us himself. When I was about 2, in 1947, he had resumed touring in Europe, having been restricted to the United States and South America during the Second World War, and was playing about 100 concerts a year. In those days, of course, transportation and communication was much more primitive, and it was not easy for my parents (my mother often accompanied him) to return to California between concerts. We saw my father primarily at Christmastime when the Messiah took over American concert halls. Once we moved to the reclaimed family home in Paris when I was 9, we saw more of him, because from there we could accompany him on European tours and he could return home more frequently.

In Paris, we had a young woman piano teacher who focused on French music. My younger brother and I—we were and are still very close—also began to play four-hand piano music, which was great fun and a good way to sublimate various sibling rivalries. We also used to compose and perform musical puppet shows. When my parents acquired an apartment in New York two years later, having decided that we should finish our education in the United States we alternated, spending seven months in New York and five in Paris until the end of high school. In New York we had two consecutive teachers, both women. As for practicing, although I have never needed encouragement to go to the piano, only in recent years have I realized the major but subtle inhibition I had about true practicing that has had far-reaching impact on my musical development. In retrospect, I don't think I ever *really* practiced, but just "played through" the music, hoping the difficult places would somehow magically fix themselves through mindless (literally) repetition. None of my teachers really taught me how to practice challenging passages properly, or if they ever did, I didn't trust that it would work, so would give up after one or two tries. My teachers also somehow managed to overlook my not really learning how to sight-read competently. Speculating about how this could have happened, I've wondered if perhaps they were themselves too in awe of my father and possibly afraid to alienate him through insisting on "disciplining" us musically.

I became aware of my childhood misconstruing of practice only in my late 50s, when I started to play chamber music. Since then I have been remedially teaching myself with occasional tips from chamber music coaches and from "how-to" books by pianists, but mostly through careful focused attention to the difficulty at hand (no pun intended!) analyzing the problem, and trying out solutions, which actually works. When I was young, I just figured that if I couldn't get past the technical difficulty with a minimal effort, there was nothing I could do, because I was convinced one had to be born with a facility I clearly just didn't have, unlike my father the prodigy. In addition, I had very small hands (still do!) and was a girl, and girls didn't become serious pianists (my father was known for the unusually large span of his hands). So I undermined my acquisition of solid, reliable technique at a critical stage of development. I find it amazing that I learned as much as I actually did, which I attribute only to my overriding love for music and the gratification I got from playing the piano myself, as well as pleasing my parents.

Typically, my father would come back from a tour and then ask to hear whatever we were working on: both my brother and I would experience enormous anxiety around these "auditions." (It was during one of these sessions that he was shocked to discover that my sight-reading was so inadequate.) He would become impatient easily, and the anticipation of an outburst of temper led to even more self-consciousness and errors, but somehow he still conveyed appreciation of my innate musical understanding. Still, I always privately felt that my father grossly overvalued my talent as a pianist, narcissistically wishing to see a reflection of himself in me in order to keep me under his control. Inevitably, I felt I had failed to perform "my best" for him (often true, because I was so anxious) and had severely disappointed him, and only recently have I come to appreciate that beyond his need to "own" me and control me, my father was also objectively responding to a real musical talent I showed that I couldn't "own" myself then out of the shame I experienced in wanting to be like him as a musician and feeling I fell so short.

I painfully recall my father's efforts, when we were teenagers, to persuade my brother to pursue musical studies at the conservatory level—"you should be a conductor"—which my brother adamantly resisted, preferring to pursue an acting career. I would sit there during these talks wishing silently that my father would ask *me* if *I* wanted to go to a conservatory, but he never did and I never said a word, assuming that in spite of his encouragement, he really didn't think I had enough talent, or simply that such pursuits were only for boys.

What was it like at home—did your father practice there or outside the home; were you exposed to his practicing all the time as a child? Is the sound of his playing in your head as you play today (or was it ever)?

My father practiced at home—when he *was* home, and in hotels on the road, but he was hardly compulsive about practicing, and really only rehearsed the technically treacherous passages in his repertoire, rarely ever playing through the entire work he would be preparing for an upcoming concert. He was, in fact, rather notorious for missing notes in concerts, compared to some of his peers. (There was some truth to this, but it was also much exaggerated). He preferred to allow for spontaneity rather than note-perfection, though this was probably partly rationalization; he was a man of many appetites—food, beautiful women, all the arts, etc., and there was never enough time to take in everything he wanted to; practice was rarely his priority. I think that attitude of his was partly the source of my conviction that if one needed to work hard to master technical difficulties one was not talented or interesting *enough* for a career, not appreciating that my father had been learned his huge repertoire in youth and had been playing in public for some 62+ years before I ever heard him play (he was 58 when I was born).

Yes, the sound of his playing is indeed still in my head today, always has been. And one result of hearing him practice at home is that I used to cringe internally when the few tricky passages he *would* go over would come up in his concerts. I even tense up when I hear those passages approaching on my father's old studio recordings as if he were about to freshly tackle them in the present! And when I hear those places traversed in live concerts by pianists today—even when those specific passages present no technical problem for that particular pianist—I still flinch involuntarily. (Most pianists today, like Olympic athletes, have reached standards of technical perfection even in live performance, thanks primarily to recording technology, which were not as common in my father's heyday.)

When I hear a work from his repertoire played on the radio, I always feel compelled to figure out if it is he playing (usually very easy for me).

When I hear another pianist perform any such work, I reflexively compare it to his interpretation. It often takes only one phrase (a few measures, even a single measure) for me to identify his playing. And in "live" recordings (e.g., tapes of live radio broadcasts), he feels particularly "present" primarily because he was always energized by a live audience in a way that wasn't so true in a studio, and this comes through in the playing. (I've had the job, for years, of authorizing releases of some of these radio broadcasts, which is for me an often conflicted task, given that my father stipulated that they were to be played only one time on the radio (the original "live" broadcast), and never again. I feel torn because most frequently I ignore his wish and have okayed quite a few of those live radio broadcasts, in order to expose young musicians to his artistry and to preserve his legacy for history and for my family.) There's also the fact that the performances are rarely note-perfect as are studio recordings (spliced here and there, though my father did this minimally compared to some others), and finally, even eerily, that his actual *breathing* along with the musical phrasing is sometimes quite audible. That's a little spooky, as was the one time a friend took me to hear the piano-roll collection of a friend of his, and I heard a roll of my father while watching the keys of the piano move up and down all by themselves. My father used to jokingly say he'd "haunt" us all after he died; and so he does, both psychologically and through his continued aural presence.

How did you feel about having so famous a father as you were growing up and how did you relate (perhaps in your fantasy life) to that fame?

Like most children, when I was very young I didn't have any basis for comparison and didn't really "get" that he was a world-famous concert pianist. Of course, the kind of total media exposure we have today didn't exist at all, though in Hollywood many of the other children we knew also had famous parents, even if most were in the movie business. My parents' friends in Los Angeles were all in the arts; mostly other European émigrés who'd fled from the Nazis and also ended up there—film directors, actors, writers, musicians, painters, and so on.

Because my father was away so much of the time it was always special and exciting when he was home; plus he was a very charismatic, passionate, impetuous, and opinionated man who dominated most settings, and always seemed larger-than-life to me. In California, we had a large map on our bedroom wall on which our nanny would stick pins indicating where my parents were in the world, and they'd send postcards, usually tinted façades of old hotels with one window marked with an X—"we are here!" But my father was mostly a Godlike figure in my fantasy—my Catholic maternal grandmother had taught us to say the bedtime prayer, "Now I lay me down to sleep, I pray the Lord my soul to keep, and if I die before I wake, I pray the Lord my soul to take." I remember connecting this powerful "Lord/God" person with my mostly absent and somewhat intimidating father who seemed to be all over the world and yet invisible. My little brother, meanwhile, confused him both with Santa Claus, who also became visible only at Christmas, and also with the infamous tailor my grandmother told him about who would appear and cut off little boy's thumbs if they sucked them, which my brother did. The implication seems obvious, and I myself anxiously wondered (and surely wished) that this would indeed happen to my brother, who I felt had supplanted me and seemed so favored by my grandmother and so much more like my father than I. I felt I was very insignificant to my father as a young child, hardly even on his "radar screen." My world revolved around school and my brother, and the housekeeper, and my father (and even my mother) seemed almost like dreamlike figures to me, even when they *were* home.

I was five or six I think when I first was taken to see my father perform in public. I particularly recall seeing him play at the huge Hollywood Bowl, which seats 17,000+ people. I'm sure we were sitting close to the stage, but I remember it feeling distant and like a dream, I know I dozed off at times, and only intermittently connected that tiny man at the piano with my father. But I began to get a clearer picture of what he did when he was away. My older sister was a dancer and actress, and it seemed as if performing was what one did as a grown-up, but I already was (or became) quite shy after my brother was born, and couldn't imagine myself performing anything. I felt I was only in the background as his older sister. This feeling was reinforced by the arrival of my maternal grandmother to live with us exactly one week after my brother's birth when I was a year and ten months old. A reserved and prudish woman who'd spent the war trapped on her family's land in Lithuania, she'd grown up in a patriarchal society, so treated my father deferentially and doted on my brother, while keeping me and my sister at an emotional arm's length.

I became more aware of my father's stature and fame as a pianist in the whole world once we moved to Europe, and spent more time in his presence and on his tours. We were included in many adult events as children in Europe. Being with him in his milieu, I saw this amazing man who seemed to speak every language, knew everyone, played the piano so thrillingly and excited audiences and friends and was always the center of attention and it did made me feel that I too was privileged, by association. I yearned to attract his interest in me and thereby affirm my self-worth—in addition to playing the piano, by learning languages, being a patient listener (he was a big talker and *raconteur* even at home) and especially, by never disagreeing with him—he couldn't tolerate disagreement. I would often feel critical of what I saw as my mother's hypocrisy, when she would express *sotto voce* impatience with his self-centeredness while simultaneously teaching me that because he was a great artist, his needs always came first. This supported my father's own attitude that he was an exception to the rules that applied to everyone else, which I also came to believe was justified, having come under his thrall. I so wanted his approval and admiration and wanted to lead the charmed life I thought he had.

In New York, I remember feeling both proud and embarrassed by my connection to him at the same time; I was extremely anxious the one or two times he actually came to a school event, as I watched my revered teachers' uncharacteristic excitement, acting like schoolgirls themselves in his presence, but also feared he would say something that would embarrass me there (like the time he expressed disapproval of a group of six-year-old kindergarteners because they sang a Christmas carol off-key at a school pageant). In the present I've more-or-less come to terms with my complex feelings about being his daughter, though I'm still amazed when his admirers ask for *my* autograph as if I *were* he! But now I am more gracious about such requests, and no longer feel compelled to inform fans that I'm *not* my father—as if they didn't know. I suspect I needed to convince myself more than them, since a big part of me did want to "be" (just like) him.

Did you look forward to a career as a concert pianist? You play beautifully today, but do not generally perform. Why? Did you feel any sort of (internally imposed) pressure to maintain the legacy by becoming a pianist yourself?

In my mid-teens, talk arose about my playing a concert in public in New York. I truly don't know who originated that idea or why (certainly not me nor my teacher!) I remember my piano teacher telling me that I had been invited play a recital on a monthly series featuring teenaged performers at a small concert hall in the city (it might have been the current Merkin or Abraham Goodman Hall). My teacher (a child prodigy from San Francisco who'd abruptly given up her promising career at age 19 after a bout of intense performance panic before an orchestra concert) decided what I would play (perhaps in consultation with my father?), and I began to intensely "practice" those works, while feeling more and more overwhelmed with anxiety and dread and conviction that I could not do it. Ultimately, I confessed my fears and begged to withdraw my name from the already-printed program, and they let me, a few months before the date I was to have played.

It was typical of me then to keep all my thoughts and feelings to myself until I was at a breaking point. I recall that when this was first been decided I silently went along with it without feeling I had a choice—and when it was enough in the future also did fantasize about the special bond this would create with my father. But as the date grew closer, I could only think about the shame and humiliation that I would experience and cause my father, too. By then I had developed intense performance anxiety both at the piano and in speaking as well as writing, on top of a considerable amount of shyness/self-consciousness in general. (It's probably not an accident that my father thought I should be, like many of his closest friends, if not a pianist, then a writer.)

Furthermore, I'm pretty certain I was the only girl on the list, and definitely the only "child-of-a-famous-musician." And perhaps most saliently, I didn't feel my technical skills were up to such exposure at that point, and my piano teacher conveyed ambivalence about the whole enterprise as well. I suspect her personal experience as a performer, which she openly shared with me, colored her views; perhaps other conflicts came into play as well. Also, in those days, the fact is that there were few women with major careers as concert pianists and I felt daunted by that and certainly not pioneer material.

How did your playing when your father was alive affect your relationship with him? Did playing make you feel closer to him? Did you identify with him/internalize features of him through your playing?

My playing certainly did make me feel closer to him, especially because of his validation of my musicality and specifically, my talent for the piano, his chosen instrument. I did clearly identify with him and internalize essential features of his playing, because, now that I have overcome to some degree (though not entirely!) my detrimental performance anxiety, I have played for many musicians and others who knew my father's music well and who invariably tell me that I have his touch and sound, and essentials of his phrasing, especially in Brahms and Chopin, among the composers to whom he himself he felt closest. My father particularly loved my playing of a Schubert *Impromptu* and gave me for my 21st birthday a volume of Schubert piano music and another of Bach's *Well-Tempered Clavier* writing some very meaningful words to me on the cover page. I promptly went through an intense Schubert phase, reading through all his Lieder and much of his chamber music (I had already been immersed in Bach).

Years later, during a short visit to Switzerland, when he was dying and I was an overworked medical intern, he asked me to play it for him, and, fearing I wouldn't do it justice, I demurred. He died not long after, and my refusal haunted me until I offered to play it at the memorial service for a dear friend who died at age 44. That seems to have released me from the remorse I felt about withholding it from my father (who loved Schubert, and had always requested that his C Major two-cello String Quintet be played when he died). My father used to comment that my musically talented younger brother "played the piano like a composer" but "I played like a *pianist*." This "left-handed" (and I'm left-handed!) compliment felt like a partial compensation to me for his having encouraged me to get the professional training to make the most of his talent. My father dealt with his own performance anxiety by selecting a specific person in his audience who he could see, and playing for that person. At times, he would tell me that he was playing a certain work for me—and I would feel it.

One can't help but notice you are the child who has your father's initials (and yet you are not the eldest of his children or a son). What is the significance of that? If none was consciously intended on the part of your parents (father?), did it have significance (conscious or unconscious) for you? Did it bear on your becoming a pianist? Was there some intention in giving you his initials to have to be the ongoing bearer of his gift?

No. I was actually named Alina for my maternal great-grandmother and, unfortunately, so was a much-disliked and crazy older sister of my mother. Consciously, the fact that we shared initials has only been significant to me as an adult. My mother's given name was Aniela so she, too, shared the initials, although she always went by her much more familiar name of Nela except on a few official documents. My (Polish) first name was a source of mixed feelings for me growing up because it was rarely spelled or pronounced correctly, and my middle name, Anna, I avoided using, mostly because it was my maternal grandmother's name and seemed extremely old-fashioned to me, like her. As a computer-literate adult, however, I identify myself as "AR" in iTunes, under the rubric "Artist," when recording my solo or chamber music performances and my father as, simply, "Rubinstein" to differentiate us. As for Anna, when I began (in college) to read about the relationship between Freud and his daughter I very much identified with her in that relationship, but it evoked anger and criticism in me. Anna was also the name of Mozart's older sister, who accompanied him on his prodigy tours playing the piano with him, but is only of interest as an historical footnote to her brother, and when I was young I identified very much with *her* "second-banana status" as well, having devoured Mozart's three-volume *Collected Letters* when they were first published and were given me by my mother.

And now that he is deceased? Does playing now (or at any time since he died in 1982) reconnect you with him? If so, can you describe/explain how?

Whenever I'm playing the piano at home alone, and now also the cello, which I took up four years ago, I find myself frequently aware of my father, and actually have a silent conversation with a portrait of him as a young man which hangs next to my piano which he left me in his will, along with all his "annotated" music scores. At the piano, I think, "Would this interpretation convince you, transport you?"—especially, of course, when I play certain pieces, including that Schubert

Impromptu that he particularly loved and often played himself. And I enjoy addressing him in casual American vernacular speech that I never would have dared use in speaking to him in life, e.g., "Whaddya think, Pops??" At the cello, I often think, "Can you *believe* that I can actually play this?" (My father had adamantly rejected learning the violin as a child.) But now I'm curious about what he would have thought when I play works he *didn't* play, at least, not in my lifetime. I feel comfortable now entertaining interpretations different from his, and liking music he didn't like or understand.

Now that I am so much more involved with making music at the piano, both solo, and even more, playing chamber music with friends (my father loved, played, and recorded a great deal of chamber music himself and I feel particularly connected to him through that), I frequently find myself wanting to ask him a question about a work, a technical issue, phrasing, interpretation, or even the composer himself (he knew most of the early 20th-century composers personally), and regret enormously that I have come to this level of comfort so long after his death, though I think that unfortunately it probably couldn't have happened sooner. I don't think I could ever have had the kind of personal and musical relationship with him that I imagine now, because it would have required overcoming my inhibitions about practicing and playing which were based on comparing myself to him and feeling my only chance to be loved was to be whatever *he* wanted, rather than coming to terms with my own musical gifts and trying to do whatever I needed to do to maximize them. And truthfully, my father's music really represented much more to me than a shared passion. At the piano he could convey the most intimate direct expression of love and a range of other intense feelings of which I felt quite deprived in general in our relationship, so it meant literally everything to me. I can experience his playing of a Mozart or Brahms phrase, say, as a loving caress, or as if he were holding my hand when I was frightened (as he did only once, in my lifetime, during a particularly scary flight when I was already *19*, and I've never forgotten it!) Of course, the irony is that everyone in his audience had a similar response—that's what made him a great interpreter, of course—so while it made me feel specially close to him, as his daughter, it was only an illusion of intimacy that I always had to share with complete strangers.

Were you competitive with your father? Did you worry about not being a good player enough to please him? Did you ever truly feel you could find your own voice as a pianist with a world-famous pianist father?

I never *consciously* appreciated my "competitive" feelings because I was so clearly a "loser": I was a woman, and I wasn't a prodigy. My father was God at the piano as well as in my personal fantasy life. I knew that he had been a child prodigy, and learned a piano concerto of Brahms (his first love) in a week at age 15. Not I! In those days women weren't expected to achieve as men did in many professional fields of which classical music was one. They were discriminated against to various degrees (the late Constance Keene, an exceptional pianist, spoke about such experiences). Those who did have careers were mostly restricted to playing Mozart, Haydn, Schubert, some Chopin, but not the big "demanding" concertos or solo works by Beethoven, Brahms, Bartok, Prokofiev, Tchaikovsky, Rachmaninov, etc. thought to require masculine strength; reviews would typically include phrases like "For a woman, she played with surprising power." Then the fiery Argentinean pianist Marta Argerich came along and proved them all wrong. Now we certainly have a number of first-rank female pianists, and more coming, I'm sure; obviously times have changed from 40 years ago. But then I was convinced that, as a girl, I didn't have and could never acquire the technical skills and stamina to manage and maintain the large repertory one must have to be a successful concert pianist.

In this regard, I remember vividly the dream I had the night before beginning my training psychoanalysis: My father and I walk into the so-called "Green Room" at Carnegie Hall (long before it was renovated in the 80s). It was a small, unattractive room with an upright, up a flight or two of stairs. The management always left the program on the old coffee table for the performer to check before the concert. In the dream, I pick it up while my father takes off his hat and coat, reads it, and says, correctly, that he would play Beethoven's 4th Piano Concerto. However, instead of Arthur Rubinstein being listed as the pianist, it says "Alina Rubinstein, pianist." I point this error out to him and he says, "*You* must play it then!" Having never played it in my life (though I felt as if I knew every note) I respond, "But I can't! I've never played it in my life!!" My father responds, "You know I believe one must always play what the printed program says, even if it's in error." He nudges me towards the stage door. I remember waking up in a state of enormous anxiety. (In fact, my father did believe that, and did act on it when, occasionally, mistakes were printed. He felt that otherwise he might arouse the audience's suspicions that he wasn't giving them—or possibly couldn't give them—what he had promised and "owed" them.)

I imagine this dream says something about my unconscious wish to get his approval (it was both his and my "favorite"—to the extent that we had favorites—piano concerto of Beethoven). Since my younger brother preferred the famous "Emperor" concerto, #5—it felt like a sibling victory for me in terms of gaining my father's approval! But it obviously also had me replacing my father at Carnegie Hall (according to own his rules, which conveniently hid my own unconscious wish to do so). Luckily, my anxiety woke me up in time to be spared the punishing humiliation that would have ensued if I'd been forced to walk out on stage to play it. In addition, my father was not keen on psychotherapy of any sort, especially for anyone in his family, so I felt guilty about my desire to become a psychoanalyst, a rebellion from my domination by him, as had been my going to medical school and specifically, becoming a psychiatrist. The dream also reminded me of my having reneged on the recital opportunity at age 16, which had felt like a major failure all my life. (Playing at the request of the organizer of a conference on art and psychoanalysis held in Florence a few years ago was, for me privately, an unexpected opportunity to finally overcome my disappointment in myself for my lack of courage at 16.)

I give myself credit for knowing the difference between being musically talented, as I am, and having the kind of *prodigious* musical gift my father had. In addition to natural musicality and technical skills, one must also have a certain presence, or charisma, a desire to share that with others un-conflicted enough to overcome common performance anxiety, pleasure in being the center of attention, while simultaneously being able to completely forget the audience and totally immerse oneself in the music—and an outsize "ego" (in the lay sense), among other attributes which I didn't feel I had, not to speak of the constant traveling, hotel rooms, practicing, and perhaps isolation of touring. I didn't have the motivation to practice as much as I would have needed to, in order to overcome my physical limitations. Though, I'm no longer so sure about that last statement. I've learned how negatively affected I was by my distorted internal and actual relationship with my father as well as my sense of being inferior as a woman in a man's (musical) world.

I definitely wanted my father's approval very badly. I was very much influenced by his love for certain composers, e.g. Brahms, Mozart, Schubert, Chopin, and specific works—Wagner's *Meistersinger*, which he played most of on the piano (by heart) before taking us to see it at the Met for the first time; *Carmen*, *Don Giovanni*, Tchaikovsky ballets, Mahler's First Symphony, many other works. I can still clearly visualize my first time hearing such works, exactly where I was sitting, even, partly because my father was actually sitting in the audience with me (and my brother) a very rare and special occurrence!

Can you say something about the "pleasure" of playing the piano today? What does that pleasure consist in?

Sharing music I love with others is so pleasurable and compelling to me it now overrides the performance anxiety which I still have. As I've said, I was always shy of public exposure, but no longer avoid openly acknowledging how much I enjoy touching other people emotionally with my playing. Also, I am no longer terrified of and humiliated by mistakes, but am forgiving of myself if a few were sacrificed to passion and spontaneity, but not inadequate practicing!—like my father, I guess, though at a much lower level, of course …

I am passionate about music in general, and love the music I play. It feels essential to me, like breathing. My musical talent (the ability to "make music" out of the notes rather than just play them, to pour my feelings and love for the music into my interpretation, to create and convey a coherent structure, a "world" in the music that I could communicate with others; and to try to produce the sound that I heard in my head—in essence, a close approximation of my father's sound) was so gratifying to me that I never stopped playing even after deciding at 17 that I never wanted another piano lesson, a decision I've actually stuck with. I stopped after a few lessons in college with a man who actually, I think, was trying to teach me for the first time how to practice effectively to develop technique, but I found his particular approach so deadening, I began to hate the music! I think I just wasn't ready to make learning to play the piano entirely for *me*, as I have in later years.

The biggest pleasure is to feel I've succeeded in directly transmitting what I hear and love in the music to another person. This feels like a kind of intimate connection, maybe it's a sort of musical projective identification (and related to my fantasy that my father was directly communicating to me when I heard him play). But it does have some basis in physical reality, since music does arouse emotions (which can only be experienced physically in our bodies). I want others to be "on the same wavelength" as I am while playing. Even during all the years when I was too inhibited to play for anyone else (most of my life, from early on, till quite recently), I still fantasized that someone was hearing it and connecting with me. For example, if I was aware that there were strangers in another room when I was playing a piano, I would immediately want them to be "enchanted" by the music through the walls. Most of my life, I only felt comfortable playing for such a kind of "accidental" or literally invisible audience. I needed to imagine that listeners weren't paying attention, but that I would capture their attention with my music. My father said he always found himself "performing" as soon as a maid would arrive and begin cleaning his room while he practiced in a hotel, so I relate to that wish to "capture" and captivate.

Did you have a fantasy of pleasing your father by playing? Was there an effort to gain closeness to your father by playing?

I wished to please him, but never felt I played well enough to succeed in doing so, in spite of his positive comments and pride in my love for the piano. I always dismissed those as a narcissistic need to see in me an extension of him, as I was the only child with a special affinity for the *piano*, the specific instrument he played, though, as I've said, we were all very musical. Also, and significantly, for years before my sister and I were born, my father had proclaimed widely his conviction that only *daughters* really understood and appreciated their fathers because sons would inevitably want to compete with them! My younger brother, but not my older, only escaped this because he too was musically talented and worshipped my father as a young boy.

With regard not to technique, but style, how do you think you have been consciously or unconsciously influenced in your playing by your father's? And are there images of him playing or do you hear his playing as your practice?

Up until the last eight years or so, I was of course both consciously and clearly unconsciously very influenced by his playing. Consciously, I was so transported and moved emotionally by his phrasing, judicious use of rubato, un-mannered approach to music, that it always just seemed "right" to me, as if there couldn't be another way to play the same music, as if his interpretation *was directly coming from* Chopin, or Brahms, or Schubert. As I said, I was quite uneducated in music history theory, etc., etc., and rarely exposed to other pianists' interpretations when I was young. In addition, the music critics' laudatory comments after his concerts reinforced my own sense that his playing had a naturalness and unmannered quality that was unlike the work of some other virtuosi of his era.

My father died when I was 36 (on December 20, 1982), and his death felt like the end of a certain inner world for me, even though I was almost finished with my medical training by then. I recall listening over and over to certain recordings of his—mostly chamber music, and Brahms in particular—because of one or two phrases which always brought tears to my eyes. It was such a consolation. Whenever I would visit my mother, I began to play the piano a lot, and it meant a great deal to me that she loved hearing it. I began to learn music I loved that my father played, wanting to make it *physically* part of me (that's what learning a piece of music feels like, and actually is! It literally becomes encoded in your neurons and your motor memory, and that allows you to bring it back to life whenever you want).

Eventually, I began to listen to other pianists, and gradually became able to let myself be "convinced" (i.e., transported) by a different interpretation. It was easiest with composers I had never heard my father play, and later with specific works he didn't play by familiar composers (even though I would usually try to *imagine* how he would play them), since every composer has such a unique "voice" and I knew so well how my father understood those composers. But I came to be able to hear interpretations of works he played frequently interpreted very differently by other pianists, and to appreciate what they brought to the works without feeling disloyal or as if I was losing my own bearings.

Just over eight years ago I began to play chamber music, a week after 9/11 and a few months before my mother's death on December 31, 2001. I had only ever played with other amateurs once, in medical school, at their invitation. I am aware of how my father might or would have emphasized something in the music, but while playing, I am now fully *attentive* and immersed in the music and if I'm practicing, the problem solving at hand. When I play through a piece, I am attentive and in a slightly altered state, the so-called "zone"—when I am totally immersed in the music and feel inspired. (Of course, inner and outer distractions are always there to cause one to slip out of that timeless, in-the-moment state and into self-consciousness, and potentially derail one technically.)

Would you talk about your creativity at the piano and your sense of self*? Is your sense of agency in any way enhanced by playing?*

Yes, my sense of agency is much enhanced. Paradoxically, I find that by immersing myself in music when I'm playing (which feels as if one's so-called "self" disappears or dissolves into the music), paying attention only to the composer's written instructions, I actually find *my own* voice somehow. I love playing Bach, who left little to no written interpretative instructions, so much is up to the performer and the extent of one's research into (and wish to adhere to) Baroque performance practices. Unlike the plastic and visual arts, music (and dance, of course) is only "alive" in real time while being performed, so one can attempt to reproduce it as it was "presumably" originally played in the composer's time, or imagine that the composer would have adapted to new instruments and technology if they had lived longer. Beethoven famously did this during his lifetime as the piano was being actively developed then.

At the same time, I also am aware that this attitude itself is an identification with my father's attitude, since he proclaimed (with the exception of a few technically effective encores) that he could only play works he felt fully directly emotionally connected to, and thereby directly in contact with the composer. As I think I've said, his desire was not to have his technical virtuosity or special gimmicks draw attention to him as performer, which would distract from the "pure message" of the music. Of course this was and is impossible, since each performer's subjectivity is unavoidable in bringing a piece of music to life, and is surely a complicated fantasy for any interpreter.

So what I guess my "creativity" at the piano might consist of (though I've never really thought of it as creativity before) is that paradoxical process of trying to imagine what the composer was wanting to communicate and then trying to communicate it. In that process, there are always many questions and the inevitably subjective solutions that arise—what inner voices to bring out, perhaps, or to downplay. Often technical solutions are necessary to convey what one has decided is the composer's intent—better fingering that will make it easier to bring out an emphasized note or theme, a judicious dropping of a too-difficult-to-reach written note when you have small hands. (More of such decisions have to be made to preserve the spirit of the music and avoid communicating technical struggle to the listener when the music is not *meant* to be conveying a sense of struggle or turmoil.)

Even as a mere amateur pianist, I feel personally expanded/enhanced when I'm playing something that I feel deeply, and when I am aware that I've succeeded in causing an emotional effect (and affect) in a listener. I can't tell you what it feels like to bring someone to tears with a musical performance, or, for that matter, to a happy smile, or whatever. There's a sense of power, aliveness, agency, whatever you want to call it. I often think, afterwards, "so this feeling is what drove my father to perform," even when he was 89 and blind. Beyond the narcissism of gaining public attention, there is this deep and very strong sense of creating emotion, of activity, of bringing something to life.

I play chamber music with and for many amateurs of all ages (17–86!) and abilities, but we are all passionate and clearly motivated by the effort and desire to feel that sense of power, aliveness, agency. As I probably already said, I imagine that what goes into performing with one's own body in real time (surely it's true for athletes, as well, but different) is for me vitally connected to a sense of agency, since one *must* make the music (or dance, etc.) part of one's physical self in order to share it with others. It's an amazing experience, which I wish I had been able to embrace un-conflicted when I was younger, and when my father was alive, but I know that his outsized presence made that almost impossible for me.

Alain Malraux

In addition to being a writer of non-fiction (*Les Marronniers de Boulogne*, his portrait of André Malraux, won the prestigious Saint-Simon Award in 1990), a playwright, and translator, Alain Malraux is an accomplished pianist like his mother, Madeleine. He is the adopted son of his uncle André, who married Madeleine upon his biological father's death in the Second World War, but it was his relationship as a pianist to his pianist mother that is the focus of this discussion

Where does the pleasure of piano playing come from for you?

From my mother. I cannot separate my very first remembrances from her piano playing. That was the most beautiful thing in the world to me and, in a way, I haven't changed my mind. I am not a religious person, but I have to say that music has something of the divine. Playing Mahler's *Urlicht*[1] is for me like saying morning prayers. This is not religious propaganda, but it is something that is overwhelming; it takes me somewhere else and gives me the greatest pleasure in the world. I am now 64, and I have spent more than half a century running everywhere in the world to hear concerts and to discover this pleasure.

Can you say more about what that pleasure is?

It's sensorial, voluptuous.

Can you say anything about your sense of self in relation to your piano playing?

Playing is a sort of direct and indispensable link with the world. You have to work hard at it to have it bring you closer to your feeling, to your longing.

Is there anyone else in your family who is musically inclined?

Yes, my aunt, my mother's younger sister who is a violinist. She started at 20. And my grandfather, their father, was a singer. My mother, who started piano very young, already accompanied him at age nine or ten.

Was your talent at the piano recognized early?

Yes, definitely, immediately: By four or five. It is still the only real gift that I have.

Did you have musical talent in any other area?

No, none, not ever! I could not have played any other instrument. The only other thing I might have done, that came naturally to me and that I adore, would have been singing. I love song, *le chant*. I couldn't have been a composer either.

Do you have any particular sensitivity to other kinds of sound?

I do; I really do. I always feel very strongly this line by Verlaine: "*Ô, bruit doux de la pluie*" [Ah, the soft sound of rain]. I adore the sound of rain. It's marvelous.

What kind of pleasure is it?

Happiness; it's thrilling.

To return to music, would you say that it has a commemorative quality to it?

Definitely. It connects to my mother and is an enormous part of my life.

Is that connection to your mother, that commemorative quality, something that is always there whether it is conscious or unconscious?

1 The fourth movement of the Symphony No. 2 in C minor known as the *Resurrection*.

Yes, it is in both registers. It is on both sides of the mountain, the one I see and the one that lies behind.

Did your mother's music have anything to do with bedtime?

No, nothing to do with bedtime. She was often at the piano. I still have extraordinary memories of her at the keyboard working so hard at Beethoven's *Appassionata*, Chopin's *La Berceuse*, or the *Passions d'Or* of Debussy.

How do you feel about yourself while playing?

I am very critical of myself in all areas of my life, but maybe not enough when I am playing. The keyboard is touch, it's very sensuous for me. But I have the illusion that it is enough for me when it should be better. I do correct my playing, but not enough.

"Enough" by whose standards?

By professional standards. And by comparison with my mother. I always compared my piano playing to my mother's and was always discouraged. She was the origin of my gift genetically speaking. And she was my teacher until I was 12. Then she understood that she couldn't be my best teacher and she got someone else.

Why couldn't she be your best teacher, because of your relationship?

She was a most indulgent mother in every way except piano teaching. I couldn't find myself within that discrepancy. I was always scared that I wasn't clear enough as everyone always told me I was confusing to everyone.

How were you "confusing" to others?

I had a certain facility with words. I had no difficulty shuffling words, concepts, and images and was in a permanent state of having them boiling up within me. I wasn't focused.

And how does this relate to your music?

I didn't work enough at a specific piece. I didn't have to make a big effort with the piano; I could play a very advanced piece without much effort. But I didn't work at it. I was a third-rate student and there was no pressure to be better. And I was so bad at reading music that it was a permanent handicap.

Anything else?

I always felt I would never be able to make it; I'll never be good enough because I am not clear enough. And I always compared my playing with my mother's. I always felt I would never be good enough because she was always so much better. I was born with a gift given by her genetically and then I had to develop it by myself and I did that, but I developed it very well as an auditor—an operagoer, a concertgoer, a listener, but insufficiently as a player. I had no self-discipline or demands from the outside. Nothing was ever expected from us. The four Malraux children—Florence, Pierre-Gauthier, Vincent, and myself—we simply had to be present. We had to be dignified in terms of the big picture, but we didn't have to add anything. The specific way of being neurotic in my family was not having anything expected from us; it was enough just to be ourselves.

What does the concept of "feeling" in music mean to you?

It's the most precious thing in the world. If I hear music I like, it is instant pleasure and I plunge right into it. There is nothing like it. If I don't like it, I turn it off immediately. Between music and my perception, there is nothing, no intermediary. It's a total fusion.

What these interviews attest to is the power of the artistic process in a working through of what was, and continues to be, a "*reciprocal process* of *active involvement with the states of mind*" of another person, as Bromberg (2009, p. 357) has put it with regard to the psychoanalytic process. As in analysis, making art allows for the internalization of "otherness" in a new and *stronger* way. It allows for mastery of longing, managing of wounding, while engaging the viewer in their own imaginative associations. Fantasies of internalization, however reflective of the triad of incorporation, introjection, and identification, are evident throughout the interviews and are as varied as the individuals interviewed. Yet from these fantasies, from these internalizations of a larger-than-life parent, a single question persistently emerges: How, under the weight of such a parent, is the child *to be*?

Each of the interviewees chose to make art as had that parent. Each chose to make art in the medium (or a related medium) of the parent (albeit some more tenuously, fearfully, or ambivalently than the others). There are consequences of being raised by a parent who seems not to see the child herself so much as what that child can do for the parent (Smith), or by a parent who seems not to see the child herself so much as a potential art object (Freud), or by one who, at times, is so emotionally or physically absent as to seem not to see the child at all (Ernst, Rubinstein). These include the child's seeking for ways to be together with that parent while also being herself. This is the central problem faced by all those interviewed and making art as did the parent, and even making art alike in genre to that of the parent while expressing one's own personal self-narratives, offers a powerful way. Thus is art shown in each of these interviews to be, like analysis, a means of enhancing the sense of self, the self in relation to the other and thereby the self as agent.

Annie Freud, another of Lucian's daughters, has said: "A great discovery for me was the realization that my parents are no longer my audience" (personal communication). Similar, if more extreme, is Kiki Smith's claim that she would not have become herself had her father not died. Fear of his judgment inhibited development of her autonomy. It was as if, for her, there was not room enough for both parent and child. Like Malraux, who "always felt [he] would never be able to make it," never "be good enough," and like Rubinstein who feared the shame and humiliation of failing to perform well before her father, Smith remains aware of what she considers her limited ability. She, like the others, internalized the critical parent to the point of uncertainty about her own capacities. Yet she derives great pleasure from the "struggle" making art demands of her. However difficult the investigation necessitated by the making of art, there is a "very deep payoff" in what she calls "identity." Not to be confused with self-revelation or exposure, "identity" for Smith is the way the mind organizes itself: "Art is a way of organizing and making a manifestation of one's present condition."

Jane McAdam Freud, however, poignantly rationalizes as autonomy the independence forced upon her by an uninvolved father. Feeling that her father admired her "independence of spirit," she paid the price of closeness to him by concealing her need or disclosing it only in sublimated form in her art. Indeed, it was there that her affect could be channeled and managed: "Making art is where I feel at one with the world, where my equilibrium centers. It is where I know who I am and what I think, where I feel safe and confident." In fact, the dream recounted by Freud tells the story: There we see her unable to allow herself feel need or longing and what she keeps hidden behind her heightened sense of independence. "Perhaps if the frightened child loosened her grip, I could be more confident," says Freud. Perhaps if she "owned" the frightened child, she would not have to make believe she is without need and so utterly self-reliant. Perhaps the persona she describes as existing "independently of the influence of those from whom [she] draws inspiration" would lead to a more certain identity. Clearly, however, her art is empowering.

Ernst and his father attempted mutual regulation in making art together. Taking turns at improvisation after the elder Ernst showed the younger a particular technique, they would usually end by deciding they had "gone too far" and abandon the work. Or they would engage in a "match of wills" over shared areas of a canvas swept into something neither could control. Is the dilemma not once again the same as that expressed by all the others; namely, how does one take in a giant and not feel eclipsed? How can one be close to this larger-than-life parent or even demand a modicum of his attention and still survive and even thrive autonomously?

One way is by rationalization, by protecting the parent from the child's aggressive feelings resulting from neglect or having been made to serve the narcissistic needs of the other: The absent parent (confused by Rubinstein's brother with Santa Claus!), the narcissistic parent, the self-serving parent *had* to be this way or that to be the great artist beloved by the world. Another is by fantasy: Rubinstein's fantasy that her father was communicating directly with her when she heard him play is telling and poignant, as is her realization that her fantasy of the closeness she experienced through his music was "only an illusion of intimacy that [she] always had to share with complete strangers." A third is by entering into direct competition and vying for first place.

Donald Winnicott (1958) wrote of the capacity to be alone as "the experience of being alone in the presence of someone." In the developmental frame of "ego-relatedness" a relational bond, as he saw it, is internalized in which "id-relationships occur" leading to a strengthening of the ego as opposed to its disruption (pp. 418, 420). This is precisely what takes place in the making of art as these artists' stories have shown. If I chose to interview artist offspring of artist parents it is because the enhancement of agency (which is to say, the ego strengthening in which agency resides) is particularly apparent in that situation. In making art every artist is alone, but alone in the internalized presence of the other. How the spectator *enters the picture* to reactivate that presence on his or her own turf remains to be explored. Before we can consider that, however, we need to reflect on the maladaptive potential of imagination, the capacity of creative thinking to counter the achievement of self-organization and growth as it seeks mastery over the internal and external environments.

Part III

THE "BLINDNESS OF THE SEEING EYE"

Being creative is like having a baby: You want to be there!

Joanne Greenberg[1]

1 AKA Hannah Green, pseudonymous author of *I Never Promised you a Rose Garden*.

6

CREATIVITY

Friend and foe

"The real reason that I am here is that *I can't feel my face!* Can you help me?" Such were the anguished words of a potential patient to an analyst. Recalling that the individual "could *feel* his face when he touched it with his fingers and … knew that it was *his* face when he looked in the mirror," the analyst informed his audience of colleagues that "neither of those experiences changed the fact that the patient 'couldn't feel his face.'" From where might such a phenomenon arise? Though the individual did not ascribe his sense of facelessness to any external agent, he might have. The analyst would then likely have considered it some variation of a delusion of control. But Martin Willick (2003) explained to the young man that the "loss of the feeling of having a 'self,' that integrated feeling of *who* one is," can "be manifested in many ways," for he suspected that the patient's not being "able to feel his face" was his way of expressing "what had happened to his sense of self" over the preceding few years.

The subjective experience of this individual and the analyst's interpretation point to the significance of the construct of self for our understanding of imagination: The human self, however obscure or elusive a construct it may be, is susceptible to the feeling of expansion or reduction and the making of meaning—which is what imagination serves—determines that feeling. Edward Tronick (2008) has observed that "When creating new meanings, individuals—infants, children, adults—grow in every possible way and experience joy, interest, curiosity, and exuberance." This, he adds in conformity with the analogy of art making to psychoanalysis that frames this book, is what we see "in adults when an interpretation takes hold." It is a matter of successfully "making sense of one's place in the world" (p. 7).

Imaginative activity requires the operation of multiple levels of awareness: Association, synthesis, and evaluation principal among them. It serves the self by enabling new ways of perceiving experience. But what can be said of imagination when the meaning it makes is not in the service of self-growth but diminishment? What can be said of imagination when the making of meaning brings not joy but fear? If imagination is the mental faculty that renders fantasy operational, what might be the relation of fantasy to an experience such as that suffered by Willick's patient? How can something commonly perceived, like one's own face, not be, and, conversely, how can something non-perceptual be taken as perceived? How might we understand the workings of imagination in the conflation of fantasy with the real? And what is the relation of the creative imagination, the making of art, to this disorder, this chaotic state of mind?

The principal focus of this book thus far has been the enhancement of self, the increased understanding of self, and the resultant sense of agency that creativity affords. Creativity in art has been viewed as a process comparable to creativity in psychoanalysis by virtue of the "insighting" inherent within it. The title, however, *Imagination from Fantasy to Delusion*, has a "from-A-to-Z" feel about it while, in truth, there is no linear progression implied. To be sure, what brings fantasy and delusion within proximity is the suspension of disbelief, albeit willing in the first instance (as Coleridge famously noted), while in the second not consciously so. Freud (1930) said the following of the gratification obtained from giving substance to fantasy through artistic creation or scientific problem solving and the discovery of scientific truths: "[T]his procedure already clearly shows an intention of making oneself independent of the external world by seeking satisfaction in internal, psychical processes." Another "procedure [that] brings out those features yet more strongly," that further loosens the connection with reality, is illusion. And a third is said to operate "more energetically and more thoroughly. It regards reality as the sole enemy and as the source of all suffering, with which it is impossible to live, so that one must break off all relations with it if one is to be in any way happy." This of course is delusion:

> The hermit turns his back on the world and will have no truck with it. But one can do more than that; one can try to re-create the world, to build up in its stead another world in which its most unbearable features are eliminated and replaced by others that are in conformity with one's own wishes.
>
> (pp. 80–81)

There is a fundamental irony in imagination's being the common core of each. But just how related *structurally* are fantasy and delusion? Are what Swiss psychiatrist Eugen Bleuler called a "loosening of associations" and the "vivid internal imagery" of delusion *constitutionally* akin to the play that fantasy circumscribes? Are they proportionate in severity (i.e., loss of reality) to the measure of freedom in that play? To respond affirmatively would contradict the very thesis I am putting forth; namely, that imagination, when deliberately given expressive and communicative shape in literary or visual art, promotes self-awareness and that the pleasure of creativity lies, at least in part, in the making of meaning from which such awareness ensues. To respond affirmatively would be to view those with a *diminished* sense of self, such as may be experienced by individuals with schizophrenia (like the patient just referred to), as the most highly creative of all when in actuality their creativity may be severely blunted, or at least in the service of substituting for a primary feeling of "me-ness" another kind of Being-in-the-world. In short, affirming a structural affinity between fantasy and delusion would be to perpetuate the association of creativity with madness (a term largely replaced by "psychosis" when psychiatry standardized itself as a discipline),[2] an association the Western world inherited from the ancient Greeks. Although deliberation of the question of a link between creativity and psychopathology is centuries old (extending at least as far back as Plato's inquiry into the relation between genius and insanity), I turn to the matter again here as an entry into imagination's potential both to repair and impair the mind.

The creative, the mad, and the creatively mad

Despite persistent efforts to prove otherwise, psychic disturbance and creativity are not mutually *in*clusive though psychic illness may be held in check, or better, by the creative effort. The destabilized mind may create art that aids in self-integration (the elaborate literary and pictorial epics produced by Henry Darger and Adolf Wölfli, to name but two, are cases in point), and then the making of art is in the service of mental health. But psychic disturbance, however minimal, is in no way requisite to freedom of imagination. It has never been documented that, of those confined to in-patient units, an impressive number show the need to paint, draw, make music, or write. Neither does the literature demonstrate that neurotic conflict or worse, the disorganization produced by delusional thinking or the intrusion of perceptual abnormalities, contributes to the creative imagination. This is because the loosening of ego function that allows for the freeing of associations, while a creative (adaptive) means of protection and psychic survival, cannot be harnessed to serve the communicative purpose of art when uncontrolled. This is to say that fantasy

2 Joel Whitebook (2006), citing André Green, observes "that before psychiatry set out to transform itself into a strict science, the term 'madness' had been part of its vocabulary. But as the discipline became progressively normalized, 'madness' came to be viewed as an imprecise everyday concept, associated with such dubious topics as witchcraft, possession, and demonology, topics that had no place in a mature scientific discipline. 'Madness' was therefore largely dropped from the psychiatric lexicon and replaced by the more technical 'psychosis'" (p. 326).

and delusion are unrelated in constitution, however related they may be related in form.

When asked about her own experience of schizophrenia, award-winning novelist Joanne Greenberg related that being ill is like "yelling in a language no one else can understand." Psychosis and creativity oppose each other, she continued, because emotional chaos and cognitive confusion do not produce art: "There is nothing communicative about a language that is defensive and disorganized." More poignantly, she added, "The whole self is out of joint" (personal communication). John Nash, like so many others with schizophrenia, found his ability to be creative in his thinking devastated by his illness. Yet, as we saw, his approach to mathematics was intimately related to the eccentricities of his thought processes before the disease took control of his life. And he has even expressed a feeling of loss in the idea that the creative mind is compromised by the return to conformity that improvement in mental health implies:

> So at the present time I seem to be thinking rationally again in the style that is characteristic of scientists. However this is not entirely a matter of joy as if someone returned from physical disability to good physical health. One aspect of this is that rationality of thought imposes a limit on a person's concept of his relation to the cosmos. For example, a non-Zoroastrian could think of Zarathustra as simply a madman who led millions of naive followers to adopt a cult of ritual fire worship. But without his "madness" Zarathustra would necessarily have been only another of the millions or billions of human individuals who have lived and then been forgotten.
>
> (1995)

Such a statement, however, does not link creativity to illness. Rather, it indirectly reminds us of the thinking of those who have posited a causative relation of society to psychosis (R. D. Laing, for instance), and it is strongly reminiscent of those who have condemned the Western world of the post-Enlightenment era for its construction of the very meaning of madness itself.

The French philosopher Michel Foucault, for one, denounced the modern medical/scientific concept of "mental illness" in his first major work, *Madness and Civilization: A History of Insanity in the Age of Reason*, arguing that it comes no closer to the truth about madness than the more fanciful concepts that originated in premodern times. The truth or meaning of madness, he determined, has always been veiled by the forces of history as by the specificity of a given sociopolitical milieu. In the modern era it is hidden by bourgeois values dubious in and of themselves. What Foucault would later refer to in *The History of Sexuality* as the "repressive hypothesis" is already visible here and the argument goes like this: With the rise of modern rationality came the exclusion of the mad from society and the excision of the phenomenon of madness from scientific rationality. There was thus an act of repression compounded by an act of concealment. "Once this twofold exclusion had taken place," Joel Whitebook (2006) explains, "madness became the deep disavowed truth of modern rationality, as unreason became the reason of an inverted world" (p. 318).

More to the point, though, is that the "truth" of madness for Foucault is perceptible precisely by way of its simultaneity, which is not to say identity, with art. Madness for Foucault (1988/1965) finds no place within the artwork however the artist's psychic state may be judged: "Madness is the absolute break with the work of art, it forms the constitutive moment of abolition, which dissolves in time the truth of the work of art; it draws the exterior edge, the line of dissolution, the contour against the void" (p. 286). Noting that the past two centuries bore witness to an increasing "number of writers, painters, and musicians who have 'succumbed' to madness," Foucault was insistent that no closer link between art and madness had been defined. On the contrary: "[B]ut let us make no mistake here; between madness and the work of art, there has been no accommodation, no more constant exchange, no communication of language; the opposition is much more dangerous" than in former times (pp. 285–286). In what did that danger consist? In the evidence of the world's own madness, a madness demarcated precisely by the absence of one person's pathology within the work itself:

> [T]hrough madness, a work that seems to drown in the world, to reveal there its non-sense, and to transfigure itself with the features of pathology alone, actually engages within itself the world's time, masters it, and leads it; by the madness which interrupts it, a work of art opens a void, a moment of silence, a question without an answer, provokes a breach without reconciliation where the world is forced to question itself.
>
> (p. 287)

In fact, Foucault explained:

> "Through the mediation of madness, it is the world that becomes culpable … in relation to the work of art; it is now arraigned by the work of art, obliged to order itself by its language, compelled by it to a task of recognition, of reparation, to the task of restoring reason from that unreason and to the unreason."
>
> (p. 287)

In arguing that madness is what the modern Western world seeks to silence in the name of a dubiously constructed rationale, Foucault claimed to show that madness is neither situated within the internal world of the individual nor controllable by the authoritative (whether sociopolitical or psychiatric) powers that be.

Although there appears to be no real evidence to indicate that he had read or even heard of him,[3] one finds in Foucault's cultural radicalism an astonishing convergence with the interpersonal psychology of Harry Stack Sullivan. Like Foucault, Sullivan emphasized the determining role of society and culture in psychopathology, although he did not ascribe to society the ruse of concealment in the name of a supercilious and erroneous rationality as did Foucault. Breaking with Freudian drive theory, Sullivan located in interpersonal relations the origin of the self's vision of itself, the construction of its self-system, and the justification for dispelling with the biological determinism of classical psychoanalytic (and also contemporary psychiatric) thinking. Foucault believed in the multiple historicity of every human existence, in the idea that we have not one but many histories. In Sullivan's view the integrity of personality is similarly illusory: There are as many personalities as there are interactive fields, relatedness being a "biosocial given" (the term is Edgar Levenson's, 2005, p. 153). That the forms of subjectivation to the forces of social power formed the basis for Foucault's understanding of the individual, while the emphasis of Sullivan's thinking was on the inseparability of the person from the active field of social interaction is, of course, significant. But it is the meaning that their common perspective on the individual as an inherently social being holds for the exploration of the creative imagination that is of interest to us here.

From the viewpoint of the connectedness of personality to social relations espoused by both Foucault and Sullivan (admittedly far more abstract as conceptualized by the former than the latter), sublimation as an intrapsychic explanation of creative process lacks legitimacy. Indeed, creativity as an adaptation of instinct on the part of the individual qua individual to the demands of the social environ, demands built upon the foundation of Enlightenment "rationality" so strongly critiqued by Foucault, stands in direct opposition to the Sullivanian paradigm of self-construction in which repression is replaced by dissociation as the modus operandi of every

3 Although he was enormously well read, Foucault could not have read Sullivan's work at the Bibliothèque Nationale in Paris as it was not purchased until after Foucault's death. Whitebook (2006) notes, however, that before his departure from France to take up a position in Uppsala, Sweden, "Foucault had signed a contract to write a history of psychiatry … with a small independent publishing house. When he moved to Uppsala, he had the good fortune to discover in the Bibliotheca Walleriana 'a trove of documents about the history of psychiatry.' The project on the history of psychiatry was never carried out as it was originally conceived. But the extensive research that Foucault pursued in the Swedish archives eventually took shape as *Madness and Civilization*, which he submitted as his thesis for the Doctor of Letters in France" (p. 317).

individual, healthy or not. Freud provided a profile of development based on the energies of libido and aggression and a profile of the mind structured by the id, ego, and superego. At the center of those profiles is the theory of repression, the cornerstone of civilization insofar as it is the very means by which the individual gains mastery over his most primitive desires and psychosexual urges. The creative act (like dreams, parapraxes, and so on) reveals what Freud called a "return of the repressed" in acceptable or sublimated form. Foucault challenged Freudian psychoanalysis for, in accordance with these profiles, its identification of norms, norms that, in their reliance on the supposition of science, are suspect in origin as well as marginalizing, and gratuitously "disciplining" and thereby untenable. Sullivan, too, challenged the developmental and structural profiles of classical psychoanalysis for their emphasis on intrapsychic function in the determining of the normative in human behavior. But the primary focus of his challenge lay elsewhere: As Stephen Mitchell and Margaret Black (1995) have succinctly summarized it, "Whereas the Freudian analyst is looking for repressed wishes and fantasies, Sullivan is looking for unattended interactions." In other words, it is the vertical conflict-resistance model of psychic function that Sullivan decenters by substituting for it a vision of the self that is organized horizontally; that is to say, by partitioned areas of dissociative incompatibility (pp. 63, 84). If creativity as the transformation of energy (the accession of primary process and id material in managed regression) and as freedom from repression (the *sine qua non* of creative activity in the classical perspective) has little or no place in relational thought, how might it be otherwise conceived? What might it mean to view the creative imagination from a post-Foucauldian/post-Sullivanian perspective; in fact, from a contemporary relational perspective?

Relational aesthetics

The conceptual frameworks of Foucault and Sullivan, their philosophical thinking on the sociality of mind and the interpersonal nature of psychic function, invite a rethinking of Freud's notion of sublimation and the association of creativity with mental health. The relational models of psychic constitution, however, would no more imply a unified understanding of aesthetic experience than they imply a unified understanding of the development of theory of mind. The belief in a relational core of human feeling and mentation does, though, allow for a number of speculations with regard to the creative imagination.

First, in the broadest context of what we might call a "relational aesthetics"—a model of aesthetics presupposing a cohesive sense of self and other—artistic expression would seemingly be exempt from the normalizing tendencies characteristic of the social order, tendencies that derive from communal discomfort before the uncertainties creative expression may lay before us. In other words, the unfamiliar in art, in eliciting less collective anxiety, would make experimentation and artistic "difference" more tolerable and thereby reduce the association of art with pathology. New eras of modernism, for instance, with its inherent sub-categories of -isms (forthcoming counterparts to futurism, cubism, dadaism, surrealism, abstract expressionism, and the like), would not require identification as an avant-garde to dispel the discomfort of the viewer or reader any more than the individual who thinks, feels, or behaves differently than the norm should require psychiatric labeling to quell the shared anxiety such "difference" provokes. Incongruity of social constructs, of those external to the individual (such as institutions and ideologies) with those that are internal (molded by the interrelation between subjectivities), would not be confused with or determinative of aesthetic valorization.

Second, the relation between painter and viewer or writer and reader would take precedence over the interpretation of content. Stan Coen (2009) has questioned the validity of the distinction between fiction and autobiography and noted that authors "resist (and invite)" the reader's wanting "to actually know, capture, and possess" them (p. 146). Freud and then Kris maintained that art communicates a daydream about the artist himself and that it is devoid of self-reference so as to ensure the maximum enjoyment of the recipient (Balter, 1999, p. 1297). But the importance of self-referential content becomes even more diminished in what I am calling the post-Foucauldian/post-Sullivanian relational view: Consider the French *nouveau roman*, the work most notably of the first generation of "new novelists," Alain Robbe-Grillet, Michel Butor, Samuel Beckett, Nathalie Sarraute, Robert Pinget, and Claude Simon. In all these writers, we see an obvious intermingling of fiction and autobiography ("autofiction") and the push–pull to which Coen refers is exploited to the fullest. Yet the texts' incomplete and contradictory scenes, in addition to requiring the reader's creative participation, actively engage him in a critical observation of the reader–author relation. The first word of Butor's early novel *La modification* is "You" and the character is indistinguishable from he who ultimately constructs him by reading. Beckett's monosyllabic or one-letter names further open the text for the readers' associations to the "unnamable" voices. And Robbe-Grillet and Sarraute go so far as to insert within the telling of their own identifiable stories more than either singular (personal) or collective (historical and universal) reference; they bring to the surface the intentionality of consciousness, the perception of the object by the subject, and render it so semiotically transmittable as to make the relation between author and reader the very subject at hand. What emerges is an intersubjectivity that is the basis for the very writing itself, the creation of the text being read.

In fact, this focus on author–reader intersubjectivity has led not only to a reduced emphasis on content interpretation but to a lessening of generic distinction. In Beckett, we have a writer for whom performance is as much about the shape of the words that are uttered, their rhythmic and lyrical quality, as how they are said and the fictive texts have the dramatic force and tension required for the stage. The distinctions between poetry, novel, and drama are blurred because what is at stake is not the well-made character developed in accordance with the traditions of literature and theater, but the relation of the spectator to the voice of the playwright himself (cf. Brater, 1987, p. 17).

Third, and more to the point, however, a post-Foucauldian/post-Sullivanian relational perspective might be said to support the idea that anterior to the interpersonal relation of the artist and the viewer or reader is the dialogic relation between the artist and his or her art. If art is to resist the discursive limits imposed by cultural and aesthetic conformity, it must remain astutely self-aware, as painting of the early 20th century aimed to show. Indeed, if Beckett's own voice in its relation to the reader or viewer is at stake in his work, it is not that there is a complete identification of the playwright with his work, but that there is not. Implied is a clearly defined distinction between two relational entities (artist/viewer and artist/art), which amounts to a non-identification of the artistic fantasy with the artist himself. This, in fact, is what differentiates fantasy (whether daydream or art) from delusion: *The former implies an ability to play while experiencing the self of that play as the self one currently is; the latter implies a loss of that separation.*

But the question arises: Can such an aesthetic paradigm truly be conceptualized outside of any significant overlap with the sublimatory model? The concept of sublimation is based on the notion that the imagination may be harnessed to prevail over the exigencies of the drives. For Freud, the ego, which serves to integrate and defend against the disorganizing propensities of the id, is enlisted in the effort to attain higher goals focusing the endeavor on multiple capacities of the individual. Understood in accordance with the relational model, aesthetic experience also implies reciprocity of thought and emotion in the shaping of ideas and the giving of aesthetic form, but inter dominates over intra to the extent that thought and emotion emanate from the mind–brain as an inherently social entity. Creativity implies expression of a self-organization not unitary but multiple, determined both by the many early relational configurations that make up the psychic structure and by lacunae in that structure resulting from dissociative mechanisms (healthy or unhealthy) used to avoid pain associated with those relational prototypes. *From this perspective the creative imagination is viewed as aiming to increase self-coherence through the dialogical interaction between the multiple self-states, diverse subjectivities, and identities that are socially embedded.* Needless to say, sublimation remains today a somewhat ambiguous theory, one that has been formulated differently over the years by a number of psychoanalysts, and the measure of its success in achieving its generalized goals of differentiation, self-integration, and gratification, among others, is therefore variable.

Anna Freud (1957), for instance, stressed the developmental component. She located the origin of creative capacity in the ability to sublimate acquired early in development and situated creative inhibition in a fear of the "emotional surrender" that characterizes the dependency of childhood (p. xv). Melanie Klein saw reparation or restitution of object relations as the motivating force behind what she too conceived of as sublimation. For Klein, the need to repair faults in the early subjective organization and internalization of the emotional environment was the source of the creative impulse. In a word, restoration of the lost object, the recreation or reparation of an inner world fragmented by aggressive desires, was seen as the basis of the sublimatory act. Hanna Segal, Klein's most faithful follower, went so far as to claim that awareness of this need is present in the unconscious of every artist, that art is its symbolic expression, and that the ability to overcome the anxiety and guilt aroused by aggressive urges, the ability to "work through" that developmental phase referred to by Klein as the "depressive position," is essential to creative expression. For ego psychologists Heinz Hartmann, Hans Loewald, and Ernst Kris, the emphasis, as noted earlier, was placed on the neutralization of drive at play in the regressive service paid the ego by the creative endeavor. Common to each of the above, however, was the notion that sublimation involved the working through of resistances, the overcoming of repression.

Given the wide range of understanding of what constitutes the relational perspective on the mind, any notion of a relational paradigm of aesthetic experience would also need to be conceived as exceedingly diverse. Already, the etiology and meaning of dissociation, a concept so fundamental to the relational orientation (dissociation as interpersonal failure was initially delineated by Sullivan) renders the paradigm problematic. It generally refers, as Elizabeth Howell (2005) succinctly puts it, to "the separation of mental and experiential contents that would normally be connected." But as Howell has further noted, it can be adaptive or maladaptive, considered taxonic or of a continuum, in process or dispositional (p. 18). Thus, how a paradigm reliant upon dissociation, much as the sublimatory model is reliant on repression, might inform the agency-enhancing feature of aesthetic experience is not only complex in and of itself, but how it might overlap with the classical theory of sublimation is all the more ambiguous. Indeed, the principal difficulty lies in the schism between dissociation and repression. Citing the work of Donnel Stern, Howell observes that dissociation most often refers to unformulated experience while repression refers to experience that is formulated. "Dissociation," moreover, "refers to states and systems of states, which are often mutually exclusive," whereas "repression usually refers to a piece of information that was accessible at one time but not at another" (p. 198).

At the same time, however much the two theories differ with regard to our understanding both of the psychology of the individual and of social interaction (especially as related to trauma), aesthetic experience, as is my thesis, enhances agency precisely by being a phenomenon of assimilation and integration. As noted at the start of this volume, Camus asked his reader to imagine the philosophical "hero" of *The myth of Sisyphus* happy. This implies imagining him *whole*. Whether conceptualized as increased dialogue between relationally constituted, segregated self-states or as transformed drive, whether conceptualized on the order of resolution of horizontal splitting (dissociation) or that of vertical splitting (repression), aesthetic achievement, "the struggle toward the heights [that] is enough to fill a man's heart," is, as aptly named by the French, *jouissance*—rapture, the sublime. *The models converge, then, in the somato-psychic charge of affect, whether through the generation by fantasy of somatic excitement that becomes the object of creative thought or the transformation of drive into fantasy.* As does the theory of sublimation, the relational perspective on aesthetic experience would recognize the *affective* significance of creativity as a mode of amalgamation emanating from within the body.

I return, though, to the association of creativity with madness from which neither model of the creative imagination, neither the relational nor the sublimatory, is immune. Throughout much of the 20th century, creativity was viewed as requiring a certain measure of mental health while implicating, simultaneously, the reverse. Lest we forget, Freud's thinking on sublimation was founded upon the belief that the "healthy" use of imagination shapes the primitive wishes and desires of the human psyche that might otherwise demonically ("unhealthily") rise to the fore. Indeed, contextualized by libido or by deinstinctualized energy, since the early days of psychoanalysis the creative imagination has been explained by the capacity to tolerate regression that the privileging of primary process implies; the *generation* of creative imagery and thought has traditionally been posited as derivative of *managed degeneration*. And if object relations theorists (and even self-psychologists) departed from drive theory to seek an alternative context in which to explain creative effort, if the idea of creativity as a defense of the ego against unacceptable, somatically derived urges of the id fell somewhat into disrepute, creativity and psychic disturbance have nevertheless remained indisputably linked. This is because, as Stern (1997) says, "We treat art as if it *is* what is *does*" (p. 18). To the extent that "what it does" is as a corrective, it is linked with need and it is that need that then becomes pathologized and this by virtue of convention and norms.

What I am calling a contemporary relational model of creativity falls prey to the same association, however intersubjective its post-Foucauldian/post-Sullivanian core: The point has often been made that certain sounds, visual images, and stories are "art" because we say they are; but Stern goes further in showing that what has meaning is always interpretation,

interpretation that is necessarily contextually and relationally embedded. Moreover, the *practice* of making art, he claims, is not to be confused with its meaning: Artistic praxis is the actualization of possibility, and *how* that potentiality passes from what is experienced as unformulated to formulation, from chaos to order, is a function of a socially constructed perspectivism that also implicates convention and norms. Theory deriving from social construction, as does the relational (whether in the psychoanalytic or aesthetic arena), conceives meaning as the consequence of consent. We can, however, conceive of a "truly unconventional form of experience" that arises by the constant reworking of meanings, the reinterpreting of experience, that, like artists, we do throughout life: "We are always trying to know ourselves and the people around us, and to do so, we interpret and reinterpret, and then we reinterpret again" (p. 21). New forms appear on the canvas replacing old ones as the artist works, just as new understandings replace earlier ones in the psychoanalytic setting. And this is just as the growing child reworks or re-encodes relationships in accordance, in part, with his internalized objects to the point where consensually validated meanings are attenuated to become less significant in one's inner life. In other words, the individual is in relation with himself as he is with others; so too the artist with his art. Yet the relational perspective, I would also suggest, puts before us a significant irony not to be ignored.

The fundamental paradox of the relational aesthetic

I have located in affect—in the rapture of the creative moment—the overlap of the classical and relational perspectives on aesthetic experience. Nonetheless, it remains that in the former fantasy is conceived as a transformation of libidinal desire while, in the latter, it is fantasy itself that provokes affective response. This distinction between the somatopsychic generation of fantasy and somatopsychic reactivity to it is epistemologically significant for it reveals within the relational frame a paradox that deepens the analogy between psychoanalysis and art.

In a recent paper Nancy Chodorow (2010, p. 216) has called upon psychoanalysts to rethink the current emphasis on the analytic dyad. The inner world of the patient, she reminds us, "enables transferences that go between unconscious and preconscious, rather than from self to other." The intrapsychic life of the patient should not be the price paid for recognition of the sociality of the dyad; while not to be undervalued, the dyad should not, she maintains, replace the analysand as the focus of attention. But keeping the patient's internal and external life at the center of analysis is not Chodorow's only concern. What she suggests is that the emphasis on the dyad goes further than the search for a more authentic empirical reality in the consulting room. The dyad, in truth, is not a "thing apart," a "self-contained unit"; rather, it "is itself part of a set of practices and tacit assumptions that go beyond and produce that reality." To be sure, the consulting room is inhabited not only by fantasies and wishes, but also theory. Beyond its clinical implications, Chodorow's argument is important for articulating *the recursive feature* of the relational experience. By this I mean it demonstrates the validity of the dyad's status as a social phenomenon and that of our reflection upon it as interactive as well. That relation is not, however, to be conceptualized apart from the non-relational forces that contribute to its constitution: "The analyst's activities are shaped by her training, her professional identity, her taken-for-granted assumptions and reflexive location as analyst, and by her conscious and preconscious ideas about what being an analyst is." *The legitimization of the dyad as inherently relational is also, therefore, something else: a coming together of both the inter- and intrapsychic worlds of analyst and analysand* (pp. 216, 217, 226).

The paradox of relational psychoanalysis—a function of the recursive nature of the dyadic exchange itself—extends to its subsidiary, the relational aesthetics I have aimed to conceptualize here. For it is as endemic to the modernist sensibilities of philosophy and art as much as to the modernist psychoanalytic orientation that is the relational perspective. Husserl's post-Enlightenment theory of intentionality, which offered a resolution of the subject–object dichotomy the pre-Enlightenment Descartes had bequeathed the Western world, is a case in point. Under the influence of Brentano, Husserl's phenomenology of consciousness, and that of his early-to-mid 20th century Continental followers, opened the monolith of Cartesian mindfulness to a fusion of subject with the object of its perception and in so doing, *it revealed awareness of consciousness as the object of its own perceptual function*.

The valorization of polyphony, the interplay of individual voices that act upon and shape each other, as put forth by Mikhail Bakhtin decades earlier but popularized in the 1970s and 1980s, made a similar philosophical, if also rhetorical and aesthetic leap. His literary analyses of Dostoyevsky and others depicted the imagination as *itself* dialogic and attributed the meaning it makes to the self-referential, intertextual underpinnings of the literary use of language and the imagination's *inherently relational constitution*. Within the lineage of Francophone modernism and postmodernism, Bakhtin's thinking on discourse was much allied with that of Foucault and was confluent in this country with the dialectics of intersubjectivity championed by Sullivan and the adherents to his interpersonal theory.

In the art world, modernism took its creative impulse from an equally radical self-reflexivity. It needs hardly be said that avant-gardism was a reaction to the academic expectations associated with 19th-century romanticism, realism, naturalism, and symbolism. But it was the congruent self-reflection, the particular mark of originality to which the aesthetic of non-conformity gave rise, that defined the parameters of the course modernism would run. It began with the self-interrogation at the heart of impressionist painting and extended to the fragmentation and dehumanization ensuing from a heightened self-awareness that are now platitudes of the discourse on visual and literary modernism, and of the discourse on the subversion wrought by modernism's offspring: Deconstruction.

This self-consciousness has been likened by Louis Sass (1992) to the structure of consciousness found in some severe psychic illnesses, a structure he refers to as "hyperreflexivity." Sass has argued that madness, not to be equated with irrationality, with the antithesis of reason, long the defining feature of mental health, derives rather from an *increase of conscious awareness* and from an "*alienation not from reason but from the emotions, instincts, and the body*" (p. 4; emphasis added). Emphasizing the epistemological over the instinctual, he likens "the mind's perverse self-apotheosis" (1994, p. 12) such as it appears in schizophrenia and related disorders to the excessive self-preoccupation characteristic of modernism. Seeking neither etiology nor influence, Sass focuses on affinities, on likenesses in which I find a clear endorsement of my own thinking that the association of psychopathology with the creative imagination is valid only as analogy and not causation.

In the kinship between modernism and madness that Sass outlines, excessive self-awareness is identified with abstraction and withdrawal. From cubism via conceptualism to abstract expressionism, the history of the visual arts tells the same story of hyperreflexive exclusion or self-removal told by the epistemological account of schizophrenia and related psychoses. I would now suggest that in its rejection of drive, of instinct, of the somatic tensions that classical psychoanalysis acknowledges as having the upper hand in psychic illness, relational thinking ironically reveals its own affinity with the parallelism between modernism and madness. *An abstractionist hermeneutic, relational theory—which objectifies the subjectivity of self to view it in a primordial relation to the other—"reflexively produces a dyad whose features include that which goes beyond and helps constitute it,"* as Chodorow has eloquently said (2010, p. 219; emphasis added). *It too is an epistemology of "hyperreflexivity," a seeing of itself seeing. But where it falls short in practice, if not in theory, is that it does not see itself as constituted of a whole greater than the sum of its parts. What is obscured by the centrality of the dyad (analytic or aesthetic) is, paradoxically, its own subjective (if not its intersubjective) constitution.*

Sass (1992) cites the work of Nathalie Sarraute to exemplify the objectification of introspection that he finds analogous in modernism and madness and with which I find a concomitant parallel in the dyadic centricity of relationalism, or more precisely, in the paradox underlying it both in psychoanalysis and art. Scrutinizing internal experience as though it were external led Sarraute in her novels to the "infinitesimal interior stirrings that seem to occur with an almost vegetable automaticity," as Sass depicts them, "the subtle driftings of an inner life that usually go unnoticed yet for her constitute the true essence of human existence." These are the "tiny and virtually anonymous events" that make up human consciousness, events that "are at once exterior *and* interior": "[T]he fleeting memories, half-remembered phrases, and semiconscious urges and sensations that move independently across one's field of awareness like water bugs across a pond" (p. 224). Sarraute calls them "tropisms," playing as much on the biological phenomenon as on the tropes of narrative and the excess connoted by the French *trop*.

The process of objectifying introspection is more visually portrayed by Beckett, particularly in his penultimate work *Stirrings still* (1988). There the opening passage reads: "One night as he sat at his table head on hands he saw himself rise and go. One night or day" (p. 1). And shortly thereafter we come to this:

> One night or day then as he sat at his table head on hands he saw himself rise and go. First rise and stand clinging to the table. Then sit again. Then rise again and stand clinging to the table again. Then go. Start to go. On unseen feet start to go. So slow that only change of pace to show he went. As when he disappeared only to reappear later at another place. Then disappeared again only to reappear again later at another place again. So again and again disappeared again only to reappear again later at another place again.
>
> (pp. 2–3)

Self-observation becomes increasingly hyperreflexive as this short text continues: "So all eyes from bad to worse till in the end he ceased if not to see to look (about him or more closely) and set out to take thought" (p. 18). Before such self-awareness—indeed, the perception of self-perception that is the Beckett text—the creative endeavor "goes on," continually threatening to overcome itself, to reach the finish, but unable to do so: "Such and much more such the hubbub in his mind so-called till nothing left from deep within but only ever fainter oh to end" (p. 22). The result, as has so often been said, is a fragmentation or de-integration of self, but the point is that it originates precisely in a subjectivity that spirals out into vivid externalization of all that is normally felt to be internal (see Sass, 1992, p. 225).

Already in Paul Valéry's 1896 *La Soirée avec Monsieur Teste*, a remarkable illustration of postmodernity well before modern turned post, the excesses of hyperreflexivity were stunningly portrayed, though both the personified mentation (as suggested by Valéry's title) and the writing itself are undone in that work by the very self-consciousness that impedes the Beckettian text from achieving its conclusion. This is to say that the text is its own rapid undoing just as the hyperreflexive M. Teste is the immediate undoing (he could live but three-quarters of an hour) of his own self-conscious reflection. Faced with the extraordinary dissolution of both character and author, we are, as Sass says in a somewhat different context, "left with a peculiar contradiction: a subjectivism without a subject, narcissism without Narcissus" (p. 226).

Thus has subjectivity in the form of narrative engagement with the world been superseded by hyper-awareness, the artist's awareness at play *within the work* of the work's aesthetic precariousness, its fragility as literary or visual art. Filmmaker Alain Resnais has said he wanted "to make films that describe the imaginary" (cited by Dargis, 2010, p. 14). Like other mid- and late 20th-century cineastes, particularly in France, his interest has been in portraying the making of film and the functioning of imagination. Michel Butor wrote theoretically of the novel as "*le laboratoire du récit*" (the laboratory of narrative; p. 9), but fictively explored its construction in *La Modification*, *L'Emploi du Temps*, and elsewhere. Alain Robbe-Grillet similarly analyzed the need for the past to release its hold on contemporary fiction in his essay collection *Pour un Nouveau Roman*, and in his novels (the metaphorically entitled *Dans le Labyrinthe* perhaps most notable among them) depicted the maze through which the writer makes his way in the act of writing. This diversion of focus within the work of art from narrative engagement to narrative structure, from the actuality of creation to the how-it-is-done (and also to viewing and reading), was hardly restricted to film or literature, as we know from the audacious escapades of Yves Klein and other visual artists centered in Paris in the 1950s and 1960s. Klein's monochromatic paintings, his gallery 1958 exhibition of nothing ("The Void"), like Arman's assemblages of rubbish and Jean Tinguely's scrap machines, displayed the objectification of introspection that deconstructs while constructing. The apotheosis of self-referentiality, whether the work's self-awareness or the excessive self-consciousness of those depicted within it, extended as well to the performing arts. Critic Ruby Cohn has written incisively of the "theaterreality" characteristic of Beckett's dramatic work noting that the buzzing sound and glaring lights spoken of in the 1972 play *Not I*, for example, are the very noise of the audience and the lighting of the performance that permits the audience to see what it is watching.

One finds, then, in modernism—early, high, late, or post—the dominant mode of creative praxis, hyperreflexivity, to be akin to that of the perspective on art, relational aesthetics, in which the centricity of the intersubjective dyad that animates the work in all its self-consciousness, precludes recognition of anything exterior to it. Situating the constitution of the work within the dyadic interaction, that of author/reader, painter/viewer, or any other, *is* phenomenologically legitimate. Yet locating it *solely* therein simultaneously deconstructs the constructive impulse, for—as in the (post)modernist heightened awareness of its own genericity—the work of art creates the author and reader or painter and viewer as much as they create the work. Indeed, as Roland Barthes showed us, "the text desires a reader who desires an author," to cite Carla Locatelli (2008) on the critic. "The author is thus the result of the wish of the reader, who creates him or her, by way of his understanding" (p. 78). The text itself generates projective mechanisms upon the reader whose own are operative upon the desired author. Listen to Barthes: "The text chooses me, by a whole disposition of invisible screens, selective baffles: vocabulary, references, readability, etc.; and lost in the midst of a text ... there is always the other, the author" (cited by Locatelli, p. 78).

Neither author nor reader, neither artist nor viewer, is reducible to a sole representable identity. No more, that is, than the text is reducible to a single construction (or the analytic dyad to an intersubjective relation irrespective of external influences upon it). This is precisely what Beckett so powerfully conceptualizes and artfully captures in his 1973 play *Not I*, a monologue in which the speaker refuses to use the first-person pronoun ("what? ... who? ... no! ... she!" is the play's persistent refrain). In so doing, however, she necessarily reveals her identity as the very I she refutes, for who names the *not* I if not I herself (Locatelli, 2008, p. 72)? This "subjective gap" "reinforces the evidence of the insurmountable distance between *I* and *self*." The same deconstructive mechanism was already articulated in the better known *Krapp's Last Tape* (originally published in 1958), a play in which the sole character, aiming to reconstitute his identity by reflecting on the past with the aid of recordings made at various moments of his life, "finds himself," to cite Locatelli, "only as a residuum of vanishing selves" (p. 74). Self-expression, then, in both these and other works by this author, is an unrealizable fantasy, a fantasy doomed to failure, but one that cannot be relinquished insofar as the very articulation of its failure is the achievement of its success.

This is precisely the *aesthetic unknowing* that the *nouveaux romanciers*, the *nouveaux réalistes*, and even practitioners of the *nouvelle vague knowingly* put on the page, the canvas, and the screen. It is the "blindness of the seeing eye" (as Freud, 1893–1895, p. 117, called the state of contemporaneous knowing and not knowing) that is the consequence of consciousness' recursive interiority whose endpoint can only be an ironic exclusion of its own subjective experience, an exclusion not unlike that of those whose hyperawareness renders them unable to maintain continuity of self.

Disorders of the imagination

Art, fantasy, delusion: All are imaginative efforts to make sense of subjective experience. Structurally speaking, fantasy is of the order of wishful thinking, delusion of the order of misbelieving. Either may serve a defensive or protective function; either may be seen as creatively adaptive. So, too, the making of art, as we saw with the aesthetic of hyperreflexion; that is, literary or visual art that disengages from the subjective through awareness of itself as aware of itself ad infinitum. Modernist art tends toward avoidance of the subjective grounding that narrative engagement with the external world once offered. Not quantitatively more imaginative than any that preceded or followed it, only differently so, like both fantasy and delusion it strives for cohesiveness of self however much it displays the lack thereof. Freud (1893–1895) spoke of a "strange state of mind in which one knows and does not know a thing at the same time," of the "perception [that produces] no psychical effect" (p. 117). This was the state of mind experienced by Willick's patient who did not feel his face despite seeing it, just as it was the state of Ms. P. who could not psychically see her paralysis though she visually perceived it. Hyperreflexive art is similar: It too (and paradoxically so) "loses sight," so to speak, of its own subjectivity to the extent that it objectifies itself in self-consciousness.

Art is imaginative in giving literary or visual form to fantasy, itself already imaginative, and in numerous ways, not least of which is its simultaneous potential for defensive withdrawal and creative adaptation, it resembles madness, also imaginative. I am reminded here of Freud's notion of symptom itself as symbol: The *symptom* for Freud *symbolizes* both what has and what has not occurred. It symbolizes, as Freud wrote (1917), "an ingeniously chosen piece of ambiguity with two meanings in complete mutual contradiction" (p. 360). The symbolic representation is a distortion bearing within it, at once, withdrawal, the presentation of the return of this withdrawal, and what has been called "a *fraught equivocation* between the withdrawal and its presentation" (Didi-Huberman, 1990, 2005, p. 179). In this way, the visual image functions uncannily as a symptom, as we know from Freud's 1919 paper on E. T. A. Hoffmann's story "The sandman." Freud (1908) further elegantly articulated the uncanny paradox of figuration when he described the hysterical symptom of a patient who, and I quote:

> [P]ressed her dress up against her body with one hand (as the woman) while she tried to tear it off with the other (as the man). This simultaneity of contradictory actions serves to a large extent to obscure the situation, which is otherwise so plastically portrayed in the attack, and it is thus well suited to conceal the unconscious fantasy that is at work.
>
> (p. 166)

Where art and madness differ is in art's apprehension of the imaginary as a distinctly new, fantastical form of reality. Consider the young woman who imagines herself in a romantic relationship with the man next door. While engaged in that fantasy, she remains cognizant of the nature of fantasy and that she is a player therein. In a word, she remains self-observing. She is like the artist whose knows that the world he imagines through his creative capacity is not identifiable as his own. But what happens when she loses sight of the connection to who she is in relation to her fantasy? She loses the "relative capacity to make room at any given moment for subjective reality that is not readily containable by the self that [she] experiences as 'me' at that moment" (Bromberg, personal communication). She separates the self of the fantasy from the self of the here-and-now with the result that fantasy is no longer fantasy but, by virtue of its very different structure, delusion.

Another way of saying this is that fantasizing is figurative exploration of a particular kind: It is a way of Being-in-the-world, but virtually; as such, it is playing at knowing without experiencing that knowing. Conversely, art making transcends the virtual in (real) form. While repeatedly and consistently revirtualized so as to be further acted upon, it is unlike unarticulated fantasy (that is, fantasy not given communicative aesthetic form) in provoking reflection upon the very process that brings it forth. Fantasizing and art making are alike in engaging the self beyond the here-and-now while retaining a subliminal awareness of the self as, precisely, in that here-and-now. When the self as maker of fantasy or of art (whether by fantasy we mean daydreaming or what generates the aesthetic work) loses its sense of separateness from the self of the here-and-now, a delusory state results.

Such is the nature of dreaming. It is by no means a new idea that psychosis is dreaming in a wakeful state. Indeed, that the positive symptoms of schizophrenia (the perceptual abnormalities that are delusions and hallucinations) are those of the dreaming but not sleeping brain has been proffered by many: The model of psychosis as wakeful sleep extends from Kant to contemporary neuroscientists via Hughlings Jackson, Schopenhauer, Jung, Bleuler, and even Freud (who noted in a 1911 paper that common features are sometimes shared by dreams and episodes of acute psychosis). Claude Gottesmann, in a 2006 paper entitled "The dreaming sleep stage: A new neurobiological model for schizophrenia," traced the neuronal pathways and activation patterns that link dreaming and psychosis and articulated the convergence of data derived from current research into dreaming and psychosis. And in 2008 Rodolfo Llinás wrote of psychosis, "If a small part of the thalamus gets permanently stuck at low frequency or part of the cortex fails to respond to the wakeup call, an abnormal rhythm is generated, a so called thalamocortical dysrhythmia. The goal is to wake up parts of the brain that have fallen into low frequency mode."[4]

Dreaming is not only thought by some to be both comparable to and explanatory of madness, but an analogue of the making of art. By way of the defocusing of attention, the associative mode of thinking, and the simultaneous activation of a significant number of mental representations that is the state of consciousness in which wakeful dreaming occurs, Allan

4 I owe this overview of the pertinent literature to Desmond Heath (2009).

Hobson and Hellmut Wohl (2005), for example, have linked dreaming to the state of consciousness from which creative insight emerges (p. 108). In an intriguing volume entitled *From Angels to Neurones: Art and the New Science of Dreaming*, they have defined the formal features shared by the universal process of dreaming and the creative endeavor of making art: "Regardless of their content," dreams are "internally generated percepts, primarily visual but also motoric"; the same may be said of art. While we are not deluded as to the reality of art's depiction, whereas we do believe in what we dream while we are asleep, and while dreams are generally characterized by a strangeness by no means necessarily found in art (although, to be sure, it may be), "the meaning of both works of art and of dreams stems from [the] integration of perception and emotion." As the authors explain: "Whatever emotions are evoked by a work of art, they must be so seamlessly integrated with its content as to render the work's content as plausible and compelling as our dreams; and the capacity of a work of art to engage the viewers' perception is enhanced by its capacity to engage the viewers' feelings" (pp. 16, 18). I strongly take issue with the position espoused by Hobson and Wohl that art and dreams are further alike in being fundamentally uninterpretable and that they do not reveal transformations of drive motivations however diverse their meaning as teased out by individual dreamers and viewers. I strongly take issue with their belief that dreaming is not regressive, defensive, or, as Freud further maintained, the guardian of sleep. I do subscribe, however, to their forcefully made argument regarding the comparability of dreaming and art making as means of self-organization.

Let us look at the developmental dynamic they outline: "We consider the evidence to be overwhelmingly in favor of the idea that ... the reliable, the redundant, and recursive running of sensorimotor programs in dreaming sleep is itself autocreative because it constantly contributes to the development of our brains and our minds." Most critical in fetal life and early childhood, this dynamic is ongoing through middle age and into the later years. Dreaming, moreover, is said to be "the subjective experience of a progressive program designed in a failsafe manner to help us maintain and improve our behavioral repertoire." Additionally, the self-organization that occurs during sleep is at once formative, as in the interconnection of cells that function concomitantly in the visual cortex when images are perceived; cognitive; and narrative, as in dreaming. In what they term their "new scientific brain/mind model," Hobson and Wohl attribute an important role to "historical antecedence" but only "insofar as biological history has brought our brain/minds to their capacity for self-organization" (pp. 182, 184, 188, 193).

Yet Hobson and Wohl maintain that: "It is not so much that we are demented in our dreams (though in a formal sense we are), as that we are surrendering one level of control (the cortical brain) to another (the sub-cortical brain)" (p. 184). Is that not simply another way of saying that dreaming is a function of primary process? Certainly dreaming and psychosis are alike in the inhibition of the prefrontal cortex, the loosening of associations, and the weakening of the ego's mechanisms of control. Certainly the creative process is dreamlike and therefore *like* psychosis; it may even be linked at times to psychic disturbance (mania and creativity, for instance, are often concomitant). But frequently such disturbance is an impediment to creative expression precisely because primary process thinking (a concept Hobson would be loath to recognize as such) is creative only when the loosening of ego function is controlled. Indeed, the lack of such control impedes creative activity which requires the manipulation or shaping of metaphoric, metonymic, and other forms of symbolic association. The creative act, in short, displays the condensations and displacements we find in dreaming; to be sure, the visual and literary image, like the dream, is uncanny in being impervious to inconsistency. But in abstracting from the concrete to the representational, in transforming feeling and sensation into another modality, the creative act—unlike dreaming and unlike the withdrawal from reality that characterizes psychological disturbance—implies *a capacity for their (unconscious) interpretation*, without which there is limited, if any, play of similarity and difference (see Modell, 2003, pp. 146–147).

At the same time, however, withdrawal from reality is not without meaning, and therefore not unimaginative, though the imaginative source of the meaning is constricted. I return for a moment to Oskar Kokoschka. Following the breakup of his three-year long relationship with Alma Mahler, the artist had made for him a doll with features resembling hers. Companion and muse, the doll was meant to satisfy his need for the ideal woman. Kokoschka was determined that it be made in such a way that he could wholly believe in it, that its likeness to life be such that it would, as he wrote in a letter of 1918, "radiate feeling" and recall for him in moments of great despair "all the delicate and intimate gifts of nature displayed by the female body." Kokoschka not only supplied detailed instructions for the making of the doll, but made elaborate preparations for its arrival. As Edith Hofman described the situation:

> At first he trained a surprised maid to wait upon a lady of distinction whose imminent arrival he announced to her in mysterious terms. Then he instructed a coachman to drive through the town in such a way that all the most important monuments could be shown, stopping here and there where the lady might like to take a rest, take the air or enter into a shop. He also had a box at the opera reserved for himself and his doll, from which she could see best and also be seen by a crowded house. And finally he invited his best friends to celebrate with him the arrival of his doll.

The excitement was palpable when the box containing the doll arrived and Kokoschka was certain that his ideal was now to be unveiled as a living being. "The anti-climax was terrible," Hoffman tells us, as:

> [F]rom the careful packing emerged a monster, studiously constructed according to Kokoschka's most extravagant demands, exactly corresponding with his detailed orders, covered with the most delicate silks and skins, softly padded where softness was desired, movable in all its limbs, carefully painted and neatly dressed—yet a monster, ghostly in its faithfulness to life, grotesque in its lifelessness. Kokoschka was stunned. His dream had become literally true, only to die with its realization. The doll, whom he had endowed with all the attributes of grace, attractiveness and the glamour of a love-thirsty heart, was still a doll.
>
> (pp. 147–149)

Whether or not it is true that the artist was seen in public with the doll, that it accompanied him to gala nights at the opera, for instance, or this was pure rumor, stories of his madness proliferated (p. 149). The irrational acting out of his fantasies—the degree to which he denied reality in favor of his idealization of this inanimate object—rendered the fetishized doll the object of a delusion.

This real-life account is reminiscent of others that are fictive: Balzac's *Le Chef-d'Oeuvre Inconnu* (The unknown masterpiece) relates the transformation of a painting such that the subject (Mary of Egypt) is seemingly brought to life from within it, Ovid's Pygmalion myth tells of a sculptor who falls in love with a statue of his creation, and closer yet is the 2007 film *Lars and the Real Girl*, written by Nancy Oliver, that plays on a similar theme. The story is that of a young man who, by choice, lives alone in a garage behind the home he and his brother have inherited. Fearful of relationships and particularly of being touched, his solution to the problem posed by a burgeoning interest in love and sex is a lifelike doll ordered over the internet. Taking the doll for a real woman, he soon falls in love. It is the advice of the family physician (also a psychologist) consulted by his concerned brother and sister-in-law that enables Lars to forsake his delusion: The doctor suggests the doll be treated by all concerned as if it were, in fact, a real person. She counsels entering the delusional space, which allows Lars to begin to trust her and develop the strong transference that will therapeutically empower him to explore the internalized relationships that are the source of his difficulties.[5]

5 I am grateful to Joan Wexler for her elegant summary of the value of the transferential relationship for the character in her discussion of a paper I presented at the Western New England Psychoanalytic Institute, April 10, 2010.

What these tales of delusion have in common is, obviously, their manifest content. But how are they meaningful? In each case, the doll served as an imaginative remedy. With regard to Kokoschka, it would appear that the delusion was a means of denying the narcissistically injurious abandonment. It may also have been a means of protecting himself from his aggressive wishes insofar as the doll was, as Joan Wexler has noted, "an already lifeless body he could not kill." In a sense, it represented, as Wexler put it, a compromise, "a rigid but life sustaining solution at the time." Harold Blum (2011) has speculated that, possibly, the doll "unconsciously represented [Kokoschka's] dissociated feminine self, identified with Alma, and earlier his mother" (p. 304) or, alternatively, that "the doll may have had genetic antecedents in an infantile transitional object, a childhood imaginary companion and/or a childhood puppet or adolescent fetish and masturbation object" (p. 305) Eventually, the doll had wreaked upon it a violent "death" by the artist: Its head was smashed and, with red wine poured on it, it was beheaded. Kokoschka experienced as traumatic Mahler's abortion of their fetus as he did her bringing to a close their tumultuous affair, but recalling other traumata of the painter's life—his having witnessed a brother's bloody birth (an older brother having also died in infancy) and having himself suffered nearly fatal wounds in war—the delusion was seemingly multiply determined. All told, though, it "imaginatively" allowed Kokoschka to replace his own victimization (in war and in love) with an enactment in which he was the agent of devastation. Of course, it was not only the delusional interactions with the doll that served him therapeutically, but the creative reproductions he made of it as well. They too contributed, as Blum (2011) has similarly affirmed, to Kokoschka's "recuperation and the restoration of his nearly shattered self" (p. 306). Both Kokoschka's repeated painting and drawing of his ideal woman and the delusions turned what was initially profoundly regressive into "a long delayed and derailed mourning process, and reparative recovery from massive trauma" (p. 306). By augmenting his sense of agency, by empowering himself and having control over what he felt and its intensity, he was able to achieve reorganization of his psyche.

Common to each of these stories is the value the doll—which is to say the delusion—had as a mode of relatedness. Not merely a denial of reality, it was a way of transforming it to maintain or produce contact. The delusion in each of these instances was a creative object-relational strategy. Roy Schafer has spoken of the conventionalized use of the word *withdrawal* in the context of patients who retreat deep within themselves to a private cocoon-like space that protects them from intolerable dysregulated affect. We tend to lose sight of the fact that such patients may also "be contriving to maintain a special kind of contact with those around them." When Kokoschka was designing the doll's construction and then, early after its arrival, displaying it in public (whether maximally, as rumored, or even minimally), the delusion may have been the only way he could, to cite Schafer (2008) on delusion more generally, "retain some integration and creativity, and in that way be enabled to stay in the world." In the case of the character in the film and that of the myth of Pygmalion, what is significant is the adaptive function served by the delusion: The creative purpose served a failed self-system in need of re-constituting in another (albeit irrational) form of relatedness. Of course, the deeper question to be asked concerns the nature of the fantasy harbored by the withdrawal into delusion, a question posed most explicitly in the film where the physician/psychologist was able to uncover it, for insofar as the delusion has a self-protective and/or self-constructive relational content, it must embody a fantasy that renders the adaptive potential meaningful. While I am not suggesting any sort of congruence between the generation of meaning in delusion with that in artistic process, I am calling attention, on the one hand, to the idea that the meaning of psychic mechanisms such as delusion is far too easily subsumed by the overzealous taxonomy of psychiatry and, on the other, to the function of creativity therein. Indeed, those inhabiting the "imaginary"—as opposed to those whom the imaginary inhabits—are, more likely than not, to be creatively, in the artistic sense, impoverished. It behooves us to explore why.

Psychosis, dissociation, and the creative imagination

"When you are seriously mentally ill," Joanne Greenberg once said explaining what psychosis feels like, "it's hard to tell the difference between the wall and doors" (personal communication). Two kinds of serious mental illness were differentiated in the latter half of the 19th century and the early 20th by Eugene Kraepelin: manic depression and dementia praecox. Kraepelin's belief that the etiology of each of these psychiatric disorders was biological is very much in favor today dominating, as it does, academic research in psychiatry, although his idea that dementia praecox (premature dementia) was necessarily degenerative was soon proved false. (It was for this reason and to distinguish life experience from what he saw as the organic deficit at the core of the illness that it was renamed "schizophrenia" by Bleuler, his German contemporary.) Among Kraepelin's most significant contributions was the finding that psychiatric symptoms overlap. This, in fact, became the basis for the American Psychiatric Association's *DSM-IV* (*Diagnostic and statistical manual of mental disorders, fourth edition*) and the World Health Organization's *ICD-10* (*International classification of diseases and related health problems, 10th revision*), the primary diagnostic systems in use today.

The *DSM-IV-TR* (the text revision published in 2000 that updates the 1994 *DSM-IV*) defines delusion as a "false belief based on incorrect inference about external reality that is firmly sustained despite what almost everyone else believes and despite what constitutes incontrovertible and obvious proof or evidence to the contrary." Intelligence, religion, and cultural background in no way account for the tenacity with which a person holds to a false belief and delusions may be found in any number of psychiatric or non-psychiatric disorders, from schizophrenia to bipolar disorder and from substance abuse to dementia. Delusional thinking differs from overvalued ideas—ideas that are seen, for instance, in obsessive-compulsive disorder (OCD), anorexia nervosa, body dysmorphic disorder (BDD), and hypochondriasis—in the degree of impairment in reality testing, although the range of severity, dimensionality, is not currently a feature of psychiatric classification. Only of late, in fact, has more attention begun to be paid to pre-psychotic states, which may or may not evolve into full-blown illness, but from which much, no doubt, is to be learned about the potential for deterioration, both biological and psychosocial.

Interviews and testing done with high-risk subjects voluntarily participating in a four-year cohort study of youths at heightened clinical risk for psychosis have revealed a lack of "motivation and courage to keep on moving forward," as one such subject put it, and confusion wrought by certain affective states: "I didn't understand the depression and anxiety and ... felt confused." An inability to comprehend the environment, the *meaning* of things said, and the function of objects in the world have been reported as leading to a lack of emotional safety: "There is no place that feels to me really safe or where I am fully comfortable," another participant reported. "I alienate myself and feel defeated because of that."[6] Alienation is indeed common to the schizophrenoform disorders, with the loss of sense of self a major feature once the prodromal phase has converted. Gavin McCabe, of England, described the phenomenon as "particularly acute in the early years after breakdown." It was "experienced by me," he said, "as a 'deconstruction' of my ability to use, or understand, language itself."[7]

6 This study was undertaken by the Center of Prevention and Evaluation (COPE) at the New York State Psychiatric Institute, Columbia University Department of Psychiatry, under the direction of Dr. Cheryl Corcoran, whom I thank for my appointment as Visiting Scholar in 2008, which gave me access to this material.

7 Gavin McCabe, who has been interviewed on his recovery in the press, shared his experience with me by email. Most interestingly, he told me of how recovery was facilitated for him by the "the care in the community" offered by treatment such as it is practiced where he lives, but also by the social interaction that came with his playing violin in three London orchestras (where he meets others at weekly rehearsals with whom he also travels on tour) and by gardening, which fostered a "connection with the earth and experience of the natural progression of the seasons." I am most appreciative of all Mr. McCabe chose to reveal to me.

What we tend to think of as schizophrenia, some of whose primary symptoms (as previously noted) are found in bipolar and other disorders as well, is diagnosed with difficulty. This is because we are inclined to think of it as a single psychic malady, with a predictable course and outcome. The criteria outlined in the *DSM-IV* and the *ICD-10* do not account for the growing evidence that schizophrenia is best understood as existing on a continuum, that it is, in fact, a number of overlapping disorders with heterogeneity of clinical presentation, course, and, in all likelihood, disease processes: Just as "correlates of fever will not support a case for similar disease class among infectious illnesses," William Carpenter (2008) has written, "correlates of anxiety ... or, for that matter, reality distortion" are attributable to a variety of nosological classes:

> The neural processes and genetic vulnerability for anxiety may be similar among persons experiencing anxiety without suggesting diagnostic unity. Hallucinations and delusions caused by lysergic acid diethylamide, amphetamine, temporal lobe epilepsy, bipolar disorder, delusional disorder, and schizophrenia may share correlates of final common pathways of expression without suggesting similarity of core pathology.

But why enter into this discussion of psychosis, generally, and schizophrenia, more specifically? Why at this point? In claiming that artistic creativity is a mode of self-enhancement, a means toward growth and increased agency whose primary feature is "insighting" (which emanates from within the dialogic interaction of the artist with his or her art much as it does within the psychoanalytic setting), I set aside any real consideration of the meaning of self and its constitution. From schizophrenia and related illnesses, however—where there is most often a diminution in the sense of self and personal agency, an understanding of self-experience that is disordered, and significant isolation—we have much to learn about the self's de- and reconstruction.

Contributing to the difficulty of definition and diagnosis is the complexity of the relationship between psychosis and dissociation, a relationship with a long and thorny history. Dissociative disorders are traditionally viewed as psychotic. But some today, in affirming trauma as their source, claim the dissociative processes to be both consistent with the positive symptoms (delusion and hallucination) of schizophrenia and precisely what saves an at-risk individual from psychosis. Andrew Moskowitz explains the very essence of delusion by the inability to metabolize experience that is overwhelming in its violation of selfhood and attributes the hallucinatory hearing of voices to a form of dissociated identity and other hallucinatory phenomena to decontextualized flashbacks. Delusions, which may also be driven by dissociative flashbacks according to Moskowitz and his colleagues, are said to derive from "early intense affective experiences that are hidden under the veil of infantile amnesia." So, too, disorganized behavior (such as catatonia) and disorganized speech are attributed by him and his colleagues (2009) to dissociative processes insofar as "information about its traumatic or affectively charged context is not conveyed to the listener/observer" (p. 529).

The trauma-dissociation-psychosis paradigm may be described as the overpowering of the mind–brain with information deemed toxic, information that must be dissociated for the sake of self-preservation. Whether on the horizon of identity, affect, or memory, the dissociative objective is the same: the disavowal of behavior or feeling. We recall in this regard Mark Solms' patient, Ms. P.: Whereas the neurological model of her poor insight would be used to explain it as deficits in executive and frontal lobe function, as an organic neglect disorder (anosognosia) preventing the mental registration of the clinically apparent paralysis, the psychological model would account for it as dissociation, a defense of her self-esteem and ego ideal. Preserving the integrity of selfhood, the dissociative mechanism, in its most extreme form, does so at its own expense.

By extreme I refer to the pathological or maladaptive multiplicity of selves at one end of the continuum of the dissociative processes. At the other end, and this is stressed by Bromberg, there is normal adaptive differentiation. In fact, for Bromberg, who goes even further than in defining delusion as dissociative in essence, delusional thinking, wherever it falls on the continuum, is not insanity at all. What *is* madness is loss of self-continuity which is precisely what delusion, with dissociation at its core, at least temporarily, prevents. Attributing delusion, traditionally a core concept of psychosis, to dissociation (an ideational cornerstone of relational theory) and deeming it non-psychotic is antithetical to the regressive context in which it has long been situated by classical psychoanalysis. Interestingly, Moskowitz questions whether the concept of psychosis should not be abandoned altogether given the lack of evidence of a true differential diagnosis between psychotic and dissociative disorders. That he would favor referring to those with delusions simply as "delusional" is supported, ironically enough, by the 1919 paper "The uncanny" in which Freud describes a number of circumstances whereby something hidden from conscious awareness re-emerges to render the familiar frightening. Although, in this essay, Freud saw anxiety as the result, rather than the origin, of repression (a notion to be reversed in his 1926 paper "Inhibitions, symptoms and anxiety"), the link between the uncanny in its "unhomeliness" to anxiety—in other words, the moments when *das Heimliche* extends into and becomes *das Unheimliche*—lends credence to the claim that the origin of delusion lies, as Moskowitz et al. (2008) have written, "in early affective experiences which cannot be consciously recalled" (p. 75). The "delusional atmosphere"—or affective state that may precede the development of delusions—is telling in this regard as well.

Evidence, however, for a genetic vulnerability to the schizophrenias is strong, with molecular studies showing that it is not one but multiple genes, in their interaction with each other and with the environment, that are potentially significant. The genetic expression may depend upon any number of environmental factors, prenatal and post: The development of neural pathways in the brain, obstetrical complications at birth, psychic trauma in infancy or childhood, and the heavy use of cannabis have all been implicated. At the same time, it is not, as Brian Koehler has noted, simply a matter of genes interacting with the environment in some sort of "dose–response relationship," but of "how the interplay is experienced, interpreted, responded to." This is why biology and psychology are truly inseparable. As Koehler (2008a) has put it, "The mind is embodied, but cannot be reduced to molecular interactions since the latter are significantly influenced by top-down processes (e.g., social experience, unconscious phantasy, relational configurations that have been internalized, beliefs and expectancies, intentionality, etc.)." Moreover, not everyone with a genetic vulnerability succumbs to psychiatric illness.

Although it is not known just how much protection strong ego functions—reality testing, mechanisms of defense, affect regulation, drive control, and object relations, among others—may provide against schizophrenia, it is clear nonetheless that attention to the neurobiological and neuropsychological changes of schizophrenia needs to be paid by the psychodynamically oriented. That a non-urban setting in which there is limited stress and constancy overall within the environment have proved favorable both to avoidance and recovery, and that the acquisition of compensatory mechanisms for cognitive deficits and other forms of cognitive enrichment are known to act positively upon the evolution of the illness and an individual's chances for recovery, cannot be ignored by those who would seek etiology solely in the psychological domain.[8] Martin Willick (2003) has eloquently stressed the gross underestimation by both clinical psychiatry and psychoanalysis of "the seriousness of primary cognitive impairments in patients with chronic schizophrenia." Independent of, but often interconnected with the positive and negative symptoms of the illness (the former, once again, referring to the delusional and hallucinatory symptoms; the latter to the reduction in affect and motivation), "serious impairments in working memory, attention, and executive function—that area of ego function involved with planning, anticipating,

8 With regard both to the neurogenetic etiology of schizophrenia and recovery, see postings by Brian Koehler on the website of the ISPS-US: *www.isps-us.org*.

and following through" not infrequently are part and parcel of the disorder. That, in fact, is a significant reason why people with serious mental illness have difficulty being artistically creative: Making art requires the capacity to choose from an infinite number of possibilities and the capacity to put that selection into communicable form. Delusions are adaptively, while not artistically, creative for this reason as well: Whether considered fundamentally dissociative or not, they are clearly, like obsessions and overvalued ideas, constrictive. As do dissociative processes, they reduce the imaginative realm by reducing the interaction of some self-states with others thereby reducing the capacity for articulating the wider realms of experience.

Dissociation, in fact, has been explained by Donnel Stern (1997) as the very opposite of imagination, as "the unwillingness to allow one's imagination free play." Stressing the constraint placed on associative linking, on the freedom of thought that is the *sine qua non* of creativity, Stern has argued that dissociation is by nature at the antipodes of "the particular kind of vivid and feelingful articulation we describe as imagination" (pp. 97, 94). In a sense, however, there is a sense in which the dissociative state may be said to be in itself a creative mode of being: In as much as it absents from conscious awareness the self-state known since Sullivan as "not me," it impedes the apprehension of agency. Indeed, it is a modality of subjective experience that simply cannot be recounted. As such, it is a creative (if all too often, though not uniquely) maladaptive mode of self-protection.

Rothko's geometric slabs of color are conventionally described as an expression of his feelings of solitude. Here, however, is what he reportedly told art critic Harold Rosenberg: "I don't express myself in my paintings, I express my not-self" (see Lahr, 2010, p. 80). Is this not what Beckett continually expresses as well? His is a fictive world that is often qualified as "schizophrenic," not merely because his "characters" (if such be the word) are devitalized, delusional, and distancing, but because the dissociated I is the very failure of expression he continually bemoans. Dissociated "I"s undeniably reach their apogee in *Not I* where not-me is the most sustainable of self-states figured. Of course, that Beckett, like Rothko, defeats this failure by his artistry is testimony to the separation between artist and art that allows for the dialogue and feedback that are the basis for growth. Their art pays testimony to the separation between self and non-self, self and other, self and world that Willick's patient was lacking, the differentiation that a psychodynamic treatment may well have provided.

I have said that what the creative imagination of aesthetic experience has in common with the creative dimension of madness (madness understood as chaotic dysregulation stemming from the mind's incapacity dissociatively or otherwise to contain and manage affect) is the objective to further self-cohesion. I have proposed that imagination is fundamentally adaptive in the face of fragmentation (which may or may not reach psychotic proportions) or in its absence, at which time its pleasure resides in the empowering use of the mind. Viewed relationally (as having to do with interpersonal relations in the present or internal representations of past significant objects) or in terms of sublimation (as modification of the urgency of drive), creativity in art resembles the creative dimension of delusional thinking in seeking to perpetuate and further agency.

We have seen with Louis Sass (1994) that schizophrenia, the prototype of severe psychic illness, may be considered not a loss of rationality, but an "exacerbation of various forms of self-conscious awareness" (p. 12), that self-control itself is what some who suffer from it appear unable to control. As Sass (1992) has explained, "what they cannot get distance from is their own endless need for distancing; what they cannot be conscious of is their own hypertrophied self-consciousness and its effect on their world" (pp. 240–241). This is tantamount to saying that self-regulation is over-employed in the effort to gain, ironically, self-regulation. We saw the same self-reflexive mechanism ironically at work in the (post)modernist aesthetic and suggested that, like relational psychoanalytic theory wherein dyadic centricity paradoxically results in a gap in subjectivity, it too displays a "hypertrophied self-consciousness."

Thus the question now becomes one of knowing how we might triumph over this subversive transcendentalism and do so without reverting either to a reductive taxonomy (psychiatric or aesthetic) or to an essentialism neglectful of intrapsychic forces and other influences external to the intersubjectivity undeniably constitutive of all forms of creative ideation. This is where the next chapter will take us.

7

NEUROBIOLOGIC AND PSYCHODYNAMIC CONCORDANCES

"Transference" and "countertransference" in art

If the principal conundrum faced by scientists and psychoanalysts alike in the 20th century was the opposition between nature and nurture, the conundrum of the 21st century is the alteration of the one by the other. How nurture modifies nature is the focus of the infant–parent bonding research that informs much of the current work on trauma. How nature modifies nurture is the focus of the research in epigenetics that informs much of the current interest in development. In the formation of an individual's identity, in the construction of self and object representations, in affects associated with the generation (and transgenerational transmission) of fantasy, and in the interplay between the sense of self and other (inclusive of the neural mechanisms that give rise to and maintain them) —this is where psychoanalysis and neuroscience meet.

I have situated that juncture in the drive for knowledge (Freud's *Wisstrieb*) that impels us all, for it emerges from the impulse to comprehend our environment that arises, in turn, from the need for mastery. Imagination responds to the impulse to know by filling in what is not known or what is known but not fully owned. (Confabulation, which like delusion is not intended as falsehood but is nonetheless a distortion of reality, is a far-reaching but illustrative example.) *How* the mind–brain imagines—in other words, *how* it makes use of different kinds of thinking and imaging—in the service of knowledge is the object of study for psychoanalysts and neuroscientists alike.

Neuroscience attends to the part of the brain, the prefrontal cortex, associated with the most focused or goal-directed form of thinking. It researches the regions associated with the least focused, spontaneous thought, known as the "default network" and located, for the most part, along the brain's midline and the temporal lobe where memory is processed. And it scrutinizes the networks linked with creative thought, with daydreaming and mind wandering, occurring on the continuum between the two. It does so by measuring electrical activity (on electroencephalogram) as tasks necessitating more or less attention are assigned and by deriving additional data from studies of the influence of certain chemical processes (specifically, the catecholamines noradrenaline and dopamine) on thought processes. Data obtained from such studies show that creative thinking is associated with the loosening of cognitive control (reduced arousal in the prefrontal cortical regions).[1]

Psychoanalysis was founded on the basis of clinical observation by Freud of the same phenomenon: the lessening of focused attention producing a more creative—that is to say, more associative—state of mentation. This is the state Freud was seeking for his patients in requiring that they reveal whatever came to mind, for it is one that provides easier access to primary process mentation and produces an easier flow of memories. Thus both neuroscience and psychoanalysis support the notion of creative thinking as intimately linked to decrease in cognitive control and attribute the attaining of knowledge (insight) and the enhancement of agency (mastery) to the application of higher level conceptual or secondary process thinking to unconstricted sensory and cognitive perception. But insight is obtained and agency enhanced in psychoanalysis through the interaction of modes of thinking with another significant process: transference. I have proposed that feed-forward is feed-back dependent in creative activity much as it is in the analytic setting. At stake here now, however, is the very credibility of the analogy between art and psychoanalysis to which that claim has led, for transference may be precisely where the two part ways—or not.

The patient in psychoanalysis brings to the treatment intense feelings for the analyst. Redirected from past objects, such feelings endow the analyst with attributes that are but fantasized and foster the revivification of early imagos for reasons to be harvested, it is hoped, from within the unconscious. As the transference motivations are made clear over time and the transference itself relinquished and mourned, inhibitions of one sort or another are removed and greater freedom from maladaptive functioning attained. Or so the classical analyst would have it.

Transference for the relational practitioner is more focused on the here and now than the past and is continually created and destroyed by the two participants. The patient who is relating to the analyst "as if" they were someone from their past has found something in him or her that activates sensitivities/anxieties born of the patient's history. It is observing and learning what it is about the analyst that the patient reacts to that gives both parties the opportunity to understand the patient's inner world, including those factors that keep the patient from living more fully in the present.

Countertransference, intermittent responses on the part of the analyst to what is occurring in the treatment, the resonance of an analyst's memories

1 For an in-depth and astute evaluation of these forms of thinking and references to the various studies providing the evidence cited here, see Christoff et al. (2011).

and imagination with the subjective experience of the analysand, has a history of controversy in the classical psychoanalytic domain. At one time considered a risk to the treatment insofar as it revealed the presence of the analyst's own unresolved conflicts, today it is more widely considered unavoidable in the treatment process. To the relational or interpersonal analyst, countertransference is not only inevitable but necessary (though to be managed by the self-observing analyst with considerable care). In this perspective, it refers not only to what is stimulated in the analyst through the material of a given session, but to what results from the patient's projective identifications that push the analyst to feel the inner world of the patient. In this model, in addition, the analyst is seen as inviting the patient into his or her own projective identifications, the consequence of which is the co-created relational space where what are known as enactments occur. (For instance, the analyst who forgets a patient's appointment may be enacting the "patient's unconscious fear of abandonment." And the analyst who becomes critical of the habitually late arriving patient may be enacting the "patient's unconscious wish for punishment"; Sandberg & Busch, 2007, p. 159). A form of activity in which both patient and analyst unconsciously participate, the concept of enactment is a derivative of countertransference and one that remains a strong point of contention between the classical and non-Freudian clinician: Transference being "an act of in vivo imagination" (the phrase is Joan Wexler's), for the more Freudian analyst it is the creation of the patient and active participation by the analyst in an enactment is thus anathema for the classical clinician to the objectives of treatment.

My purpose here being to explore not differences in theory or practice, however, but the relation between the central foci of psychodynamic process and aesthetic experience, I would simply say that, whether explored more as a projection from past onto present or as a mode of communicating the actuality of one's psychic interior, it is a given that transference and, increasingly, countertransference as well are sacred to the psychoanalytic mission. Which brings me to this: Neuroaesthetics has become progressively more defined as a field of science whose practitioners seek to understand the workings of art by the workings of the brain or even the reverse. Zeki looks at the way the brain, before the physically stable image of a painting such as Vermeer's "Girl with Pearl Earring," responds to ambiguity, in this case that of the expression in the face. Cognitive instability in the beholder yields to multiple interpretations rooted in memory and experience of what such a facial expression might mean. Ramachandran locates the pleasure of, say, Cézanne's "Mont Sainte-Victoire" in the lack of explicit meaning and the challenge to the brain to imagine what is not entirely there. His several universals of artistic experience are meant to explain the basis on which this accomplished. Others seek answers in vision itself, in the retina and the visual cortex: The degree to which we perceive

Mona Lisa as smiling in Leonardo's painting depends for Margaret Livingstone upon the part of the retina perceiving at any given moment that part of her face. In the simulationist theory championed by neurophysiologist Vittorio Gallese, it is empathic resonance owing to mirror neurons that explains our relation to the art we see, read, and hear. In a previous book (2005), I wrote of the homeostatic benefits of the making and reception of art. Now I would ask: Are there psychodynamic benefits in aesthetic experience—benefits to be contextualized beyond sublimation and object relation reparation—deriving from the very means we know from the psychoanalytic setting itself? Does the artist or viewer of the plastic or performance arts, the writer or reader of literature, or the composer or listener of music, in other words, bring to the work something comparable to the primary mode of therapeutic change in that setting: namely, the transference phenomenon?

"Unconscious, leftover struggles from childhood influence all of us. The opportunity to play out, observe and alter them in relation to the therapist is one of the most important contributions of psychoanalysis" (p. 19). In demonstration of this, Lawrence D. Blum (2011) studied the relationship between two people in a film, but how this influence plays out in one's relation to the film itself might well be the object of study. Transference to the institution in which they are treated is not unknown in the hospitalized patient. Transference to the institute in which the analytic candidate is educated (to supervisors, peers, and others) is part and parcel of analytic training. "To these vicissitudes," Leo Rangell (1982) wisely added "transference to psychoanalytic theory" (p. 29). Is there something relevant here to how art is made and perceived? Yet transference in psychoanalysis is a form of resistance. Is some comparable form of resistance at work in the interaction with art and, if such be the case, to what would it be? Might one go so far, moreover, as to speak of countertransference in aesthetic experience without personifying art to the point of silliness? Critic Paul de Man wrote of autobiography not as a genre but as "a figure of reading or of understanding that occurs, to some degree, in all texts." "The autobiographical moment happens," he argued, "as an alignment between the two subjects involved in the process of reading in which they determine each other by mutual reflexive substitution" (quoted in Locatelli, 2008, p. 70). A similar idea of mutual determination had previously been expressed by Roland Barthes, who wrote of the text's desire for a reader desirous of an author who desires a reader. From within this circularity of desire the author and reader emerge, much as analyst and analysand take form: from within fantasies, projections, intuitions, and perceptions. What's more, author and reader identity ultimately culminate in some measure of self-knowledge much as *this* analyst and *this* patient, brought into being by, for, and with each other, come to know themselves differently in view of what is unique to their relationship.

Writing of the "transubstantiation" of "internal objects from the deep solitude of an internal world into an altered external actuality," Bollas (1999) describes the movement in which "psychic reality leaves its home in the mind and moves into a different intelligence" and claims that the same principle of change that takes place through a given artistic medium is that which occurs in the analytic setting: "This transition is not representational. It is presentational. What the poet writes or the painter paints or the composer composes has not existed before" (pp. 174, 173, 175). So, too, in psychoanalysis the freely associating patient experiences a shift to a new mode of being. Knowing the conversational and social codes that frame the analytic setting, the patient nevertheless "creates himself in another place" and "instantiates himself in the logic of an aesthetic that differs from purely internal experience or conversation." Just as the artistic imagination creates through a given medium works that demonstrate a "peculiarly evocative integrity" (p. 175) received by the viewer or reader in terms of his or her own newly created experiencing self, free association becomes the medium through which the analysand will come to exist in a transformed way. But what is the nature of the link between the medium (be it paint, music, poetry—or free association) as a mode of self-creation and transference/countertransference?

James Breslin, Mark Rothko's biographer, is said to have changed careers from professor of English to art historian in response to Rothko's art at a time when, his first marriage having come to an end, he was depressed. The paintings by Rothko "create an empathic space in which to confront emptiness and loss; they create an environment for mourning," Breslin reportedly said (in Modell, 2003, p. 164). What Breslin was relating was an alteration in self-identity achieved through his experiencing of Rothko's work, but it hardly need be said that neither his choice of Rothko nor his "reading" of Rothko was by chance: "*We select objects in current time that will provide the meaning that will enable us to alter the experiences of the past*. We invest those objects with feeling when we perceive a metaphoric correspondence between present experiences and unconscious memory" (Modell, 2003, p. 164). Is that "investment" of feeling not "transferential"? Might it suggest the perception of something "countertransferential"? And just how visceral is the "metaphoric correspondence" between present and past? Although I raise here more questions than I will answer, as an ensemble they are reducible to two: First, insofar as, like psychoanalysis, the making or reception of art allows for the recovery of "*mnemonic inklings* of earlier subsymbolic experience" (Raphael-Leff, 2009, p. 25), does this imply something intrinsic to the artwork that would account for the linkage to memory, to associations, to change (as in Bollas' presentational as opposed to representational mode of transition)? To put it differently, does this imply that art, phenomenologically speaking, is ontologically operative as a spatiotemporal presence or is it, rather, solely a matter of the artist/viewer perceptually installing within it what Livingstone (2007) has referred to as "conscious or unconscious aesthetic trope[s]" (p. 478)? Second, does this imply something that neurophysiology—and I refer here not only to the processing systems that account for the perception of color, shape, and so on, but to the existence of mirroring mechanisms in the brain—might help us to understand?

Seeing what regards us

"*Ce que nous voyons ne vaut—ne vit à nos yeux que par ce qui nous regarde*"—a wonderfully charged expression in French whose multiple possibilities for translation into English manifest the very problematic with which its author, Georges Didi-Huberman (1992, p. 9), is grappling: "What we see is of value—lives—in our eyes only though what …" *looks at* us? *concerns* us? Therein lies but one of the several conundrums with which we are faced in considering this statement: Does the artwork in some way gaze back at us? Certainly it both "concerns" us and is "of concern" to us, but does it also, in its way, "regard" us as in "see" us? Surely, it would be foolish to subjectivise the work, but then there is that testy word, *vit*; the work of art "lives" for whoever experiences it. What might be meant by that? How metaphorically must we understand it? Art historian James Elkins (2009) has questioned whether pictures can think, whether there is some quality possessed by paintings and drawings similar to thought or to what proposes or articulates thought. Elkins' query is doubtfully more easily conceptualized than the idea that there is a sense in which art can "see." Yet both are meaningful questions, neither mystical nor irrational, that reveal how the perceiver is transformed by art much like art is transformed in being perceived.

Emily Dickinson's "Letter to the world" challenges the reader to reflect on its status as a poem:

> This is my letter to the world,
> That never wrote to me, —
> The simple news that Nature told,
> With tender majesty.
>
> Her message is committed
> To hands I cannot see;
> For love of her, sweet countrymen,
> Judge tenderly of me!

In such a non-narrative poem there is no before, no after; nothing reducible to a narrated temporality. In this way, it resembles abstract visual art, a painting or drawing, say, upon which no narrative can be superimposed, which is why I introduce it here. Even a narrative poem is irreducible to what it says, to its semantic contents, for fundamentally it is non-representational of any a priori reality that might be said to precede it. Dickinson tells us as much by writing a poem the very crux of which is a semantic void, "the simple news that Nature told," for this is news whose message is left unsaid by the words she writes. It is news whose message, "committed" to faith, is ineffable but which, as a poem, *takes place*. Transposing itself from logos to topos, this "letter to the world" is poetry's revelation of itself as an unfolding—in time as in space—of the imagining mind.[2]

Reading Dickinson's poem, we engage with this identification of itself as a transposition, a presentation or event to be negotiated: Confronted with verse that does not say of what it speaks, we are obliged to gauge ourselves as readers, to take hold of who we are in how we experience the semantic void and the spatiotemporal unfolding that defines the work at hand. Perhaps the verse's lyrical and soothing rhythm suffices before the potentially disconcerting ambiguity of the unsaid. Or perhaps not, meaning the unarticulated is felt as threat. Conceivably, we are compelled to defend against it—by intellectualizing it or having it remain an incomprehensible if disturbing curiosity. Quite possibly, we lose our self within it. In each of these responses there is something "transferential" (best written in quotes), for the comfort, threat, defense, or fusion come from our valorizing the work in accordance with what "concerns" us and what "concerns" us all, as humans, is the unknown that delimits the human condition. Indeed, transference, for Freud (1924) is precipitated for the adult as for the child by the "need for protection against the consequences of his human weakness" (p. 24).

Yet Freud also maintained that transference is the greatest source of resistance in psychoanalytic treatment. Why? And is that resistance embedded in the concept of transference as applied to aesthetic experience? Irwin Badin has claimed that the force that prevents patients from embracing the therapeutic process derives from the tension between what Stephen Mitchell referred to as "Hope and dread." That is, patients come to treatment in the hope that something new will emerge out of something old, while their internalized relational schemas (or internal working models) tell them that something bad will happen, that something old will reemerge. As from Freud's perspective, transference from Badin's relational perspective has much to do with how safe one feels, though the

2 Echoed here is the phenomenology of aesthetics (Heidegger and Merleau-Ponty's, in particular) that claims art to exist neither on the horizon of the conceptual nor as a product inert and external to the mind, but as consciousness in a pre-reflexive (or precognitive) mode. A line from Antonin Artaud's (1954) *L'olimbique des limbes* is striking in its relevance: *"Là où d'autres proposent des œuvres, je ne prétends pas autre chose que de montrer mon esprit"* ["There where others propose works, I don't claim to show anything but my mind"] (p. 51; all translations from the French in this chapter are mine).

concept for him is without the broader existential overtone given it by Freud. Badin explains:

> The safer one feels in being oneself (the more one feels able to weather rejection, shame, and mis-attunement with regard to the other), and the more "in the moment" (or mindful) one is, the less transference there will be and the less resistance to knowing oneself and the other as he or she is.
>
> (personal communication)

The term *transference* is used by some to apply only to the treatment situation. Others, however (analysts and social scientists among them), find it useful for understanding phenomena unrelated to treatment (Person, 2000, p. 83). Dickinson's "Letter to the world" is a striking example of art, as one such phenomenon, that provokes the pull toward and away from awareness transference entails. As a co-creation, every interaction has the potential for hope and dread, for projective identifications, submission, and destruction. "Whatever it is that the artist is expressing," to cite Badin further, "has to be a consequence of that which he/she can know and how much must be hidden to them, which is experienced by the viewer who comes to the artwork inclined to know some things and inclined not to know others, hoping for one thing, dreading another" (personal communication). The poet tells us as much in proclaiming that it is for the love of Nature that she should be judged "tenderly" precisely because her "letter to the world" bears what she herself cannot know or say.

It is not merely in addressing her "sweet countrymen" that the poet engages the reader and reveals the poem as something that, to use Didi-Huberman's word, "lives." All art must be negotiated precisely because, in a very real sense, it is disruptive and that is where the notion of "countertransference" comes into play. How the work disrupts is comparable to the (mostly unconscious) perceptions on the part of the analysand of the analyst's own conflicts and resistances. However much the analyst may strive to remain the "blank screen," the patient intuits something of what underlies the stance of neutrality. Much like the energy that emanates from within the artwork (indeed, *is* the artwork), much as it acts upon the reader or viewer to stimulate an affective response, the analyst stirs things up in the analysand, whether by interpreting or not interpreting, furthering the negotiation their engagement requires. Can we speak of the negotiation between Dickinson's reader and the poem as similarly intersubjective? Certainly not. Can we speak of the negotiation between her reader and the poem as interactive? Without a doubt!

Without subjectivizing art we can say it functions interactively to the degree that the "transference"-like phenomenon itself imposes upon it a corporeal existence. Sculpture is generally inanimate but only in the sense that it does not physically move. As the object of a viewer's charged perception, projections, and meaningful constitution, it is apprehended both in space and in time, which is to say that it "spatializes" and "temporalizes" as it opens itself up to view, to the valorizing grasp of the viewer by means of which it is embodied and "lives." It is not for nothing that one of Richard Serra's most celebrated large-scale installations is titled "The Matter of Time," with the dual meaning of "matter" putting the interactive negotiation in high relief. Serra's colossal works impose upon the viewer the experience of her own corporeality as dwarfed. Their material presence (often steel and other industrial materials weighing a great many tons) imposes upon her the experience of her own corporeality as lacking in strength. Meaning is made precisely from the challenge posed by the confrontation, which is to say that the interactional process arises from the sense of one entity acting upon another and the other's responding. Indeed, one may push back against the domination or yield to what may be perceived as inviting in the meandering structures, for there is something that potentially resonates most favorably with the viewer as she makes her way through their enveloping, protective even, forms. (Guggenheim Bilbao's *Snake*, to cite but one example, enfolds the viewer within its three winding sheaths of steel open at either end.) Serra's sculpted contemplation of the uniqueness of art as spatial and temporal processes, of what it "means" to view (to interactively feel) it, seems to reflect the installations' "seeing" of the viewer in the sense that art stimulates a dynamic experience that is not merely responsive on the part of the viewer but dependent upon the incarnation of the artist in her art. Consider once again the second-person pronoun used by a number of writers, the single word that implicates the reader directly in the text. It recreates, for a moment in time, the reader's self-image as the protagonist of the work. More precisely, it obliges the reader to "live" the work, to enliven it, much as Serra's installations do in obliging the viewer to negotiate, through her "regard" of them, their challenging enclosure of her. They "regard" her ("concern her" and "gaze upon" her) as she "regards" them.

Mikhail Bakhtin wrote of the energy of literature as deriving from the confrontation between discourses occurring not *within* the text but *as* the text. The dialogic nature of writing arose for him from the interactive points of view of author, character, and reader and literary meaning was a function of the *reactive quality* of both the writing and reading that constitute it. Elkins' (2007) view of seer as seen is not dissimilar: Although writing more of figural than abstract art, Elkins recognizes variations in the gaze of the subject portrayed—whether it be the figure that looks but doesn't stare; the figure that doesn't look but could; or the non-human object in human-like position but without any eyes. Identifying in "the subtleties of looking" three principal gazes that act on the viewer, he writes of "positional discourse" (that situates the viewer with respect to the gaze depicted in the painting, drawing, or other visual work), "gender discourse" (that reveals how one sees as a male or female), and "psychoanalytic discourse" ("that imagines the gaze as a field in which the self defines and redefines itself"). The last of these has more than a Bakhtinian ring to it and calls to mind as well what Daniel Stern (2010) cites as "the dynamic forms of vitality," developmental, psychotherapeutic, and artistic experience that "can arise from the arousal systems acting relatively alone" or "from the input of cognitive and emotional centers that regulate the original brainstem message to meet local conditions" (p. 71). Thus is brought to life the personal narrative that provides access to past experience dissociated or otherwise rendered non-conscious. *Self-definition and redefinition, therefore, may be seen as that renewal obtained through knowledge (sensory, emotional, and cognitive) that is interactive and reactive and that, in energizing the work, is precisely what characterizes the "living" dimension (à la Didi-Huberman) of the work of art.*

The interaction may be of the order of conceptualism, such as we have in, say, Duchamp's 1917 readymade "Fountain" (an upside down urinal). There the artist makes a point about art that the viewer reflects back upon the work contextualized by her contemplation of the visualized conceptualization. It may be of the order of provocation, aggression even—as in the Dadaist assaults on the spectator (the slitting of the eye in director Luis Buñuel's 1929 film *Un Chien Andalou* or the cannon fired at the viewer in René Clair's short film of 1924, *Entr'acte*)—that engages the viewer as she protectively looks away or courageously faces the visual attack. Or it may of another order entirely, an obtrusiveness that certain art (Henry Moore's, for example), by its largeness of scale as much as by its size, inflicts upon the beholder. Michael Fried, in "Art and objecthood," described the distancing occasioned by sculpture that exacts, by its sheer presence, a deep seriousness (Didi-Huberman's "concern") on the part of the viewer. Such distancing, Fried (1998) suggested, is not "entirely unlike being distanced, or crowded, by the silent presence of another person" (p.155). Serra attains in his work interaction of yet another order: Self-reflection. Elkins' notion of gaze as psychoanalytic discourse is pronounced in Serra's art that reflects—and stimulates reflection upon—the mutual "regard" through which "the self defines and redefines itself." What Serra achieves is the fundamental undoing of the artist and spectator's equanimity that results precisely from their co-created or, to cite Bollas as above, jointly "altered external actuality."

Sculptor Tony Smith spoke of his minimalist artworks not as objects, but as "forms with presence" (quoted in Didi-Huberman, 1992, p. 153). What the term would seem to imply is that he viewed his art as the locus of an occurrence, the site in which a process of *formation* is *presented*. Thinking of "form" in terms of "formation" and "presence" in terms of "presentation" opens the work to its organic function, to the dynamic relation between artist and viewer who interact in a way that transcends conception of the work as thing, an intervening impenetrable entity (see Didi-Huberman, 1992, pp. 161–194). Indeed, the minimalist ideal to which Smith subscribed in making *The Black Box* (1961), *Die* (1962), *The Wall* (1966), *Ten Elements* (1975–1979), or any of his other painted wood or steel creations, is itself in a dialectical engagement with closure. Moreover, considering "form" as "formation" necessarily implicates the notion of "deformation," an implication comparable to Freud's account of figuration as disfiguration: Dream work, through condensation and displacement, *disfigures* and refigures (reforms) unconscious wishes. So, too, symptoms *disfigure* and refigure (reform) unconscious fantasy. Likewise, thinking "presence" in terms of "presentation" opens us up to the site of the "formation" where the image paradoxically appears as the destruction of spatial coordinates and proximities with which we are familiar. As Didi-Huberman describes it, "*Les images—les choses visuelles—sont toujours déjà des lieux: elles n'apparaissent que comme des paradoxes en acte où les coordonnées spatiales se déchirent, s'ouvrent à nous et finissent par s'ouvrir en nous, pour nous ouvrir et en cela même nous incorporer*" (p. 194).[3]

Didi-Huberman's idea of the image and its relation to the beholder, its relation as seer responsive to being seen, is strongly reminiscent of Heidegger's in his writing on the phenomenology of art. Like the philosopher, Didi-Huberman stresses the temporal and spatial constituents of the image that are also and simultaneously an undoing of the temporal and spatial coordinates from which they derive. Like Heidegger, he speaks of the anxiety of looking—and seeing—what lies (in space and in time) before us. And, like Heidegger, he views the art image as the constitution of a "world," one whose lines are drawn not congruent with but as derivative of the "always already there." Yet where the art historian most closely reveals the influence of phenomenology on his thinking is in the idea of art, as expressed by Merleau-Ponty as well as Heidegger, as incarnation of the perceptual activity of the mind. The embodied configuration that the phenomenological aesthetician envisions when speaking of the work of art implies something more than the sublimated manifestation of bodily instinct and drive. More obviously, it also implies something other than the codification of signs (signifier and signified) in material form. What is meant by aesthetic embodiment, rather, is the instantiation of lived experience, experience felt in the mind–body of the beholder as a result of art's being by nature interactive and communicative.

3 "Images—visual things—are always already places: they appear only as paradoxes in act where spatial coordinates tear themselves apart, *open themselves up* to us and finish by opening themselves within us, in order to open us and, in so doing, even incorporate us."

Already in Kris (1952) we find the idea that art's inherent communication is a function of our kinesthetic reaction to art. The viewer responds to any representation of the human figure with her own body: Perception, recognition, identification are all brought into play through the sensory pathways in which are embedded memory traces of the earliest modes of communication (tactile and other) between infant and mother, traces that ultimately relate to the development of body image. Lacking any real evidence for kinesthetic empathy, Kris (citing psychologist Rudolf Arnheim in this regard) was aware, however, of the limitations of this theory. Yet phenomenology, particularly that of Merleau-Ponty, picked up the slack in taking the idea of empathic embodiment beyond the response of a beholder to the representation of the human figure to the idea that there is never an absolute division between subject as perceiver and object as perceived. This is due, of course, to the intentionality of consciousness (referred to in chapter six), but also to the potential for reversibility: "Looking at" can always be construed as "looked at" in Merleau-Ponty's "chiasmic" phenomenology of art. The whole notion of alterity, in fact, resides for Merleau-Ponty, particularly in his late work, in the intertwining of self and other, the overlapping that comes from the gestalt with which something is perceived: There being no such thing as perception without association, without recollection, expectation, correlation of whatever kind, there is never perception of an object as purely "in itself." Merleau-Ponty's well-known example of two hands touching each other drives home the point:

> [W]hen I touch my right hand with my left, my right hand, as an object, has the strange property of being able to feel too. When I press my two hands together, it is not a matter of two sensations felt together as one perceives two objects placed side by side, but an ambiguous set-up in which both hands can alternate the roles of "touching" and being "touched."
>
> (1962, p. 106)

In the same way, before the work of art there is a "chiasmic" reciprocity between seer and seen.

Giacometti's *Cube* (whose original plaster execution dates to 1934) would appear to provide a sure illustration of the inaccessibility of the object as other, a perfect instance of the dichotomy erected by a mass (later produced in bronze) that gives up nothing beyond its status as tangible but silent object before a perceiving subject. Didi-Huberman (1993) finds in *Cube*, however, a Merleau-Pontyian case in point:

> *[P]ar sa clôture même il se sépare, il demeure seul; par sa clôture même il nous sépare, il nous laisse seuls devant lui. Mais il se rend capable pour*

> *cela, alors même qu'il se donne "aveugle" de* regarder *l'humain qui sur lui pose les yeux.*
>
> (p. 57)[4]

Like the divergence between the two hands touching each other that resides in their never concurrently being felt as touching and being touched but, rather, with the delay of but an instant in which is anticipated the incarnation of the other hand, there is in the relation of viewer to Giacometti's *Cube* a gap that makes for the intertwining that allows us to conceive of the reciprocity between viewing and being viewed:

> *Le rapport au visuel, le face-à-face imposé par le* Cube *deviendrait alors celui d'un sujet venant à éprouver sa propre altération ou division dans l'objet altéré—voué à l'altérité—qui lui fait front. Comme si lever les yeux sur cet objet revenait à se sentir "regardé," c'est-à-dire clivé. Comme si l'altération interne à l'objet devenait aux yeux de son spectateur l'image d'une altération interne à l'acte même de lever les yeux.*
>
> (pp. 57–58)[5]

But in what does this reciprocity originate? Might we speak of it as a projection of ways of relating emanating from the past as transference and countertransference do? Elkins (2006), describing Jacques Lacan's theory of vision, writes of the echo of one's gaze that is found in the object upon which one looks: "I see and I can see that I am seen, so each time I see I also see myself being seen." But to this reflection of the perceiver in the perceived and its play back onto the looker he adds, "Each object has a certain force, a certain way of resisting or accepting my look and returning that look to me" (p. 70). The point is that literary and verbal art subtly elicit associations, generate images, and reawaken memories and modes of being.

Bollas (1978), in fact, refers to the memories evoked by aesthetic experience as "existential" in that "memory is conveyed not through visual or abstract thinking, but through the affects of being" (p. 385). Such memories, he explains, "are registered through an experience of being, rather

4 "By its very closure, it separates itself, it remains alone; by its very closure it separates us, leaving us alone before it. But in so doing, even showing itself as blind, it renders itself capable of *regarding* he who looks upon it."

5 "The relation to the visual, the face-to-face encounter imposed by the *Cube*, would then become that of a subject having come to experience its own alteration or division within the altered object—bound to alterity—which confronts it. As if setting one's eyes upon the object amounted to feeling oneself "looked at" by it, that is, split. As if the alteration within the object had become in the eyes of the viewer the image of an alteration residing within the very act of seeing."

than mind, because the epistemology of the aesthetic moment is prior to representational cognition, and speaks that part of us where the experience of rapport with the other was the essence of being" (pp. 385–386). At the crux of the reciprocal relation, for him, is the communication of infant with mother, that moment where the mother's "handling and the infant's state of being are prior to the infant's processing his existence through mentation." Thus "the uncanny pleasure of being held by a poem, a composition, a painting, or, for that matter, any object," stems from those moments "when the infant's internal world is given form by the mother." Moreover, as "this first human aesthetic informs the development of personal character (the utterance of self through the manner of being rather than the representations of the mind) and will predispose all future aesthetic experiences that place the person in subjective rapport with an object," he argues "that each aesthetic experience is transformational," a search for "a transformational object" that holds the promise, through the form it provides, of self-integration (p. 386). If one concurs with Bollas, the path from "existential" memory to transformation can be seen as what I would term *existential knowledge*, but the question remains: *How* is it obtained? What allows us to experience the deep rapport and interaction defining of aesthetic experience, and of psychoanalytic experience as well, where it is even more evident in the transference and countertransference to which the memories and associations give rise? I turn now to the recently developed theory of embodied simulation to see if it might further our understanding of *how* this reciprocity occurs.

Embodied simulation

Simulation theory, called by Gallese "embodied simulation," is a model for how we have knowledge of another's feelings or apprehend their intentions. As contrasted with what is referred to as "theory theory"—which holds that sense data are rapidly assembled, matched with an inner template, and by way of inference recognized or known—embodied simulation is based on the idea that, automatically and unconsciously, a copy is made in the brain that resembles the phenomenon or object perceived (Olds, 2009, p. 555). Thus empathy, according to this model, is rooted in the body and dependent upon those systems in which mirror neurons are engaged.

Mirror neurons were initially described in the early 1990s by Gallese and Giacomo Rizzolatti who identified in non-human primates (macaque monkeys) single cells activated not only by the performance but the observation of an action performed by another. Since that time there has been much speculation about the role of mirror neurons in humans with researchers focusing on how they contribute to the acquisition of language and to development of theory of mind (the ability to understand mental states in others both as they relate to and differ from those in oneself). As a theory of empathy, embodied simulation has had also to explain empathic failures, among which autism and related disorders, and the idea that reduced activity in the human mirror neuron system could account for an autistic spectrum individual's impaired capacity to recognize and apprehend the emotions of others quickly spawned considerable interest. Needless to say, treatment becomes better defined when one attributes the failure to develop theory of mind to deficiencies in a neuronal system marked as responsible for empathy (see Bird et al., 2010; Gallese, 2009; Moriguchi et al., 2009). Work in this area may also have significant implications for a number of other cognitive and psychiatric disorders. Yet the concept of mirroring mechanisms in humans remains controversial.

Alfonso Caramazza and Ilan Dinstein, among others, are skeptical of the morphing of the clear identification of a mirror neuron system in monkeys to the equivalent in humans. Dinstein et al. (2008) have expressed deep concern with the experimental protocols of various studies using functional magnetic resonance imaging (fMRI) and numerous other scanning procedures for their failure to isolate and measure mirror neuron activity to the exclusion of other neurons. "Visual recognition, visual motion perception, working memory, movement planning, and movement execution (in the case of imitation)" are all implicated in the tasks assigned study participants. "How then," they ask, "can one know if the fMRI response exhibited by a particular brain area is generated by the activity of mirror neurons or by the activity of any of these other neural populations?" (p. R14). Douglas Watt (2007) has argued for a bottom-up view (as opposed to Gallese's top-down perspective) of empathy, claiming that affective processes interdigitate with cognitive processes only on a broad continuum extending from theory of mind to mechanisms of resonance (or "contagion") as yet poorly understood. And Jeanine M. Vivona (2009) has questioned the testing of assumptions about mental activity by means of data obtained on the brain. Leaving the controversy over the validity of the concept to the experts, however, I will direct my attention to its appropriation by aesthetics and psychoanalysis to determine if support for the analogy between the two may be found therein.

"Bracketing" (à la Husserl) the artistic dimension of a given work, focusing solely on the neural mechanisms activated by its contemplation, Freedberg and Gallese (2007) aimed to demonstrate how art evokes empathy via motor simulation in the brain of the viewer. Substituting for the disembodied (cognitive) perspective privileged by much art criticism an approach steeped in the ontology of the phenomenological tradition, they attempted to show, more precisely, that empathy is induced in the viewer by the very musculature of his or her own body experiencing what is visually observed in the content of the work. They cite as an example how looking at *Prisoners*, a sculpture by Michelangelo, a spectator would feel activation within muscles depicted as activated within the sculpture. Similarly, they note how the feeling of physical imbalance and responses in those parts of the body lacerated in the image would empathically be felt by the viewer of Goya's unbalanced and mutilated figures in *Desastres de la guerra*. Where narrative and object are absent, "traces" of physical movements used to make the brush marks—or drippings even, as in the case of a painter like Jackson Pollock—are claimed by Freedberg and Gallese to evoke such simulation in the beholder. Thus when no emotional component is manifest in the content, bodily resonance nonetheless arises, they maintain, for there is *implied* emotion or movement and remnants of the making of the art.

Further investigation of embodied simulation was undertaken by Fortunato Battaglia, Sarah H. Lisanby, and Freedberg (2011) in a study devoted specifically to the significance of movement in a painting (Michelangelo's *Expulsion from paradise*) on motor output in the observer. Increase in cortical-spinal excitability was found in the viewer, although, interestingly, not in the observation of a photograph replicating the same action, which indicated for the investigators that the effect was due to the talent of the artist in portraying the feeling of movement. Felt imitation in the perception of art, the effect on the corticomotor system and the relation of this effect to emotional arousal, needs now to extend to studies of more abstract visual art as well as non-visual art like music and dance.

While the argument for embodied simulation and the physical engagement with art is compelling, a number of questions come to mind: One has been posed by Stern (2010) in his work on "dynamic forms of vitality": "We know that actions as means–ends operations are well handled by mirror neurons. But what about the vitality forms of those actions?" These, Stern argues, raise different anatomical issues with regard to the virtual feeling of another's action within the self: "Only part of the mirror neuron system is understood. Could some of the unknown part be responsible for dealing with the dynamic experiences of vitality?" (p. 48). The "dynamic qualities that give the impression of an 'inhabited body'" (p. 124) are as significant for our understanding of the interactive space shared by psychoanalyst and analysand as how we experience art. They are what allow for the experience of a "vital human being behind the words that are being said" (p. 124).

Three other questions come to mind: First, what is to be made of the anticipatory knowledge intimately linked to perception by the synthesizing function of the brain (as noted in Chapter 1)? Next, what of the psychological processes that mediate empathy over and beyond its neurobiological substrates? And third, *if proved as a tenable theory of empathy applicable in this way to creativity, would embodied simulation not imply that those with deficits in mirroring mechanisms—those with decreased ability for mentalization and shared emotion—have less capacity for making and responding to art?*

With regard to psychoanalysis Gallese, Eagle, and Migone (2007) have proposed the hypothesis that "both patient and analyst bodily internalize aspects of each other's behavior and emotional expressions." As they further explain, "as far as general neural processes are concerned, there are as good grounds for positing the patient's empathic resonance with the analyst as for the analyst's empathic resonance with the patient" (p. 163). Elsewhere, Gallese (2009) writes of transference and countertransference as "instantiations of the implicit and prelinguistic mechanisms of the embodied simulation-driven mirroring mechanisms" (p. 519). One wonders about the association of "empathic resonance" with internalization. Empathy has been defined and redefined in the psychoanalytic literature. As explicated by William Meissner (2010), it "is a cognitive-affective form of experiencing that attunes the subject to communications from another person, leading to some intimation of the state of mind or inner experience of that other" (p. 424). Understanding similarity, whether in the treatment setting, when reading a novel, or watching a drama, does not imply internalization in the present. The empathy felt by the analyst (or, for that matter, by the analysand), as by the reader or spectator, is related to one's internal organization. As Meissner has argued, the sadness felt by the analyst in response to the grief of a patient who has experienced great loss is not the patient's but his own.

The difference between empathic attunement and countertransference reaction lies in the impact of a patient's transferential projection on the analyst. An analyst projecting feelings or fantasies onto a patient is reacting countertransferentially, whether or not he feels empathy as well. A "victimized stance" on the part of an analysand "is an open invitation and stimulus to the potential aggressor to become more aggressive and victimizing," Meissner offers by way of illustration. Such an enactment would be countertransferential, not empathic, and not the result of an internalization but the consequence of what already exists in the participants (p. 461).

As though in response to my first question regarding the synthesizing function of the brain, Meissner concludes "that the mirror neuron system is a fundamental part of a more comprehensive neural organization involved in the perception, reception, recognition, and initial responsiveness to sensory and emotional stimuli" (p. 440). As if in response to the second, what mediates empathy over and beyond its neurobiological underpinnings, he determines that, insofar as mirror neurons are not themselves inferential and that the "'understanding'" ascribable to them "is limited only to knowing and recognizing that a stimulus of a certain quality has been experienced as coming from the object," another process is at play: "Contrary to Gallese, Eagle, and Migone's (2007) assumption of an automatic, unconscious, and noninferential understanding, it seems to me that any further understanding would require an inference or interpretation based on the presumed analogy between my inner experience and that of the other (p. 440)."

My third question regarding the application of simulationist theory to aesthetic experience—namely, the implication that those with deficits in mirroring mechanisms are less creatively inclined than others—is perhaps more problematic still. Is this implication not tantamount to saying that impaired mentalization diminishes the motivation to master (underlying the drive for knowledge) and, thereby, the chances, through the creative imagination, for enhancement of agency? Surely this is not the case any more than the distortions of reality that characterize the breakdown of mental health, that is, the delusions that, while not structurally related to fantasy, share with it the common objective of mastery through imaginative (if delusional) thinking. Indeed, it is possible, as Michael Fitzgerald (2005) has demonstrated, to have significant social problems stemming from empathic failures of various kinds and be highly creative or even possess artistic genius. People on the autistic spectrum, for instance, may not know how to form or maintain relationships, but this need not hinder their curiosity and ability to write creatively, say, about them. In fact, qualities most often associated with Asperger's syndrome—high levels of energy, an extraordinary capacity for concentration, and perseverance (p. 12)—are traits we find also in the very gifted. Those with autism, in other words, may certainly be highly imaginative and creative, as Fitzgerald's investigations of a large number of exceedingly successful writers, composers, philosophers, and painters show.

Too quickly we assume that the child who is seemingly unresponsive to a crying playmate is so because she does not feel what the other child is feeling, how it is like what she at times feels or how it may be different. More likely, the child does not *know* what to do. Might the same not be said of the individual with deficits in mentalization as regards the work of art; in other words, that she is as deeply responsive to the visual or aural perception but that she simply may not "get" what is subtly implied on a higher cognitive level? She may affectively resonate (and deeply) with a figurative painting (such as Andrew Wyeth's "Christina's world"), an expressionist painting (like Edvard Munch's "The scream"), or even a highly abstract work (the muted rectangles and ovals of Robert Motherwell or the architectonic strokes of Franz Kline); where she would predictably have difficulty would be in understanding why Magritte's "Ceci n'est pas une pipe" has congruent verbal and visual meaning. It would appear that we need to rethink the value of simulated embodiment for our understanding of various kinds of affective experience, social and cultural, quite simply for what deficits in mirroring mechanisms may be thought to imply.

That said, I would now add that the notion of embodied simulation as applied to aesthetic experience is not without value and, furthermore, that it does illuminate the notion of reciprocity in art as in psychoanalysis.

In *Philosophy in the flesh*, Lakoff and Johnson (1999) revealed the grounding of mentation in our perceptual and motor systems and how subjective experience is delimited by the activation of neural connections automatically acquired by our sensorimotor functioning in the world. They further showed how spatial relations and various other image schemas are neurally modeled on, which is to say comprehended through, the body. Their work on "embodiment of mind," like Modell's (2003) "biology of meaning," supports the idea of empathic resonance (with its bodily origin) in the aesthetic context. Already from Freud's thinking on the ego as fundamentally of the body and from a multitude of academic disciplines—women's studies, queer studies, linguistics, and the social and biological sciences—we know that disembodied subjectivity is an indefensible concept. Transference projections and countertransference reactions are concepts exemplifying subjectivity as affectively embodied and, in art as in psychoanalysis, these "as-if" situations are consistent with the neuroscience of mirror neuron systems (cf. Sandberg & Busch, 2007) to the extent that these systems are qualified as only partially understood and not (yet?) explanatory of the dynamic features of experience—those qualities that Freud described in terms of somatopsychic energy; that Sartre, Heidegger, and others described ontologically as Being-in-the-world; that, on our own time and in not necessarily in opposition to what came before, researchers are describing in terms of development and early intersubjective attunement.

A central point of this book is that the reception of art, like the perceptual processes involved in its making (feed-forward being, as I have repeatedly said, feed-back dependent), is intrinsically creative. Another is that creativity furthers self-cohesion, an increase in mastery attained through (sensory, emotional, and cognitive) knowledge. Embodied simulation and the discovery of mirroring mechanisms in the brain contribute to our understanding of how this is so, if they have yet to provide a truly comprehensive picture. Didi-Huberman (1992) has eloquently articulated the interaction emblematic of aesthetic experience:

> *Nous ne pouvons dire tautologiquement* Je vois ce que je vois *que si nous dénions à l'image le pouvoir d'imposer sa visualité comme une ouverture, une perte—fût-elle momentanée—pratiquée dans l'espace de notre certitude visible à son égard. Et c'est bien de là que l'image se rend capable de nous regarder.*
>
> (p. 76)[6]

6 "We cannot say tautologically *I see what I see* unless we deny the image the power of imposing its visuality as an opening, a loss—however brief—exercised in the space of our visible certainty with respect to it. And this is surely where the image renders itself capable of regarding us."

The same may be said of psychoanalytic process in which what emerges in the course of observation (of self, other, and the relation between them) is a phenomenon that "regards" the dyad—at once relational and individual subjectivities—whether it be called with Thomas Ogden "the analytic third" or something else.

CONCLUSION

I have emphasized in this book the idea that imagination generates knowledge. Our sensory systems, like our higher cognitive functions, give the human brain knowledge to maintain the homeostatic balance required for survival and to enrich the sense of self required for agency. And, I have suggested, imagination is a function of their doing so. I have explored the construct by which we apprehend the workings of imagination—fantasy—and considered in what the mental imagery that endows it consists, how fantasy may be transmitted transgenerationally, and how the *unwilling* "suspension of disbelief"—delusion—can be an impediment to imagination while also being a product of it. Moreover, I have likened psychoanalysis to the making of art as a process of "insighting," the acquiring of knowledge actively from within (as well as from without), and I have looked at creativity itself as a coming-to-know.

Throughout this study, however, there run several opposing threads. The first is that of the intra- and interpsychic psychoanalytic paradigms. This theoretical contrast bears on our understanding of aesthetic experience as sublimatory versus object relational, on our understanding of the construction of meaning. A second opposition resides in the notion of agency (with its implication of self-cohesion) that has everything to do with ego function and, seemingly, little place in the context of a (Sullivan-derived) multiplicity of selves. The third concerns fantasy itself; specifically, the usefulness of "unconscious fantasy," a cornerstone of psychoanalysis now thrown into question by the postmodern favoring of dissociation over repression and other mechanisms of defense. Last, but no less significant, is the contrast interwoven throughout this volume between the empiricism of neuroscience and the metaphysics of philosophical thought. My underlying effort has been to explore the validity of these oppositions for it seems to me that they simply do not hold as steadfastly as we tend to suppose. Indeed, modern conflict theory, in focusing on intrapsychic function, relies on the concepts of sexual and aggressive drives while relational and interpersonal theories attempt to devalue the notion of drive. Yet what relationalists and interpersonalists substitute are interpsychic constructs that (however conceived and whatever we call them) are descriptive of motivational forces. This has been convincingly argued by Mervyn Peskin (2011) who claims, and I would agree, that drives are innate within the mind and whether sexual, aggressive, object relational, or organizational (the drive for self-cohesion), all are not only motivational but adaptational in nature and pleasure seeking in essence. As theories of knowledge, moreover, neuroscience and philosophy reflect the fundamental crossroad at which Freud arrived: the juncture between the *kinds* of knowledge afforded by fantasy and the *levels* of knowing determined by the regulation of affects associated with what is (consciously or unconsciously) known.

With regard to the former, I think of Michael Wood's (2003) deft differentiation between the *kinds* of knowledge generated in a novel by Henry James: "[K]nowing that something is the case," knowing "what other people think" and "what you yourself feel or believe," knowing in the sense of "having been introduced" to or recognizing others, knowing "in the sense of deep intimacy," the knowing of inference, and so on. All are extracted by Wood, along with an even more substantial list of kinds of not knowing, from within James' story. But some knowing is not expressible in words and this is the knowing the novel itself knows (and here I depart from Wood's interpretation of just what that is): the knowing of intersubjectivity (writer and reader, artist and spectator) and of the reciprocity between artist and the work of art itself. No work of art exists independently of either kind of shared knowledge.

With regard to the latter, *levels* of knowing, a discussion by Dori Laub and Nanette C. Auerhahn (1993) of traumatic memory comes to mind. From not knowing consciously (a level of knowing nonetheless) to knowing as conscious remembering, depth of knowledge as memory is defined. Fugue states, fragments, overpowering narratives and, ultimately, metaphorical expression, among other progressive, while not mutually exclusive, breakthroughs of the known represent levels of integration, steps toward the experience of "I" within memory, that are the measure of knowledge as more or less subjectively owned.

The neuroscientific perspective on knowledge may summarily be gleaned from the following quote from Zeki (2009): "To obtain knowledge of the world, the brain must categorize objects and situations and form a concept of them" (p. 42). Two kinds of concept, the inherited and the acquired, he explains, are used for the creation of meaning, with ambiguity itself dependent upon the formation of concepts. At variance with its commonly accepted definition of "vagueness" or "uncertainty," ambiguity is taken by Zeki to means "the certainty of different scenarios, each one of which has equal validity with the other" (p. 88). In a work of art, then, we may see ambiguity while, in fact, there is none, but rather "the possibility of multiple interpretations projected by the brain onto the painting. Each of these projections is a brain reality and each has a validity and a certainty for a limited time" (p. 89). I said at the outset that a premise of this book was that *the imaginary is not illusory*, neither in art nor in fantasy or even delusion. For such a notion ignores the reality of the brain, the reality that, for neuroscience, is the only reality there is.

Opposing such a perspective, however, is that which extends from the phenomenology of Husserl, Heidegger, Sartre, and Merleau-Ponty to the deconstructionism of Derrida and the phenomenologically informed practice of art history by Didi-Huberman and others. Categories of thinking, the alignment of concepts, determine for the so-called continental philosopher, as much as for the neuroscientist, *how* the mind comes to know. No less than for the neuroscientist, knowledge for the phenomenologist is *brain real*. But in any form of knowledge there is an additional dimension for the metaphysician that resides precisely where the coordinates of sensorial perception and cognitive function recede, a dimension situated beyond mental representation in the apprehension of the object of perception in its own act of self-revelation. Familiar to us through the ontological preoccupations of Heidegger and Sartre (in particular, their reliance on the notion of intentionality), it is there that the image is apprehended *not merely in its visible proximities, its perceptible form, but in its opening before—and within—the viewer and in its incorporation of the viewer within the viewed.*[1]

How is it that I subscribe in this book to both? Some three decades ago Gilbert Rose (1980) wrote that "Creativity is not just a vicissitude of id drives discharging themselves." His justification for that observation was that "Conscious and unconscious ego interests figure prominently. Since the ego is the organ of adaptation, orientation in an evolving reality is a central issue" (p. 10). Implicit in Rose's statement is both the dynamic interrelation of self and other—who together make up the "evolving reality"—and the recognition that missing from the classical notion of sublimation is agency, the artist as agent, as a being *in the world*. Continental philosophy articulated early in the 20th century what psychoanalysis and neuroscience alike have only recently begun to acknowledge: the experiencing of the other as other, called by psychoanalysts "mentalization" and by cognitive neuroscientists "theory of mind." This, in fact, is a primary ingredient in agency, whether construed in terms of ego function or the adaptation of self to the relational environment.

Ironically, psychoanalysis developed from within the very same philosophical frame that led Freud and others of his time, namely, Brentano and

1 Didi-Huberman (1992) references Heidegger's "L'art et l'espace" (1962), a segment of which concerns, as Didi-Huberman puts it, "*des choses comme de* lieux, *de la sculpture comme jeu de* l'ouverture *et de* l'incorporation, *et enfin de vide comme 'le jumeau de la propriété du lieu'*" ["things as *places*, sculpture as a play of *opening* and of *embodiment* and, finally, of emptiness as 'closely allied to the character of place'"] (p. 194, fn 30).

Husserl, to overcome the subject–object schism left the modern world by Descartes. Freud's initial concerns were with the meaning of "mind" and at one time he intended to pursue a doctorate in philosophy. In his early work on aphasia, he grappled with the impasse addressed by Husserl but a few years later in his theory of intentionality. Indeed, if Husserl's phenomenology would unite subject and object in the spatiotemporal projection of consciousness, in an "intentional" relation, it was that he was deeply influenced by Brentano, with whom Freud also studied in his first year at the University of Vienna.

But as Freud developed his theory of drives, in which motivations were seen as biological in origin and thus of a fundamentally impersonal nature, his resolution of the Cartesian impasse took a decisively Darwinian turn (not to deny its Lamarckianism), which meant that evolution of the individual psyche was analogous to that of the human species as a whole. The phenomenological tradition, as perpetuated by Heidegger and Sartre however, was decisively anti-determinist and its most primordial concept, human freedom, was constructed upon the relation of self to other that defines the condition of every human as Being-in-the-world. Thus the shift in psychoanalysis toward a relational paradigm would appear to emanate precisely from the phenomenology that appealed so early in his education to Freud.

In fact, Sartrean existentialism (having come to France via the Germany of Husserl and Heidegger) emphasized, like the interpersonal relational psychology of Sullivan, our "situation" in the world. It formulated the idea that how we live our lives is based upon our connection to others and it was not for nothing that the very concept of human freedom would impose a moral imperative, the political commitment Sartre called *engagement*, in recognition above all of the relational nature of human existence. Even if the interest on the part of post-Freudian psychoanalysts in the significance of the relational bears the mark of the phenomenology that paradoxically was Freud's initial passion, the meaning of "self" and the import of "personal agency" is no less ironically linked to the same philosophical origin. That is to say that the intentionality of consciousness by which Husserl overrode the Cartesian schism of subject and object was a forerunner of the embeddedness of self in the social matrix so determinative of psychic function for the relational analyst. Yet it was also what defined the self as immediate experiencer of that social reality.

What makes for enhancement of the sense of self as agent is the apprehension of self through imagination—representation of the self as in-relation—whatever the aesthetic, cognitive, or behavioral vehicle of its expression. This coming-to-know, or *knowledge*, is what clinical and artistic praxis have in common. Recognition of the short-sightedness of the dichotomies referred to earlier allows for greater appreciation of just how enabling aesthetic experience, like the analytic endeavor, is of that increase in capacity that is agency. Only from agency can real freedom, and with it moral responsibility, ensue. Did Sophocles not tell us as much when he had Oedipus reveal the source of his blindness? "It was Apollo, friends, Apollo that brought this bitter bitterness, my sorrows, to completion. But the hand that struck me was none but my own." From the "blindness of the seeing eye" to the seeing of the blinded—such is the itinerary of imagination.

REFERENCES

Abelson, R., & Margolis, J. (1978). A further exchange on psychotherapy, personal dignity, and persons. *Psychoanalysis and Contemporary Thought*, *1*, 227–235.

Abend, S. (2008). Unconscious fantasy and modern conflict theory. *Psychoanalytic Inquiry*, *28*(2), 117–130.

Abrahams, J. (2005). My intuitometer: Experience and inference. *Psychoanalytic Review*, *92*, 237–248.

Abrams, S. (1971). The psychoanalytic unconscious. In M. Kanzer (Ed.), *The unconscious today* (pp. 196–210). New York: International Universities Press.

Abrams, S. (1984). Fantasy and reality in the Oedipal phase: A conceptual overview. *Psychoanalytic Study of the Child*, *39*, 83–100.

Abrams, S. (1996). Offerings and acceptances: Technique and therapeutic action. *Psychoanalytic Study of the Child*, *51*, 77–86.

Abrams, S. (2004, February). Coordinating the developmental process with clinical psychoanalysis. Paper presented at the Psychoanalytic Association of New York.

Abrams, S. (2008). Transformation: Identifying a specific mode of change, descriptive and conceptual considerations. *Psychoanalytic Study of the Child*, *63*, 312–320.

Abrams, S., & Neubauer, P. B. (1976). Object orientedness: The person or the thing. *Psychoanalytic Quarterly*, *45*, 73–99.

Albee, E. (1965). *Tiny Alice*. New York: Atheneum.

Alexander, F. (1926). Neurosis and the whole personality. *International Journal of Psychoanalysis*, *7*, 340–352.

Anderson, H. H. (Ed.). (1959). *Creativity and its cultivation*. New York: Harper & Row.

Anscombe, R. (1986). The ego and the will. *Psychoanalysis and Contemporary Thought*, *9*, 437–463.

Arlow, J. A. (1969a). Unconscious fantasy and disturbances of conscious experience. *Psychoanalytic Quarterly*, *38*, 1–27.

Arlow, J. A. (1969b). Fantasy, memory, and reality testing. *Psychoanalytic Quarterly*, *38*, 28–51.

Artaud, A. (1954). *L'olimbique des limbes*. Paris: Gallimard.

Ashton, D. (2005). Rothko's frame of mind. In G. Phillips & T. Crow (Eds.), *Seeing Rothko* (pp. 13–24). Los Angeles, CA: Getty Research Institute.

Balter, L. (1999). On the aesthetic illusion. *Journal of the American Psychoanalytic Association*, *47*(4), 1293–1333.

Bass, A. (2007). When the frame doesn't fit the picture. *Psychoanalytic Dialogues*, *17*(1), 1–27.

Battaglia, F., Lisanby, S. H., & Freedberg, D. (2011). Corticomotor excitability during observation and imagination of a work of art. *Frontiers in Human Neuroscience*, 5:79. doi:10.3389/fnhum.2011.00079.

Bazan, A., Shevrin, H., Brakel, L., & Snodgrass, M. (2007). Motivations and emotions contribute to a-rational unconscious dynamics: Evidence and conceptual clarification. *Cortex*, *43*, 1104–1105.

Beckett, S. (1965). Imagination dead imagine. In S. E. Gontarski (Ed.), *Samuel Beckett: The complete short prose 1929–1989* (pp. 182–185). New York: Grove Press, 1995.

Beckett, S. (1970). *Proust and three dialogues with Georges Duthuit*. London: Calder & Boyars.

Beckett, S. (1984). Letter to Axel Kaun. In R. Cohn (Ed.), *Disjecta* (pp. 51–54). New York: Grove Press.

Beckett, S. (1988). *Stirrings still*. New York: Blue Moon Books.

Bell, D. (2009). Is truth an illusion? Psychoanalysis and postmodernism. *International Journal of Psychoanalysis*, *90*, 331–345.

Ben-Ze'ev, A. (1993). *The perceptual system: A philosophical and psychological perspective*. New York: Peter Lang.

Beres, D. (1960). Perception, imagination, and reality. *International Journal of Psychoanalysis*, *41*, 327–334.

Berland, R. (2008). The exploration of dreams: Kokoschka's *Die träumenden Knaben* and Freud. *Notes in the History of Art*, *27*, 25–31.

Bion, W. R. (1962). *Learning from experience*. London: Tavistock.

Bion, W. R. (1965). *Transformations*. London: Karnac.

Bird, G., Silani, G., Brindley, R., White, S., Frith, U., & Singer, T. (2010). Empathic brain responses in insula are modulated by levels of alexithymia but not autism. *Brain*, *133*, 1515–1525. doi:10.1093/brain/awq060.

Bloom, H. (1973). *The anxiety of influence*. Oxford: Oxford University Press.

Blum, H. (2001). Psychoanalysis and art, Freud and Leonardo. *Journal of the American Psychoanalytic Association*, *49*, 1409–1425.

Blum, H. (2011). Oskar Kokoschka and Alma Mahler: Art as diary and as therapy. *Psychoanalytic Study of the Child*, *65*, 293–309.

Blum, L. D. (2011). "The king's psychotherapy," Commentary published in *Psychiatric Times*, p. 34, May.

Blumenberg, H. (1983). *The legitimacy of the modern age* (R. M. Wallace, Trans.). Cambridge, MA: MIT Press.

Bollas, C. (1978). The aesthetic moment and the search for transformation. *Annual of Psychoanalysis*, *6*, 385–394.

Bollas, C. (1999). *The mystery of things*. London: Routledge.

Bollas, C. (2009). *The infinite question*. London: Routledge.

Brater, E. (1987). *Beyond minimalism*. New York: Oxford University Press.

Breslin, J. (1993). *Mark Rothko: A biography*. Chicago, IL: University of Chicago Press.

Bromberg, P. M. (1998). *Standing in the spaces; Essays on clinical process, trauma, and dissociation*. Hillside, NJ: Analytic Press.

Bromberg, P. M. (2003). On being one's dream: Some reflections on Robert Bosnak's "embodied imagination." *Contemporary Psychoanalysis*, *39*, 697–710.

Bromberg, P. M. (2006). *Awakening the dreamer: Clinical journeys*. Mahwah, NJ: Analytic Press.

Bromberg, P. M. (2008a). "Grown-up" words: An interpersonal/relational perspective on unconscious fantasy. *Psychoanalytic Inquiry*, *28*, 131–150.

Bromberg, P. M. (2008b), "Mentalize this!": Dissociation, enactment, and clinical process. In E. Jurist, A. Slade, & S. Bergner (Eds.), *Mind to mind: Infant research, neuroscience, and psychoanalysis* (pp. 414–434). New York: Other Press.

Bromberg, P. M. (2008c, April). "The nearness of you": Navigating selfhood, otherness, and uncertainty. Paper presented at the annual meeting of APA Division 39 (Psychoanalysis), New York.

Bromberg, P. M. (2009). Truth, human relatedness, and the analytic process: An interpersonal/relational perspective. *International Journal of Psychoanalysis*, *90*, 347–361.

Bunce, S. C. et al. (2001). Neurophysiological evidence for implicit memory formation under adequate general anesthesia [Abstract]. Proceedings of the 5th International Conference on Memory, Awareness and Consciousness under Anesthesia, New York.

Butor, M. (1969). *Essais sur le roman*. Paris: Gallimard.

Byrne, A. (2010). Recollection, perception, imagination. *Philosophical Studies*, *148*, 15–46.

Camus, A. (1942). *The myth of Sisyphus and other essays* (J. O'Brien, Trans.). New York: Vintage Books.

Camus, A. (1992). Préface à l'édition américaine. In *Bernard Pingaud commente L'étranger d'Albert Camus* (pp. 193–194). Paris: Gallimard.

Carpenter, W. (2008). A few methodologic issues of note. *Schizophrenia Bulletin*, *34*(6), 1003–1005. doi: 10.1093/schbul/sbn125.

Casey, E. S. (1976a). *Imagining: A phenomenological study*. Bloomington, IN: Indiana University Press.

Casey, E. S. (1976b). Comparative phenomenology of mental activity: Memory, hallucination, and fantasy contrasted with imagination. *Research in Phenomenology*, *6*, 1–25.

Caws, M. A. (1989). *The art of interference: Stressed readings in verbal and visual texts*. Princeton, NJ: Princeton University Press.

Charles, M., & Telis, K. (2009). Pattern as inspiration and mode of communication in the works of Van Gogh. *American Journal of Psychoanalysis*, *69*, 238–262.

Chávez-Eakle, R. A., Graff-Guerrero, A., Garcia-Reyna, J. C., Vaugier, V., & Cruz-Fuentes, C. (2007). Cerebral blood flow associated with creative performance: A comparative study. *NeuroImage*, *38*(3), 519–528. doi:10.1016/j.neuroimage.2007.07.059.

Chodorow, N. J. (2010). Beyond the dyad: Individual psychology, social world. *Journal of the American Psychoanalytic Association*, *58*(2), 207–230.

Christoff, K., Gordon, A. M., & Smith, R. (2011). The role of spontaneous thought in human cognition. In O. Vartanian & D. R. Mandel (Eds.), *Neuroscience of decision making* (pp. 259–284). London: Psychology Press.

Clark, A. (2008). *Supersizing the mind*. Oxford: Oxford University Press.

Coen, S. J. (2009). Reading memoirs of childhood. *International Journal of Psychoanalysis*, *90*, 145–156.

Coles, P. (2007). Transgenerational conflicts between sisters. *British Journal of Psychotherapy*, *23*, 563–574.

Colombo, D. (2008). How much can analysis be discovery, not suggestion? Panel report. *Journal of the American Psychoanalytic Association*, *56*(2), 611–622.

Dargis, M. (2010, June 18). Balancing levity and heft in an exploration of desire. *New York Times*.

Davidson, L. (2003). *Living outside mental illness: Qualitative studies of recovery in schizophrenia*. New York: New York University Press.

Davoine, F., & Gaudillière, M. (2004). *History beyond trauma* (S. Fairfield, Trans.). New York: Other Press.

Didi-Huberman, G. (1990). *Devant l'image*. Paris: Minuit. (John Goodman, Trans (2005). *Confronting images: Questioning the ends of a certain history of art*. University Park, PA: Penn State University Press.)

Didi-Huberman, G. (1992). *Ce que nous voyons, ce qui nous regarde*. Paris: Editions de Minuit.

Didi-Huberman, G. (1993). *Le cube et le visage: Autour d'une sculpture d'Alberto Giacometti*. Paris: Editions Macula.

Dinstein, I., Thomas, C., Behrmann, M. & Heeger, D. J. (2008). A mirror up to nature. *Current Biology*, *18*(1), R13–R18.

Downey, T. W. (2008). Review of *The center cannot hold* by Elyn Saks. *Journal of the American Psychoanalytic Association*, *56*(4), 1361–1371.

Edelheit, H. (1978). On the biology of language: Darwinian/Lamarckian homology in human inheritance (with some thoughts about the Larmarckism of Freud). In J. H. Smith (Ed.), *Psychoanalysis and language* (pp. 45–74). New Haven, CT: Yale University Press.

Elderfield, J. (2005). *Transformations*. In G. Phillips & T. Crow (Eds.), *Seeing Rothko* (pp. 101–122). Los Angeles, CA: Getty Research Institute.

Elkins, J. (2006). *The object stares back: On the nature of seeing*. New York: Simon & Schuster.

Elkins, J. (2007). The end of the theory of the gaze. Unpublished essay. Retrieved from http://www.jameselkins.com/images/stories/jamese/pdfs/the-visual-gaze.pdf.

Elkins, J. (2009). Can pictures think? Paper presented at the Academy of Art, Maastricht, April 2006. Retrieved from http://www.jameselkins.com/images/stories/jamese/pdfs/Can-pictures-think.pdf.

Erikson, E. H. (1956). The problem of ego identity. *Journal of the American Psychoanalytic Association*, *4*, 56–121.

Faimberg, H. (1988). The telescoping of generations: Genealogy of certain identifications. *Contemporary Psychoanalysis*, *24*, 99–117.

Faimberg, H. (1997). Misunderstanding and psychic truths. *International Journal of Psychoanalysis*, *78*, 439–451.

Faimberg, H. (2005). Après-coup. *International Journal of Psychoanalysis*, *86*, 1–6.

Faimberg, H., & Corel, A. (1990). Repetition and surprise: A clinical approach to the necessity of construction and its validation. *International Journal of Psychoanalysis*, *71*, 411–420.

Fitzgerald, M. (2005). *The genesis of artistic creativity*. London: Jessica Kingsley.

Foucault, M. (1988/1965). *Madness and civilization: A history of insanity in the Age of Reason* (R. Howard, Trans.). New York: Vintage.

Frances, A., Sacks, M., & Aronoff, M. S. (1977). Depersonalization: A self-relations perspective. *International Journal of Psychoanalysis*, *18*, 325–331.

Frayze-Pereira, J. A. (2007). Psychoanalysis, science and art: Aesthetics in the making of a psychoanalyst. *International Journal of Psychoanalysis*, *88*, 489–505.

Freedberg, D., & Gallese, V. (2007). Motion, emotion and empathy in esthetic experience. *Trends in Cognitive Science*, *11*(5), 197–203.

Fried, M. (1998). *Art and objecthood: Essays and reviews*. Chicago: University of Chicago Press.

Freud, A. (1957). Foreword. In M. Milner, *On not being able to paint* (pp. xiii–xv). New York: Penguin.

Freud, A. (1960). Discussion of Dr. John Bowlby's paper. *Psychoanalytic Study of the Child*, *15*, 53–62.

Freud, J. M. (2006). Lénárd Kata interjúja Jane McAdam Freuddal [Lenard Kata's interview with Jane McAdam Freud]. *Thalassa*, *17*(60), 133–139.

Freud, S. (1893–1895). *Studies on hysteria*. In J. Strachey (Ed. & Trans.), *The standard edition of the complete psychological works of Sigmund Freud* (Vol. 2, pp. 1–181). London: Hogarth Press.

Freud, S. (1895). *Project for a scientific psychology*. In J. Strachey (Ed. & Trans.), *The standard edition of the complete psychological works of Sigmund Freud* (Vol. 1, pp. 281–391). London: Hogarth Press.

Freud, S. (1892–1899). Extracts from the Fleiss Papers: Letter 69 (September 21, 1897). In J. Strachey (Ed. & Trans.), *The standard edition of the complete psychological works of Sigmund Freud* (Vol. 1, pp. 173–280). London: Hogarth Press.

Freud, S. (1905). *Three essays on the theory of sexuality*. In J. Strachey (Ed. & Trans.), *The standard edition of the complete psychological works of Sigmund Freud* (Vol. 7, pp. 123–246). London: Hogarth Press.

Freud, S. (1908). Hysterical phantasies and their relation to bisexuality. In J. Strachey (Ed. & Trans.), *The standard edition of the complete psychological works of Sigmund Freud* (Vol. 9, pp. 155–166). London: Hogarth Press.

Freud, S. (1909). Family romances. In J. Strachey (Ed. & Trans.), *The standard edition of the complete psychological works of Sigmund Freud* (Vol. 9, pp. 235–242). London: Hogarth Press.

Freud, S. (1910). Leonardo da Vinci and a memory of his childhood. In J. Strachey (Ed. & Trans.), *The standard edition of the complete psychological works of Sigmund Freud* (Vol. 11, pp. 57–138). London: Hogarth Press.

Freud, S. (1912). The dynamics of transference. In J. Strachey (Ed. & Trans.), *The standard edition of the complete psychological works of Sigmund Freud* (Vol. 12, pp. 27–108). London: Hogarth Press.

Freud, S. (1913). The disposition to obsessional neurosis. In J. Strachey (Ed. & Trans.), *The standard edition of the complete psychological works of Sigmund Freud* (Vol. 12, pp. 311–326). London: Hogarth Press.

Freud, S. (1916/1917). *Introductory lectures on psychoanalysis.* In J. Strachey (Ed. & Trans.), *The standard edition of the complete psychological works of Sigmund Freud* (Vol. 15 & 16, pp. 1–463). London: Hogarth Press.

Freud, S. (1918). From the history of an infantile neurosis. In J. Strachey (Ed. & Trans.), *The standard edition of the complete psychological works of Sigmund Freud* (Vol. 17, pp. 1–124). London: Hogarth Press.

Freud, S. (1924). *The future of an illusion.* In J. Strachey (Ed. & Trans.), *The standard edition of the complete psychological works of Sigmund Freud* (Vol. 21, pp. 1–56). London: Hogarth Press.

Freud, J. (1926). Inhibitions, symptoms and anxieties. In J. Strachey (Ed. & Trans.), *The standard edition of the complete psychological works of sigmend freud* (Vol. 20, pp. 87–172). London: Hogarth Press.

Freud, S. (1930). *Civilization and its discontents.* In J. Strachey (Ed. & Trans.), *The standard edition of the complete psychological works of Sigmund Freud* (Vol. 21, pp. 57–146). London: Hogarth Press.

Freud, S. (1938). *An outline of psycho-analysis.* In J. Strachey (Ed. & Trans.), *The standard edition of the complete psychological works of Sigmund Freud* (Vol. 23, pp. 139–208). London: Hogarth Press.

Freud, S. (1939). *Moses and monotheism.* In J. Strachey (Ed. & Trans.), *The standard edition of the complete psychological works of Sigmund Freud* (Vol. 23, pp. 7–137). London: Hogarth Press.

Gallese, V. (2007). Commentary on "Toward a neuroscience of empathy: Integrating affective and cognitive perspectives." *Neuro-Psychoanalysis*, *9*, 146–151.

Gallese, V. (2009). Mirror neurons, embodied simulation, and the neural basis of social identification. *Psychoanalytic Dialogues*, *19*, 519–536.

Gallese, V., Eagle, M. N., & Migone, P. (2007). Intentional attunement: Mirror neurons and the neural underpinnings of interpersonal relations. *Journal of the American Psychoanalytic Association*, *55*(1), 131–176.

Gardner, H. (2006). A blessing of influences. In J. A. Schaler (Ed.), *Howard Gardner under fire* (pp. 1–32). Chicago & La Salle: Open Court.

Garelli, J. (1966). *La gravitation poétique*. Paris: Mercure de France.

Garelli, J. (1982). *Artaud et la question du lieu*. Paris: Librairie José Corti.

Garrett, M., Singh, A., Amanbekova, D., & Kamarajan, C. (2011). Lack of insight and conceptions of "mental illness" in schizophrenia, assessed in the third person through case vignettes. *Psychosis*, *3*(2), 115–125.

Gershenowitz, H. (1979). The influence of Lamarckism on the development of Freud's psychoanalytic theory. *Indian Journal of the History of Science*, *14*(2), 105–113.

Gerson, S. (2008). Unconscious phantasy and relational reality. *Psychoanalytic Inquiry*, *28*, 151–168.

Greenacre, P. (1957). The childhood of the artist: Libidinal phase development and giftedness. *Psychoanalytic Study of the Child*, *12*, 47–72.

Greenberg, J. (1964). *I never promised you a rose garden*. New York: Holt, Rinehart and Winston.

Grossman, W. I. (1982). The self as fantasy: Fantasy as theory. *Journal of the American Psychoanalytic Association*, *30*, 919–937.

Grossman, W. I. (1991). Discussions of "Contemporary perspectives on self: Toward an integration." *Psychoanalytic Dialogues*, *1*, 149–172.

Grynsztejn, M. (2005). Kiki Smith: A Gathering, 1980–2005. Online publication of Resource Library, San Francisco Museum of Modern Art. Retrieved from http://www.tfaoi.com/aa/6aa/6aa177.htm.

Hanly, C. (1990). The concept of truth in psychoanalysis. *International Journal of Psychoanalysis*, *71*, 375–383.

Hanly, C. (2009). On truth and clinical psychoanalysis. *International Journal of Psychoanalysis*, *90*, 363–373.

Heath, D. (2009, May). The psychoanalytic treatment of psychosis, part II: The dream, break through model for diagnosing, treating and understanding psychosis. Paper presented to the Works in Progress group at the New York Psychoanalytic Society and Institute.

Heidegger, M. (1971). *The origin of the work of art: Poetry, language, thought* (A. Hofstadter, Trans.). New York: Harper & Row.

Heilman, K. M. (2005). *Creativity and the brain*. New York: Psychology Press.

Hobson, J. A., & Wohl, H. (2005). *From angels to neurones: Art and the new science of dreaming*. Fidenza, Italy: Mattioli.

Hodin, J. P. (1948). Style and personality: A graphological portrait of Oscar Kokoschka. *Journal of Aesthetics and Art Criticism*, *6*(3), 209–225.

Hodin, J. P. (1966). *Oskar Kokoschka: The artist and his time*. New York: New York Graphic Society.

Hoffman, E. (n.d.). *Kokoschka: Life and work with two essays by Oskar Kokoschka*. Boston, MA: Boston Book and Art Shop, Inc.

Holland, N. (2009). *Literature and the brain*. Gainesville, FL: PsyArt Foundation.

Howell, E. (2005). *The dissociative mind*. Hillsdale, NJ: Analytic Press.

Hut, P. (1999). Theory and experiment in philosophy. *Journal of Consciousness Studies*, 6(2/3), 241–244.

Ikonen, P., & Rechardt, E. (1984). On the universal nature of primal scene fantasies. *International Journal of Psychoanalysis*, 65, 63–72.

Inderbitzin, L. B., & Levy, S. T. (1990). Unconscious fantasy: A reconsideration of the concept. *Journal of the American Psychoanalytic Association*, 38, 113–130.

Jeannerod, M. (1994). The representing brain: Neural correlates of motor intention and imagery. *Behavioral and Brain Sciences*, 17, 187–245.

Jeannerod, M. (2003). Modulating the experience of agency: A positron emission tomography study. *NeuroImage*, 18, 324–333.

Kafka, J. S. (2011). Chestnut Lodge and the psychoanalytic approach to psychosis. *Journal of the American Psychoanalytic Association*, 59, 27–47.

Kahn, M., & Sutherland, J. D. (1968). Introduction. In C. Rycroft, *Imagination and reality* (pp. vii–ix). London: Maresfield Library.

Kandel, E. (2001). Psychotherapy and the single synapse: The impact of psychiatric thought on neurobiological research. *Journal of Neuropsychiatry and Clinical Neurosciences*, 13, 290–300.

Kaplan-Solms, K., & Solms, M. (2000). *Clinical studies in neuro-psychoanalysis*. London: Karnac.

Kaufmann, J. (2009). In the shadow of suicide: Lessons from mental health professionals who have been there. Paper presented at Institute on Psychiatric Services Conference.

Kaufmann, J. (2011). In the shadow of suicide. In B. Willock, L. C. Bohm, & R. C. Curtis (Eds.), *Loneliness and longing: Conscious and unconscious aspects* (pp. 176–186). London: Routledge.

Kessler, R. (2010, January). Freud's brain: Under construction. Paper presented at the American Psychoanalytic Association annual meeting, New York.

Knize, P. A. (2002). Growing up with art: Kokoschka in my life. In T. G. Natter (Ed.), *Oskar Kokoschka: Early portraits from Vienna and Berlin 1909–1914* (pp. 67–70). New York: Neue Galerie.

Knox, J. M. (2001). Memories, fantasies, archetypes: An exploration of some connections between cognitive science and analytical psychology. *Journal of Analytical Psychology*, 46, 613–635.

Koehler, B. (2008a). Posting to the to the U.S. listserv of the International Society for the Psychological Treatments of the Schizophrenias and other Psychoses (ISPS-US) on 6/29/08.

Koehler, B. (2008b, March). The eclipse of the person in contemporary psychiatry: Challenging neurobiological reductionism—An integration of neuroscience, psychosocial and phenomenological perspectives. Paper presented at meeting of ISPS-US, New York University.

Kokoschka, O. (1971/1974). *My life* (D. Britt, Trans.). New York: Macmillan.

Kokoschka, O. (n.d.). On the nature of visions (H. Medlinger & J. Thwaites, (Trans.). In E. Hoffman, *Kokoschka: Life and work* (pp. 285–287). Boston, MA: Boston Book and Art Shop, Inc.

Kris, E. (1952). *Psychoanalytic explorations in art*. New York: Schocken Books.

Kuspit, D. (1991). Visual art and art criticism: The role of psychoanalysis. *Annual of Psychoanalysis*, *19*, 1–16.

Lahr, J. (2010, April 12). Escape artist: Mark Rothko onstage. *The New Yorker*.

Lakoff, G., & Johnson, M. (1999). *Philosophy in the flesh*. New York: Basic Books.

Laplanche, J., & Pontalis, J.-B. (1967). *The language of psycho-analysis* (D. N. Smith, Trans.). London: Karnac.

Larner, G. (n.d.). The rich textuality that is psycho-analysis: Review of Jacques Derrida's *Resistances of psychoanalysis*. Stanford, CA: Stanford University Press (1998).

Laub, D., & Auerhahn, N. C. (1993). Knowing and not knowing massive psychic trauma: Forms of traumatic memory. *International Journal of Psychoanalysis*, *74*, 287–302.

Lehrer, J. (2008). *Proust was a neuroscientist*. Boston, MA: Houghton-Mifflin.

Levenson, E. (2003). On seeing what is said: Visual aids to the psychoanalytic process. *Contemporary Psychoanalysis*, *39*, 233–249.

Levenson, E. (2005). *The fallacy of understanding & the ambiguity of change*. Hillsdale, NJ: Analytic Press.

Livingstone, M. (2002). *Vision and art: The biology of seeing*. New York: Harry N. Abrams.

Livingstone, M. (2007). Art, illusion and the visual system. *Current Opinion in Neurobiology*, *17*, 476–482.

Llinás, R. (2001). *The I of the vortex: From neurons to self*. Cambridge, MA: MIT Press.

Locatelli, C. (2008). Projections: Beckett's *Krapp's last tape* and *Not I* as autobiographies. In L. Ben-Zvi & A. Moorjani (Eds.), *Beckett at 100: Revolving it all* (pp. 68–80). Oxford: Oxford University Press.

Loewald, H. W. (2000). Sublimation: Inquiries into theoretical psychoanalysis. In *The essential Loewald: Collected papers and monographs* (pp. 435–527). Hagerstown, MD: University Publishing Group.

Maher, A. L. (1993). Creativity: A work in progress. *Psychoanalytic Quarterly*, *62*, 239–262.

Mahler, M. S. (1967). On human symbiosis and the vicissitudes of individuation. *Journal of the American Psychoanalytic Association*, *15*, 740–763.

Mashour, G. A. (2008). Toward a general theory of unconscious processes in psychoanalysis and anesthesiology. *Journal of the American Psychoanalytic Association*, *56*(1), 203–222.

Maude, U. (2009). "Material of a strictly peculiar order": Beckett, Merleau-Ponty and perception. In U. Maude & M. Feldman (Eds.), *Beckett and phenomenology* (pp. 77–94). London: Continuum.

McCormick, C. *Journal of Contemporary Art*. www.jca-online.com.

McGilchrist, I. (2009). *The master and his emissary*. New Haven, CT: Yale University Press.

Meaney, M. J. (2001). Maternal care, gene expression, and the transmission of individual differences in stress reactivity across generations. *Annual Review of Neuroscience*, *24*, 1161–1192.

Meissner, W. W. (2010). Some notes on the epistemology of empathy. *Psychoanalytic Quarterly*, 79(2), 421–469.

Merleau-Ponty, M. (1945). Cézanne's doubt. In G. Johnson (Ed.), *The Merleau-Ponty aesthetics reader* (pp. 59–75). Evanston, IL: Northwestern University Press.

Merleau-Ponty, M. (1960). Eye and mind. In G. Johnson (Ed.), *The Merleau-Ponty aesthetics reader* (pp. 121–149). Evanston, IL: Northwestern University Press.

Merleau-Ponty, M. (1962). *Phenomenology of perception*. London: Routledge & Kegan Paul.

Mitchell, S. A. (1991). Contemporary perspectives on self: Toward an integration. *Psychoanalytic Dialogues*, *1*, 121–147.

Mitchell, S. A., & Black, M. (1995). *Freud and beyond*. New York: Basic Books.

Modell, A. H. (1993). *The private self*. Cambridge, MA: Harvard University Press.

Modell, A. H. (2003). *Imagination and the meaningful brain*. Cambridge, MA: MIT Press.

Modell, A. H. (2008). Horse and rider revisited: The dynamic unconscious and the self as agent. *Contemporary Psychoanalysis*, *44*, 351–366.

Moriguchi, Y., Ohnishi, T., Decety, J., Hirakata, M., Maeda, M., Matsuda, H., & Komaki, G. (2009). The human mirror neuron system in a population with deficient self-awareness: An fMRI study in alexithymia. *Human Brain Mapping*, *30*, 2063–2076.

Morin, C., & Thibierge, S. (2004). L'image du corps en neurologie: De la cénesthésie à l'image spéculaire. Apports cliniques et théoriques de la psychanalyse. *L'évolution psychiatrique*, *69*, 417–430.

Moskowitz, A., Nadel, L., Watts, P., & Jacobs, W. J. (2008). Delusional atmosphere, the psychotic prodrome, and decontextualized memories. In A. Moskowitz, I. Schafer, & M. J. Dorahy (Eds.), *Psychosis, trauma and dissociation: Emerging perspectives on severe psychopathology* (pp. 65–78). London: Wiley.

Moskowitz, A., Read, J., Farrelly, S., Rudegeair, T., & Williams, O. (2009). Are psychotic symptoms traumatic in origin and dissociative in kind? In P. Dell & J. O'Neil (Eds.), *Dissociation and the dissociative disorders: DSM-V and beyond* (pp. 521–534). New York: Routledge.

Nardone, I. B., Ward, R., Fotopoulou, A., & Turnbull, O. H. (2007). Attention and emotion in anosognosia: Evidence of implicit awareness and repression? *Neurocase*, *13*, 438–445.

Nasar, S. (1998). *A beautiful mind*. New York: Simon & Schuster.

Nash, J. (1950). The bargaining problem. *Econometrica*, *18*, 155–162.

Nash, J. (1995). In T. Frängsmyr (Ed.), *Les Prix Nobel 1994*. Stockholm: Nobel Foundation.

Nash, J. (2007). Nash suggests schizophrenia may serve adaptive function. *Psychiatric News*, *42*(13), 2–4.

Natter, T. G. (Ed.). (2002). *Oskar Kokoschka: Early portraits from Vienna and Berlin 1909–1914*. New York: Neue Galerie.

Neubauer, P. B. (1987). The many meanings of play: Introduction. *Psychoanalytic Study of the Child*, *42*, 3–9.

Neubauer, P. B., & Neubauer, A. (1996). *Nature's thumbprint*. New York: Columbia University Press.

Noë, A. (2004). *Action in perception*. Cambridge, MA: MIT Press.

Noy, P. (1969). A revision of the psychoanalytic theory of the primary process. *International Journal of Psychoanalysis*, *50*, 155–178.

Noy, P. (1979). Form creation in art: An ego-psychological approach to creativity. *Psychoanalytic Quarterly*, *48*(2), 229–256.

Offen, S. (2008). Cognitive control of perceptual processing in the human brain. Dissertation submitted in partial fulfillment of the requirements for the Ph.D. at New York University.

Olds, D. (2006). Identification: Psychoanalytic and biological perspectives. *Journal of the American Psychoanalytic Association*, *54*(1), 17–46.

Olds, D. (2009). Leap carefully from brain to mind—but it can be done: Commentary on Vivona. *Journal of the American Psychoanalytic Association*, *57*(3), 551–558.

Olesker, W., & Lament, C. (2008). Conceptualizing transformations in child and adult psychoanalysis. *Psychoanalytic Study of the Child*, *63*, 273–279.

Oppenheim, L. (2000). *The painted word: Samuel Beckett's dialogue with art*. Ann Arbor, MI: University of Michigan Press.

Oppenheim, L. (2005). *A curious intimacy: Art and neuro-psychoanalysis*. London: Routledge.

Oppenheim, L. (2012). The lexicographer's nightmare. In A. Fotopoulou, D. Pfaff, & M. A. Conway (Eds.), *From the couch to the lab: Trends in psychodynamic neuroscience* (pp. 282–292). Oxford: Oxford University Press.

Pally, R. (2008, February). Regina Pally, mirror neurons and beyond: Implications for the subjective experience of self and other. Paper presented at the Arnold Pfeffer Center for Neuro-Psychoanalysis, New York Psychoanalytic Institute.

Panksepp, J. (1998). *Affective neuroscience: The foundations of human and animal emotions*. Oxford: Oxford University Press.

Person, E. S. (2000). Change moments in therapy. In J. Sandler, A. Cooper, R. Michels, & P. Fonagy (Eds.), *Changing ideas in a changing world* (pp. 77–85). London: Karnac.

Person, E. S., & Klar, H. (1994). Establishing trauma: The difficulty distinguishing between memories and fantasies. *Journal of the American Psychoanalytical Association*, *42*, 1055–1081.

Peskin, M. M. (1997). Drive theory revisited. *Psychoanalytic Quarterly*, *66*, 377–402.

Peskin, M. M. (2011, November 15). Presentation at the New York Psychoanalytic Institute.

Phillips, G., & Crow, T. (Eds.). (2005). *Seeing Rothko*. Los Angeles, CA: Getty Research Institute.

Proust, M. (1928/1970). *Remembrance of things past: Swann's way* (C. K. Scott Moncrieff, Trans.). New York: Random House.

Ramachandran, V. S. (1996). What neurological syndromes can tell us about human nature: Some lessons from phantom limbs, Capgras syndrome, and anosognosia. *Cold Spring Harbor Symposia on Quantative Biology*, *61*.

Ramachandran, V. S., & Hirstein, W. (1999). The science of art: A neurological theory of aesthetic experience. *Journal of Consciousness Studies: Art and the Brain*, *6*(6/7), 15–51.

Rangell, L. (1982). Transference to theory: The relationship of psychoanalytic education to the analyst's relationship to psychoanalysis. *Annual of Psychoanalysis*, *10*, 29–56.

Raphael-Leff, J. (2009). The "dreamer" by daylight: Imaginative play, creativity, and generative identity. *Psychoanalytic Study of the Child*, *64*, 14–53.

Rich, S. K. (2005). Staring into space: The relaxing effect of Rothko's painting on critics in the 1950s. In G. Phillips & T. Crow (Eds.), *Seeing Rothko* (pp. 81–100). Los Angeles, CA: Getty Research Institute.

Ritvo, L. B. (1965). Darwin as the source of Freud's Neo-Lamarckianism. *Journal of the American Psychoanalytic Association*, *13*, 499–517.

Ritvo, L. B. (1990). *Darwin's influence on Freud: A tale of two sciences*. New Haven, CT: Yale University Press.

Rorty, R. (1997, November 1). Think tank: Lofty ideas that may be losing altitude. *New York Times*, B13.

Rose, G. (1980). *The power of form: A psychoanalytic approach to aesthetic form*. Madison, CT: International Universities Press.

Rothko, M. (2004). *The artist's reality: Philosophies of art* (C. Rothko, Ed.). New Haven, CT: Yale University Press.

Rudden, M. (2008, December). The "secret cocoon": Fantasy and private space in analysands with a psychotic parent. Paper presented at a meeting of the Columbia University Center for Psychoanalytic Training and Research, New York.

Rycroft, C. (1968). *Imagination and reality*. London: Maresfield Library.

Sandberg, L. S., & Busch, F. N. (2007). Commentary on "Toward a neuroscience of empathy: Integrating affective and cognitive perspectives." *Neuro-Psychoanalysis*, *9*, 156–161.

Sarraute (1984). *Childhood* (B. Wright, Trans.). New York: George Braziller.

Sartre, J.-P. (1940). *L'imaginaire: Psychologie phénoménologique de l'imagination*. Paris: Gallimard.

Sass, L. (1992). *Madness and modernism*. Cambridge, MA: Harvard University Press.

Sass, L. (1994). *The paradoxes of delusion*. Ithaca, NY: Cornell University Press.

Saxe, R., & Offen, S. (2010). Seeing ourselves: What vision can teach us about metacognition. In G. Dimaggio & P. Lysaker (Eds.), *Metacognition and severe adult mental disorders: From basic research to treatment* (pp. 13–29). New York: Routledge.

Schachter, J. S. (1996). Final overview panel: Chaired by León Grinberg, Madrid. *International Journal of Psychoanalysis*, *77*, 387–391.

Schafer, R. (1968). *Aspects of internalization*. New York: International Universities Press.

Schafer, R. (1976). *A new language for psychoanalysis*. New Haven, CT: Yale University Press.

Schafer, R. (2008, December). Discussion of paper by Rudden, M. (2008), presented at a meeting of the Columbia University Center for Psychoanalytic Training and Research, New York.

Seldes, L. (1978). *The legacy of Mark Rothko*. New York: Holt, Rinehart & Winston.

Shapiro, E. (2011). Psychoanalytic institutions and treatment of resistance: Commentary on Kafka. *Journal of the American Psychoanalytic Association*, *59*(1), 71–79.

Shapiro, T. (1993). Review of *Darwin's influence on Freud: A tale of two sciences*. *Journal of the American Psychoanalytic Association*, *41*, 850–852.

Shevrin, H. (2002). A psychoanalytic view of memory in the light of recent cognitive neuroscience research. *Neuro-Psychoanalysis*, *4*, 131–139.

Shevrin, H., Williams, W. J., Marshal, R. E., Hetel, R. K., Bond, J. A., & Brakel, L. A. (1992). Event-related potential indicators of the dynamic unconscious. *Consciousness and Cognition*, *1*, 340–366.

Siever, L. J. (1997). The biology of borderline personality disorder. *Journal of the California Alliance for the Mentally Ill*. Retrieved from http://www.borderlinepersonalitytoday.com/main/clinicians/siever.htm.

Silverman, R. C., & Lieberman, A. F. (1999). Negative maternal attributions, projective identification, and the intergenerational transmission of violent relational patterns. *Psychoanalytic Dialogues*, *9*, 161–186.

Smith, K. (2006). Interview with John LeKay. Retrieved from http://www.pacewildenstein.com.

Solms, M. (2003). Do unconscious phantasies really exist? In R. Steiner (Ed.), *Unconscious fantasy* (pp. 85–105). London: Karnac.

Solms, M. (2004). Freud returns. *Scientific American*, *290*(5), 82–89.

Solms, M., & Turnbull, O. (2002). *The brain and the inner world*. New York: Other Press.

Sripada, B. (2011). Remembering Leo Rangell. *The American Psychoanalyst*, *45*(3), 28.

Stegner, W. (1967). *All the little live things*. New York: Viking.

Stern, D. B. (1997). *Unformulated experience: From dissociation to imagination in psychoanalysis*. Hillsdale, NJ: Analytic Press.

Stern, D. B. (2004). The eye sees itself: Dissociation, enactment, and the achievement of conflict. *Contemporary Psychoanalysis*, *40*, 197–237.

Stern, D. B. (2009). *Partners in thought: Working with unformulated experience, dissociation, and enactment*. New York: Routledge.

Stern, D. N. (2010). *Forms of vitality: Exploring dynamic experience in psychology, the arts, psychotherapy, and development*. Oxford: Oxford University Press.

Stolorow, R. D. (2008). A review of *Subjectivity and selfhood: Investigating the first-person perspective*. *Journal American Psychoanalytic Association*, *56*(3), 1040–1041.

Storr, A. (1972). *The dynamics of creation*. New York: Atheneum.

Sugarman, A. (2008). Fantasizing as process, not fantasy as content: The importance of mental organization. *Psychoanalytic Inquiry*, *28*(2), 169–189.

Sullivan, H. S. (1962). *Schizophrenia as a human process*. New York: W. W. Norton.

Sullivan, R., & Lasley, E. N. (2010). Fear in love: Attachment, abuse, and the developing brain. *Cerebrum*. Retrieved from http://www.dana.org/news/cerebrum/detail.aspx?id=28926.

Treffinger, D. J. (2002). Creativity, creative thinking and critical thinking: In search of definitions, Sarasota, FL, Center for Creative Thinking. In D. J. Treffinger, G. C. Young, E. C. Selby, & C. Shepardson, *Assessing creativity: A guide for educators*. Retrieved from www.creativelearning.com.

Tronick, E. (2008). Law and order taps infant–mother paradigm research. *The American Psychoanalyst*, *42*(4), 1 & 6–7.

Turnbull, O., Jones, K., & Reed-Screen, J. (2002). Implicit awareness of deficit in anosognosia: An emotion-based account of denial of deficit. *Neuro-Psychoanalysis*, *4*, 69–86.

Vivona, J. (2009). Leaping from brain to mind: A critique of mirror neuron explanations of countertransference. *Journal of the American Psychoanalytic Association*, *57*(3), 525–550.

Volkan, V. (1998). Transgenerational transmissions and chosen traumas. *International Association of Group Psychotherapy*. Retrieved from http://www.austenriggs.org/images/uploads/Opening%20Address.TRANS.TRANS.pdf.

Watt, D. (2007). Toward a neuroscience of empathy: Integrating affective and cognitive perspectives. *Neuro-Psychoanalysis*, *9*(2), 119–140.

Weiss, J. (Ed.). (1998). *Mark Rothko*. Washington, DC: Catalogue of the National Gallery of Art.

Werkner, P. (2002). Gestures in Oskar Kokoschka's early portraits. In T. G. Natter (Ed.), *Oskar Kokoschka: Early portraits from Vienna and Berlin 1909–1914* (pp. 31–36). New York: Neue Galerie.

Whitebook, J. (2006). Against interiority: Foucault's struggle with psychoanalysis. In G. Gutting (Ed.), *The Cambridge companion to Foucault* (pp. 312–347). Cambridge: Cambridge University Press.

Whitney Museum of American Art (2006, October 16). *Kiki Smith*. Retrieved from http://www.undo.net/it/mostra/44190.

Willick, M. (2003, May). Reflections on treating people with schizophrenia in psychotherapy. Freud Lecture, New Jersey Psychoanalytic Society.

Wingler, H. M. (1958). *Oskar Kokoschka: The work of the painter* (F. S. C. Budgen, Trans.). Salzburg: Verlag Galerie Welz.

Winnicott, D. W. (1958). The capacity to be alone. *International Journal of Psychoanalysis*, *39*, 416–420.

Wood, M. (2003, December 18). What Henry knew. *London Review of Books*.

Zeki, S. (1998). Art and the brain. *Deadalus*, *127*(2), 71–103.

Zeki, S. (1999). Splendors and miseries of the brain. *Philosophical Transactions of the Royal Society of London*, *354*, 2053–2065.

Zeki, S. (2009). *Splendors and miseries of the brain: Love, creativity, and the quest for human happiness*. Hopewell, NJ: Wiley-Blackwell.

Zellner, M. (2009, December 12). Neural substrates of drive, motivation and cathexis. Paper presented at the Arnold Pfeffer Center for Neuropsychoanalysis.

INDEX

www.ingramcontent.com/pod-product-compliance
Lightning Source LLC
LaVergne TN
LVHW011126300926
849160LV00008B/537
9780415875714